trotman

# Which Uni?

## FIND THE BEST UNIVERSITY FOR YOU

**2nd Edition**

D0524952

Books are to be
th

099339

ARLA FITZHUGH

*Which Uni? Find the Best University for You*

This second edition published in 2009 by Trotman Publishing, an imprint of
Crimson Publishing, Westminster House, Kew Road, Richmond, Surrey TW9 2ND

© Trotman Publishing 2009

Previously published as *The Ultimate University Ranking Guide* by
Catherine Harris published in 2004 by Trotman & Co Ltd.

**Author:** Karla Fitzhugh

ISBN: 978-1-84455-209-2

**British Library Cataloguing in Publications Data**
A catalogue record for this book is available from the British Library

Typeset by RefineCatch Ltd, Bungay, Suffolk

Printed and bound in the UK by TJ International Ltd, Padstow, Cornwall

# Contents

# List of tables

# Acknowledgements

I would like to warmly thank the staff of Trotman for all their help and advice with this book. I am also very grateful to HESA, UCAS, the *Guardian*, and *The Good University Guide* for allowing the use of their data, and to the students and staff who helped me with interviews.

Special thanks go to Doug Bryson for his patience, bright ideas and unswerving support.

# Introduction

Studying for a degree at university can be one of the most memorable and rewarding experiences of your life, as long as you choose the right course and the right surroundings. Get this decision correct and you'll soon be exploring the academic subjects that capture your interest and imagination, considerably enhancing your career prospects, and enjoying a full and varied social life crammed with new opportunities.

For many new students it's also the first time they move away from the parental home and gain more personal independence. Ideally you'll want to be as happy as possible in your new surroundings, comfortable with the people and places, and taking a course that you like and can complete successfully.

## So many choices – where do you begin?

It's a big decision and at times the sheer range of choice can seem overwhelming, but this book is a useful place to start. There's so much differing information and opinion out there that it's easy to become confused, but this guide can help you navigate through it all and pick the best university specifically for you. It will help you to decide what you want most out of your experience of student life, and show you how to compare degrees, departments and different locations so that you can narrow down your options to get the best 'fit'.

Going to university is a major investment in your future, both in terms of time and effort and, increasingly, in terms of finance. As the cost of studying continues to rise, undergraduates are under more pressure to get the best value from their courses and leisure time, and they also need to avoid making expensive mistakes. For example, one of the commonest reasons for dropping out of degree courses is that students dislike the course or subject that they've chosen – something that can often be avoided by careful comparison of the various options available before making your application.

## But enough about that, let's talk about you . . .

There's a lot at stake, and it's crucial to take the time to research a range of courses and institutions in detail so that you can make your own well-informed decision.

To begin this process you need to discover and explore your priorities for higher education, something that's as individual as your fingerprints. One person's preferences are completely different from the next person's, and this book aims to cover them all.

There's no single set of figures on which you should base your final decision, so this guide provides you with a wider range of information to give you a proper overview. It contains summaries of many of the biggest league tables and other ranking and classifications systems, with mentions of their pros and cons, and how they might relate to you specifically. There are also many other official sources of information that relate to academic excellence, ranging from entry standards to levels of student satisfaction with the quality of teaching, and some of them will hold more weight for you than others.

Of course, you'll probably want to look into much more than just the academic side of things, unless you're planning on locking yourself into the library for the whole of the next three years. That's why *Which Uni?* also contains original research that will tell you more about the atmosphere, facilities, and fitness and entertainment opportunities at different universities. Plus there's information about accommodation, student support and the cost of living.

Once you've started to gain more of an idea of the best courses and academic institutions for you, this book gives plenty of pointers to show you where to find further credible, trustworthy information so that you can follow up your own lines of research. It won't be long before you're comparing prospectuses and course guides, visiting universities during open days and narrowing down your top choices.

# How to pick YOUR perfect university

What are the greatest influences on your decisions about where to study? You will have your own unique set of preferences, some of which will probably be academic, and some of which will be non-academic. If anything mentioned below is important to you, add it to your personal checklist.

Your personal academic factors will vary, but they might include:

▶ overall entry standards for new students
▶ general academic spending
▶ percentage of students attaining high classes of degree
▶ number of students per member of teaching staff
▶ general research standards

▶ general continuation rates

▶ overall student satisfaction.

See Chapter 2 to find out more about these academic factors.

Choices about university environment are often highly personal, and what's ideal for you may be far from ideal for someone else. When you aren't studying, the general environment can make an enormous impact on your everyday life, so it pays to give it plenty of attention. The distance from your current home can be crucial, for example, do you need to study near where you currently live?

You might relish the idea of immersing yourself in completely different surroundings, or you might prefer to stick with 'more of the same', in other words a type of environment that you're already used to. For example, some people would jump at the chance to go to a large university in a busy town, while others might feel lost in the crowd and crave a smaller community where they can get to know everyone.

General environment factors include:

▶ type of university – older/traditional versus newer

▶ university site – campus (concentrated) or non-campus (spread out)

▶ setting – city, rural, small town, large town, inland, seaside, etc.

▶ general atmosphere – hectic, laid back, close-knit, etc.

For more about finding the right place, turn to Chapter 4.

From a financial point of view, you might want to consider:

▶ overall cost of living

▶ availability of part-time work

▶ average prices of university and private rents.

See Chapter 3 for further information on finance.

The range of different students can really add to a university's general atmosphere. It can be influenced by many things, including: male:female ratios, number of international students, mix of ethnicities or socio-economic backgrounds, proportion of mature students, and so on. See Chapter 4 for more about the student mix.

You will almost certainly be interested in at least some of the university's or local amenities and the leisure and social opportunities, such as:

- ▶ clubs and societies
- ▶ sports and fitness facilities
- ▶ culture – cinema, music, theatre, comedy, radio, etc.
- ▶ cafés, bars, nightclubs
- ▶ student union/political activities.

See Chapter 5 for more ways to spend your free time at different universities.

Make a note of any hobbies or interests you'd like to continue or try for the first time, and see whether any universities offer them. There really is something for everyone, whatever you're into. Generally speaking, the larger the university (or the larger the nearest town), the wider the range of leisure options there will be.

# Where will your investment lead you?

Studying for a degree means that you'll be pushing yourself, developing new skills, expanding your horizons, increasing your self-confidence and meeting diverse and interesting people. While it will be hard work at times, and take you out of your comfort zone, this can enhance your future in a variety of ways. Prospects for graduates tend to be better than prospects for non-graduates: people with degrees tend to earn more over their working lives and are significantly less likely to be unemployed for any length of time. Certain careers also demand specific degrees or postgraduate qualifications before you can work in them.

When you are choosing where and what to study, after looking at all aspects of academia and undergraduate life, you might wish to examine life after graduation more closely, since taking a degree is such a huge investment in so many ways. Aspects that you might want to consider, and which are discussed in more detail in Chapter 6, include the recruitment preferences of top employers, how many students manage to find graduate and general jobs, graduate starting salaries, and employment rates by subjects studied.

There are many career-enhancing work placements and extra-curricular activities to consider while you're still at university, too – these can make that all-important difference to any job applications you might want to make in the future, giving you an edge over the competition in a tough employment market.

Or perhaps, after graduating, you'd like to go on to undertake further study to further your knowledge or improve your CV. If that's the case then you might be interested in the number of graduates from certain courses whose next move is to begin a postgraduate degree, or how different universities are regarded when it comes to their quality of research. Research 'reputations' are mentioned in Chapter 1 (page 12), and the national Research Assessment Exercise is discussed on page 42.

# Making your 'league table'

As you read through the personal checklists and the rest of *Which Uni?*, you'll discover the deciding factors that hold the most importance for you. For example, you might only be able to study at an institution that's within a 30-mile radius of your home: this factor is unlikely to appear in any of the general UK league tables, but you can certainly make a league table of your own to compare the universities that fall into that category. Similarly, you will undoubtedly have your own unique mixture of academic requirements, career factors, non-academic interests, and perhaps support needs.

Tables 85a and b, towards the back of the book, can be used to create your own individual rankings guides, where you can compare courses at different universities using your own unique selection of academic and non-academic factors. These allow you to create quick reference tables that put the most important facts and figures at your fingertips, and aid you in the decision-making process. We've even included an example table to help get you started.

Soon you'll be turning your personally tailored research into those all-important applications for places, and with a little luck you'll be well on your way into higher education.

# Chapter 1

# How to find YOUR perfect university

Studying for a degree gives you the chance to explore an interesting subject in greater depth, to try new ways of thinking and to challenge yourself intellectually. At the same time it can also be an excellent opportunity for improving your future employment prospects. Academia and work aside, it's an ideal environment for making all kinds of new friends and trying a wide range of new activities and hobbies.

Everyone has their own unique reasons for deciding what they want to get out of their university experience. Your personal priorities may be:

- ▶ academic excellence at all costs
- ▶ employment prospects at all costs
- ▶ taking a good course in a place where you feel comfortable
- ▶ finding yourself in the centre of a social whirl and somehow managing to get a qualification at the same time
- ▶ finding somewhere that will take you even though you have fairly low predicted grades
- ▶ taking a degree close to home so you don't have to move out
- ▶ getting value for money on a course you can afford
- ▶ or something else entirely that only you can think of!

Deciding what to study, and where, is a big decision with potentially life-altering consequences, and it can be very difficult deciding where to start with this process. This guide breaks it down into smaller, more manageable sections so that you don't feel overwhelmed, and you can take it one step at a time.

**Getting the most out of this book**
*It's a good idea to make notes as you go along, either in a file or in the extra pages at the back of this book, so you know where you are and can quickly refer back to them for reminders if you have moments where you get a bit lost or stuck.*

When looking for a course and a university you need a thorough overview in order to make an informed decision. Don't look at just one list or ranking table and base your opinions on that set of data alone, and avoid making any rushed decisions or big guesses if you can help it.

# What do you hope to gain from university?

Your choices of higher education institution and course really are important, so take enough time to consider what your priorities are. There's no right or wrong answer – it's all about you, and what best suits your personal talents, situation and tastes. The time and money you spend gaining a degree are a major investment in your future, so it's worth asking some searching questions.

One useful thing to ask yourself is: *What do I most want to achieve from going to university?* The list below gives some of the commonest responses to this question.

## The main reasons for going to university

1. To gain qualifications.

2. To improve my chances of getting a job.

3. To improve my earning potential.

4. For the experience.

5. To learn more about interesting subjects.

6. I have always wanted to go.

7. It's a natural progression.

8. To stretch me intellectually.

9. To mix with different people.

*Source: UNITE Student Experience Report 2007*

Looking at this list, the top three reasons students currently give for going to university (i.e. to gain qualifications, to improve chances of getting a job, and to improve earning potential) are all to do with looking ahead and investing in their future.

It isn't all work, work, work, though – plenty of students are interested in the other rich and varied experiences they can expect to have along the way. Even if you are highly career orientated or academic, do remember that potential employers tend to prefer candidates who have social skills, well-rounded personalities and at least a few outside interests. These can all successfully be built upon while you're studying.

# Some general pros and cons

The two lists below show what current students describe as the best and worst aspects of university life, and they can help you think about things to prioritise, plan ahead for or maybe even avoid if at all possible. What might you find the most rewarding? What might be the most challenging?

As you can see, much of this list of 'positives' does relate strongly to the course and the academic environment, and these things tend to lead the decisions of most students when they're deciding what to study and which institution to apply to. For more about academia, turn to Chapter 2.

There are two other strong positive themes in this list: the social side of life; and gaining independence. The general environment and the social scene can make an enormous difference to your overall happiness and quality of life while you're studying for a degree, so it's important to find a place where you're going to be happy and comfortable too. Chapters 4 and 5 of this book are a great place to start finding out more about this.

## top ten best aspects of university life ⭐

=1. Improving my career prospects.
=1. Meeting new friends.
3. Learning more about my chosen subject.
4. Stretching myself intellectually.
=5. Mixing with different types of people.
=5. Gaining independence/ greater freedom.
=7. My studies.
=7. Meeting people with similar interests to me.
9. Doing something for myself.
10. Change in lifestyle.

*Source: UNITE Student Experience Report 2007*

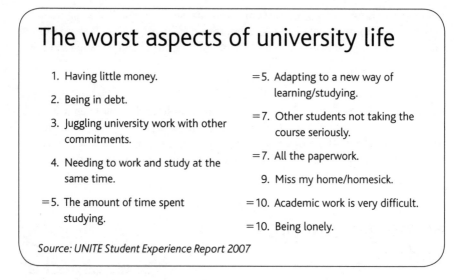

## The worst aspects of university life

1. Having little money.

2. Being in debt.

3. Juggling university work with other commitments.

4. Needing to work and study at the same time.

=5. The amount of time spent studying.

=5. Adapting to a new way of learning/studying.

=7. Other students not taking the course seriously.

=7. All the paperwork.

9. Miss my home/homesick.

=10. Academic work is very difficult.

=10. Being lonely.

*Source: UNITE Student Experience Report 2007*

While it might look like a catalogue of doom and gloom, many of these challenges, while undeniably tough at the time, can become great successes when you overcome them. Learning new academic and life skills, facing your anxieties and showing determination will stand you in good stead in the future.

However, it's a fact of life that money problems, particularly levels of student debt, are increasing. It's important to be aware of the financial aspects of university life, and you'll find more about them in Chapter 3.

If you're certain that you want to go into higher education and gain a degree, you'll need to make three main decisions.

▶ WHAT do I want to study? (See the following section.)

▶ WHERE do I want to study it? (See page 12 in this chapter.)

▶ HOW can I fund my studies? (See Chapter 3.)

# Deciding what to study

Most students start out by picking a subject area or specific type of course, and then comparing the universities that offer them.

You might have a very firm idea of your favourite subject or course already, or you might want to spend more time making this decision. Up to a third of degree students say they chose the wrong course, and picking a course or institution you find you don't like increases your chances of dropping out. However, investing in a little research and reflection should make you more confident in your decisions, and increases your chances of enjoying your course and surroundings, and staying motivated during your studies.

To begin with, think hard about your interests, talents and values, and look at broad subject areas that might suit you. At the same time you may wish to consider future career options, professions or vocations, if you already have some in mind.

Which one of these applies to you?

▶ I'm interested in a subject that I've already studied at GCSE or GCE A level, and I want to study it in greater depth.

▶ There's a new subject or issue that interests me, and think I could do well studying it academically.

▶ I have a vocation or career in mind, and need to study a specific course to qualify for a particular kind of employment.

▶ I haven't decided what to study yet – I'm a bit stuck.

The right subject, and perhaps career, for you takes into account your personality, preferences, values, talents and skills. Think your subject decision through carefully, and perhaps try a few of the following exercises or questionnaires. For example, you could make lists of your strengths and your weaknesses, your personal passions or your interests versus your dislikes.

A different perspective can help, too.

▶ Try asking several people who know you well where they think your strengths, weaknesses and talents lie.

▶ You could talk to teachers, tutors, family members, friends, or even people at your part-time job. This might make you squirm a bit, but they could come up with some perceptive comments that you hadn't expected, or even good points you'd forgotten or were too modest to mention.

▶ It's also well worth having a chat with your nearest higher education adviser or careers adviser.

## Your next question, for five points . . .

If you're still completely stumped, don't panic. Try a subject or careers questionnaire to give you a variety of suggested sectors that you can then research in greater detail. A useful tip for filling in these questionnaires is this: don't say what you *think* you should say, answer honestly about how things really make you feel. Sit quietly with nobody looking over your shoulder, and don't worry what others might say about your answers – just be true to yourself.

Questionnaires that you might find useful include the following.

▶ Directgov and UCAS both recommend the Stamford Test, an online questionnaire about your interests, attitudes and values. It makes broad course suggestions that are dependent on the way you respond to the questions, and then you can follow up the most appealing ones. It's easy and quick to fill in, and it's free to use. Find it at www. ucas.com/students/beforeyouapply/whattostudy/stamfordtest.

▶ Centigrade is another test designed to help you find the courses that will suit you best. It is administered for free by some schools, or can be taken online for a £15 fee. It contains 150 questions and the results go into far greater detail than the Stamford Test. Look at www.centigradeonline.co.uk if you are interested.

▶ You might want to try out Course Finder, which is an online resource that suggests subjects and courses, according to your personal preferences and values. Find it at www.ukcoursefinder.com.

By now you will have found some areas that interest you, and you can begin to narrow subject choices down into specific courses. Depending on your preferences, they might be purely academic, purely vocational, or a mixture of both. Either way, it's worth looking at some subject profiles and career profiles to help you discover some courses that might suit you.

## Subject overviews

Subject profiles can be a straightforward starting point from which to begin some general reading. They provide an overall feel for each general area, and give an overview of the individual courses that are available within each subject.

▶ Careers and higher education advisers may be able to help with subject choices – there are many books and leaflets about different subjects and career types.

▶ The *Guardian* newspaper has a useful guide on its website listing subject areas and relevant courses that can lead to various careers: www.guardian.co.uk/education/list/educationsubject.

▶ If you already have some idea of subject areas, try Course Discover, a searchable database of UK higher education courses. This subscription service is available via careers advisers or local libraries.

Applications for most degrees in the UK are made through UCAS, and they have a course search function on their website that's searchable both by subject and by course code. You can also narrow your search by region, institution and type of course. Courses are listed with their entry requirements, including details of the qualifications needed, and whether applicants also have to sit an additional test before they can apply: www.ucas.com/students/coursesearch/index.html.

Sometimes there are also useful entry profiles and links to brief general information about the university that's offering each course: www.ucas.com/students/beforeyouapply/whattostudy/entryprofiles.

## Career choices

Many students think about possible careers while they're deciding which subject or course to study.

► The Graduate Prospects website has a tool called What Job Would Suit Me? (Prospects Planner) that allows you to look at what would motivate you in a job, identify your skills, generate job ideas and explore jobs in greater detail. It's mainly aimed at students in higher education and recent graduates, but it can also be useful to pre-university students (www.prospects.ac.uk).

► Connexions Direct runs Jobs4U, a helpful website containing hundreds of different job profiles arranged into 'families' (also accessible in a searchable A to Z format), detailing everyday life within that profession, salary expectations, and necessary skills and qualifications. It also lists many specific jobs and careers within these 'families'. There are suggestions for further reading and research, and you can also speak to a Connexions adviser (www.connexions-direct.com/jobs4u).

► Directgov has some more general job profiles too: http://careersadvice.direct.gov.uk/ helpwithyourcareer/jobprofiles/.

If you're thinking about a specific professional or vocational course, try your nearest careers library for useful books about different careers and the qualifications needed to work in them. Your higher education adviser or careers adviser should also be able to provide you with other resources for further research, such as official websites, information agencies and professional bodies. You should be able to use these resources to identify the right courses to research further.

## What if I don't have a career in mind yet?

If your interests are mainly in an academic subject, rather than in a specific career after university, that's fine too. You might be happier simply studying a subject that inspires you academically, and you may also find yourself taking a degree that's relatively general and won't drastically narrow down your career opportunities after graduation. There are also postgraduate qualifications you can take after a first degree to enter a specific career, such as teaching or journalism.

**Read ALL the small print about a course**
*The content of a course and the way it's organised and taught can vary greatly – there's no undergraduate national curriculum so two degree courses with the same name may be completely different according to the institution where they're taught. These differences can make you love or hate a course, so it's vital to find out exactly what you could be getting yourself into with every course you're considering.*

If a single academic subject doesn't appeal, you might prefer to study two subjects within the same degree course, often described as 'dual honours', or even more subjects ('combined honours').

## In-depth course information

The most important sources of information about individual courses are university prospectuses and course guides, and university department websites. Do not skimp on reading these properly as they're likely to answer most of your questions about course formats and content, and to give various indicators of quality. Each course is unique, so don't make any assumptions: make sure you know the facts.

> **?** Did you know?
>
> *In addition to being invaluable resources when you're researching what and where to study, course guides and prospectuses are also the best places to go if you're trying to think up intelligent questions to ask during university entrance interviews or at open days.*

## Where can you find course guides?

► Pick them up at higher education fairs.

► Order via UCAS's prospectus service (http://ucas.prospectusuk.com).

► View them online via universities' own websites (see the Appendix, pages 183–211).

► Telephone university departments or admissions offices and ask them to send you printed copies.

## Looking at course structures

While you're looking at individual courses in more detail, there are a few factors that might be of particular importance to you.

► Would you prefer a course split into modules, or a non-modular course?

► Would you respond better to a traditional teaching style, or newer styles of teaching?

► Would you be happier with lots of timetables lectures/tutorials, or more free time for your own research/study?

► Depending on how well you perform in exams, what would be best for you – exam-based assessment, mainly coursework/continuous assessment, or a mixture of both?

You also need to look at the course content. Would you prefer to take a course with a broad range of content, or are there specific course areas that you're especially attracted to? Is there any sub-area you know you'd really prefer to avoid?

It's also a good idea find out whether the whole course is university based, or whether you are expected to undertake work experience or placements outside university. There may be the chance to work or study abroad, for example.

## Entry requirements

If there's a course that you like the look of, you need to make sure that you can meet its entry requirements. This might be with current or predicted grades or UCAS tariff points, with suitable experience or accreditation of prior learning (APL), or with compulsory pre-entry test results. Remember that university and college departments can re-adjust their average offers at any time, so don't assume you'll be made exactly the same offers as the ones you see in books or on websites.

As mentioned earlier, the UCAS website and the UCAS *Big Guide* both contain the complete entry requirements for each course. Alternatively, *Heap 2010: University Degree Course Offers* by Brian Heap (published by Trotman) is a comprehensive guide to entry requirements that uses official information. It lists target grades and tariff points needed to gain entry to all UK courses, and also mentions teaching quality, research ratings, number of applicants per place, graduate prospects, plus subject-specific advice for personal statements and interviews.

After researching course contents and formats you can then use the resources in this book to check course standards, quality ratings, graduate prospects, and anything else that interests you. This is also the point at which most prospective students start to match up suitable courses with suitable university environments.

## The largest and most popular subject areas

Some subject areas attract large numbers of undergraduates. Table 1 shows which subjects the most students are studying. For example, you can see that while many students are taking degree courses in subjects allied to medicine, relatively few are studying agriculture or veterinary science.

Some subjects are harder to get into than others, and there can be great competition for places. Often this makes universities raise their entry standards so that they can draw on a smaller, more manageable pool of applicants to make their selection from. If you think you can meet the course requirements then there's nothing to stop you applying, although it's a good idea to apply for an insurance place somewhere else as well, just in case.

**Table 1 Main subject areas for first degrees, ranked by total number of full-time undergraduate students**

| Rank | Subject area | Total number of undergraduates |
|------|--------------|-------------------------------|
| 1 | Business and administrative studies | 156,765 |
| 2 | Subjects allied to medicine | 143,910 |
| 3 | Creative arts and design | 129,595 |
| 4 | Biological sciences | 111,690 |
| 5 | Social studies | 110,700 |
| 6 | Engineering and technology | 80,425 |
| 7 | Languages | 78,035 |
| 8 | Computer science | 55,700 |
| 9 | Law | 54,160 |
| 10 | Physical sciences | 52,685 |
| 11 | Historical and philosophical studies | 52,560 |
| 12 | Education | 51,735 |
| 13 | Medicine and dentistry | 43,820 |
| 14 | Mass communications and documentation | 35,750 |
| 15 | Architecture, building and planning | 31,455 |
| 16 | Mathematical sciences | 22,770 |
| 17 | Agriculture and related subjects | 10,050 |
| 18 | Combined | 6,120 |
| 19 | Veterinary science | 4,080 |

Source: HESA, Students in Higher Education Institutions 2007/2008

**TIP**

**Taking a chance with high course entry requirements**

*If you're not sure whether you can meet a course's entry requirements you will have to make a tough decision – still apply even though there's a greater risk of not getting in, or play it safer and apply mostly for places where you might stand a better chance. If in doubt, talk it through with a careers adviser.*

Table 2 shows some of the most competitive subject areas, where many students apply but only a few are accepted by their chosen universities. The average number of applications per offered place is 4.8, according to UCAS, so it might be much tougher getting in to university to study these subjects.

**Table 2 Applications per acceptance by subject area, 2008**

| Rank | Subject | Applications per acceptance | Total applications | Total acceptances |
|------|---------|---------------------------|--------------------|--------------------|
| 1 | Dentistry | 8.9 | 10,707 | 1,209 |
| 2 | Medicine | 8.6 | 69,021 | 8,013 |
| 3 | Materials science | 8.1 | 57 | 7 |
| 4 | Classical Greek studies | 7.5 | 15 | 2 |
| 5 | Veterinary medicine | 7.4 | 7,007 | 943 |
| 6 | Other veterinary science-related subjects | 7.1 | 256 | 36 |
| 7 | Business and administrative studies | 6.9 | 103 | 15 |
| 8 | Subjects allied to architecture, building and planning | 6.6 | 73 | 11 |
| 9 | Biotechnology | 6.4 | 741 | 115 |
| =10 | Economics | 6.3 | 43,100 | 6,875 |
| =10 | Japanese studies | 6.3 | 1,053 | 168 |
| =12 | Combinations within biological sciences | 6.2 | 2,479 | 401 |
| =12 | Architecture | 6.2 | 26,517 | 4,247 |
| =12 | Drama | 6.2 | 44,279 | 7,085 |
| =12 | Combinations within engineering/technology/building studies | 6.2 | 980 | 159 |
| =16 | Aural and oral sciences | 6.1 | 5,559 | 909 |
| =16 | Combinations within non-European languages | 6.1 | 227 | 37 |
| =16 | Dance | 6.1 | 7,201 | 1,177 |
| =19 | Anatomy, physiology and pathology | 6.0 | 19,753 | 3,272 |
| =19 | Pharmacology, toxicology and pharmacy | 6.0 | 24,621 | 4,122 |
| =19 | Ophthalmics | 6.0 | 4,821 | 808 |
| =19 | Botany | 6.0 | 132 | 22 |

*Source: UCAS 2008 applications data*

# Deciding where to study

Although your choice of university is up to you, it's also interesting to see how previous students have narrowed their choices down to create their own personal lists of potential universities.

## top ten factors in how students choose a university

1. Overall reputation (see the following section, this page)
2. Academic reputation (see the following section, this page)
3. Quality of teaching (see Chapter 2)
4. Town/city reputation for social life (see Chapter 5)
5. Quality of learning (see Chapter 2)
6. University league table placing (see this chapter, page 17)
7. University reputation for social life (see Chapter 5)
8. Guarantee of place in halls (see Chapter 4)
9. Social facilities in town (see Chapter 5)
10. Availability of good halls (see Chapter 3)

*Source: UNITE Student Experience Report 2007*

According to this study, the overall reputation of the institution was the most important factor in students' choice of university, and the overall reputation was most strongly influenced by measures of its academic reputation. However, 'reputation', while useful to some extent, is not the most reliable factor to use when you're looking for a good university, as we're about to see.

## General 'reputation'

Where do you start if you want to look at a university's general reputation? It's tricky, because reputation is based on people's opinions, not on anything you can measure reliably or scientifically. General reputation can also remain static for many years in the public consciousness, when in reality a university may have improved drastically or gone seriously downhill. However, the reputation of many institutions continues to impress many people, including employers, so it's something many students choose to keep in the back of their mind while they're looking at other important factors.

The three lists below have been extracted from *Guide to UK Universities 2010* by Klaus Boehm and Jenny Lees-Spalding, published by Trotman. The brief descriptions represent the opinions of the authors and are intended to be used as a brief introductory guide, rather than representing an exact ranking. That's just how 'reputation' works. Let's see what the authors have to say anyway.

# World-class research-intensive universities

University of Cambridge
Cardiff University
Durham University
University of Essex
Imperial College London
London School of Economics
    and Political Science

University of Manchester
University of Oxford
University of Southampton
University College, London
University of Warwick

# Top UK research-intensive universities

University of Aberdeen
Aston University Birmingham
Bangor University
University of Bath
University of Birmingham
University of Bristol
University of Dundee
University of East Anglia
University of Edinburgh
University of Exeter
University of Glasgow
Goldsmiths, University of London
Heriot-Watt University
Keele University
University of Kent
King's College London
Lampeter (University of Wales)
Lancaster University
University of Leeds

University of Leicester
University of Liverpool
Loughborough University
Newcastle University
University of Nottingham
Queen Mary, University of London
Queen's University Belfast
University of Reading
Royal Holloway, University
    of London
University of St Andrews
University of Sheffield
School of Oriental and African
    Studies, University of London
University of Stirling
University of Surrey
University of Sussex
University of York

# Research-intensive universities

Aberystwyth University
University of Bradford
Brunel University
City University, London

University of Salford
University of Strathclyde
University of Wales Swansea
University of Ulster

*Source: Guide to UK Universities 2010, Klaus Boehm and Jenny Lees-Spalding (Trotman)*

## 'Popularity'

The 'popularity' of an institution, or overall number of applications, doesn't tell you anything specific about a university, it simply informs you that a lot of other students might like to go there, so you should be prepared to face some tough competition if you hope to get in.

> **?** **Did you know?**
>
> *The universities of Oxford and Cambridge tend to receive only around four applications per acceptance, which is close to the total UK average. This may partly be because their entry standards are so high that many students are put off applying.*

**Table 3 Twenty most popular universities, by applications per acceptance 2008**

| Rank | University | Applications per acceptance | Total applications | Total acceptances |
|------|------------|------------------------------|---------------------|--------------------|
| 1 | London School of Economics | 14.66 | 19,039 | 1,299 |
| 2 | University of Bristol | 11.42 | 42,633 | 3,735 |
| 3 | University of Edinburgh | 9.11 | 45,640 | 5,008 |
| 4 | University of Warwick | 8.68 | 33,342 | 3,840 |
| 5 | King's College London | 8.10 | 30,700 | 3,792 |
| 6 | University College London | 7.96 | 30,075 | 3,780 |
| 7 | City University | 7.62 | 20,597 | 2,704 |
| 8 | University of Bath | 7.05 | 19,990 | 2,836 |
| 9 | University of Leeds | 6.88 | 52,150 | 7,582 |
| 10 | University of Bolton | 6.74 | 4,986 | 741 |
| 11 | Aston University, Birmingham | 6.68 | 14,246 | 2,133 |
| 12 | Durham University | 6.67 | 24,335 | 3,646 |
| 13 | University of Birmingham | 6.46 | 37,398 | 5,793 |
| 14 | Brunel University | 6.35 | 22,491 | 3,540 |
| =15 | University of Liverpool | 6.22 | 27,465 | 4,417 |
| =15 | University of Sheffield | 6.22 | 30,805 | 4,953 |
| 17 | University of Southampton | 6.08 | 31,007 | 5,102 |
| 18 | University of Exeter | 6.06 | 23,784 | 3,923 |
| 19 | Cardiff University | 6.05 | 31,597 | 5,224 |
| =20 | London Metropolitan University | 6.04 | 22,728 | 3,762 |
| =20 | Queen Mary, University of London | 6.04 | 22,191 | 3,676 |

*Source: UCAS 2008 applications data*

Some universities have students queuing up to get in the door, while others are less popular. This can be because a given institution has a great overall reputation, or because it performs well academically, or it may have less to do with the academic side of things. Applicants are also drawn by other factors, for example graduate employment prospects, a relatively low cost of living, a location near the parental home, a reputation for an excellent social life, etc.

While places at some institutions are in great demand, others are slightly less popular, as you can see from Table 4.

**Table 4 Twenty least popular universities, by applications per acceptance 2008**

| Rank | University | Applications per offer | Total applications | Total offers |
|------|-----------|------------------------|---------------------|--------------|
| 1 | Glyndŵr University | 1.97 | 1,383 | 703 |
| 2 | Swansea Metropolitan University | 2.64 | 3,737 | 1,414 |
| 3 | Edinburgh Napier University | 2.67 | 10,475 | 3,920 |
| 4 | Lampeter (University of Wales) | 2.88 | 689 | 239 |
| 5 | University of Hull | 2.91 | 13,944 | 4,797 |
| 6 | Buckinghamshire New University | 3.02 | 5,090 | 1,686 |
| 7 | Aberystwyth University | 3.15 | 8,373 | 2,658 |
| 8 | University of East London | 3.16 | 14,931 | 4,722 |
| 9 | Southampton Solent University | 3.19 | 13,225 | 4,144 |
| 10 | University of the West of Scotland | 3.20 | 7,542 | 2,357 |
| 11 | Thames Valley University | 3.22 | 7,155 | 2,219 |
| 12 | University of Central Lancashire | 3.32 | 18,764 | 5,659 |
| 13 | Swansea University | 3.48 | 11,441 | 3,283 |
| =14 | University of Cumbria | 3.50 | 6,636 | 1,898 |
| =14 | University of Lincoln | 3.50 | 11,228 | 3,209 |
| =14 | University of Teesside | 3.50 | 9,709 | 2,776 |
| 17 | Northumbria University | 3.52 | 21,277 | 6,042 |
| =18 | University of Bedfordshire | 3.54 | 9,800 | 2,767 |
| =18 | Birmingham City University | 3.54 | 17,704 | 5,008 |
| =20 | University for the Creative Arts | 3.58 | 6,225 | 1,739 |
| =20 | Robert Gordon University | 3.58 | 7,524 | 2,108 |

Source: UCAS 2008 applications data

## 'To do' list – initial ideas about where you'd like to study

Try making your own top 10 list of important things you'd like in a potential university. Be as quirky or as straightforward as you like, and don't worry about what anybody else might say or think. You can always refine and change your initial 'wish list' later as you read through this chapter or look at other sources of information.

General reputation and popularity certainly influence the decisions of many prospective students. What matters the most, though, is what *you* want and what will make *you* the happiest.

### Finding out more

In addition to using this book, you can find out more about different universities by:

▶ attending higher education conventions and fairs

▶ looking at various commercial league tables

▶ finding out what current students think

▶ studying various university profiles

▶ attending university open days.

The remainder of this chapter is devoted to making the most of these sources of information.

### Higher education conventions and fairs

There are over 50 higher education conventions and fairs held around Britain each year. Most of them are of general interest and include all universities and subjects.

Conventions and fairs are an ideal opportunity to speak in depth with staff from a range of institutions all on the same day. Entry is free, and you can turn up without booking. Full listings appear at www.ucasevents.com/conventions.

You will get the most out of a convention or fair if you've already done some preliminary research into what and where you'd like to study. This should give you a 'hit list' of stands and staff to target. Pick up a floor plan of exhibitors at the front door as you arrive and work out the quickest route to take to get around all your favourites, then if you have time left over afterwards you can browse around the convention hall and find out more about other institutions that you might not already have considered. See www.ucas.com/students/exhibitions/howtoprepare for more.

You can chat to university and Connexions advisers at fairs about any of the following: entry requirements; selection procedures; course structure and assessment; self-directed learning; costs; sponsorship opportunities; facilities and support; general questions about the institution; graduate prospects; contact details; and where to go for more information. Pick up as many relevant leaflets and prospectuses as you can. You may also want to attend seminars on the day about filling in application forms, writing personal statements or taking gap years, for example.

## League tables

As you've undoubtedly already noticed, there's an enormous amount of information out there that can help you to decide where to study and what course to take. Some organisations produce league tables which put a specific selection of this information together in one place, and then rank it according to what the authors consider to be most important. Generally speaking, these tables look mainly at certain academic data, and each uses a unique formula to weight the data and calculate the 'top' universities or the 'top' courses.

League tables can give you a useful rough idea or 'rule of thumb' when looking for an academic-style university or course, and the tables probably do have quite an effect upon each university's overall reputation and public image, which in turn may influence potential employers. The creators of the different league tables do not always agree with one another over their final results (neither do many of the universities!), and the rankings may not reflect *your* personal priorities, so it's important to look at a wide variety of tables and other information as well.

Current league tables include the following.

▶ *The Times Good University Guide 2009*, by John O'Leary, published by Times Books. Rankings and subject tables available online: www.timesonline.co.uk/tol/life_and_style/education/good_university_guide.

▶ *The Guardian University Guide 2009*, edited by Alice Wignall, published by Guardian Books. Summary tables and full data set available online: www.guardian.co.uk/education/universityguide.

▶ *The Complete University Guide 2009*, online only at www.thecompleteuniversityguide.co.uk.

There are also many reliable single indicators of quality that are collected and published by official and independent bodies. Starting with Chapter 2 of this book, you'll be able to look at some of the universities that sit at the top and bottom of these different data sets.

## What the students think

The National Student Survey results are available on www.unistats.com and they are certainly worth a look. The main figure they provide is the percentage of students who say that they're satisfied with the quality of their course. The survey is also broken down into areas of finer detail, including teaching standards, assessment and feedback, academic support, course organisation, learning resources and personal development.

Unistats allows you compare subjects (but not individual courses) at universities and colleges in the UK. The information is provided by HESA (Higher Education Statistics Agency) and the National Student Survey (run by HEFCE, the Higher Education Funding Council for England). In addition to the National Student Survey, it includes official information on the following, searchable by subject and university.

▶ Student data – entry qualifications and UCAS points, continuation and achievement (see also Chapter 2 of this book).

▶ Destinations of Leavers from Higher Education (DLHE) data – destinations of leavers, job categories and job types (see also Chapter 5).

▶ Context statistics – student domicile, age, level of study, gender, study mode (see also Chapter 3).

You might also want to see what individual students have to say, or to swap messages with students or advisers. In which, case there are quite a few useful websites to try.

▶ You Go Further – run by UCAS for prospective and current students. Get official advice from trained advisers as well as comments from individual students: http://yougo.co.uk.

▶ WhatUni – a commercial site full of profiles written by current and past students. It's interesting stuff, but do remember that it's not always official data and can be very subjective: www.whatuni.com/degrees/home.html.

▶ The Student Room – very busy commercially run student message boards, plus a large wiki that contains information about university applications and so on. Again, while interesting, it's not always official data and can also be very subjective: www. thestudentroom.co.uk.

## University profiles

After you've looked at academic data and league tables, you'll probably want to find out a lot more about the atmosphere and lifestyle at different universities. You can narrow your options down by comparing lots of different university profiles, then continue your research by making visits and/or contacting the relevant students' unions at places you like the look of. The main student website addresses are all listed in the appendix of this book, and there's general lifestyle information in Chapters 4 and 5.

The *Guide to UK Universities 2010* by Klaus Boehm and Jenny Lees-Spalding (published by Trotman) is a useful guide book containing individual university profiles, and you can also find summary information pages in *The Guardian University Guide 2009*, edited by Alice Wignall, and *The Times Good University Guide 2009*, by John O'Leary.

If you want to search online, you could try any or all of these sites:

▶ the UCAS Institution Guide, which is arranged around a map: www.ucas.com/students/beforeyouapply/wheretostudy/instguide

▶ the PUSH Guide – www.push.co.uk/Uni-profiles.

## University open days

No amount of reading, emailing or telephoning can substitute for seeing the place for yourself. Universities hold departmental open days, open days for their individual colleges, and university-wide open days. Try to visit as many as your time and finances allow, and definitely visit more than one if you can. While it's important to get a general feel for the place, it's usually best to prioritise looking around departments and finding out as much as possible about courses you're interested in.

**Getting the most out of an open day**
*Write a checklist of whatever's important to you before you set off. Take a notebook with you and write down what you find out as a reminder for when you get home. Talk to students, and to academic and support staff. It's always a good sign when staff are willing and able to answer your questions – they could end up teaching you, so hopefully they will make a good impression.*

While you're attending an open day, there are many things that you should be looking out for. Think about the course, the department, the university in general, the transport links, academic and general facilities, student support services, financial aspects, graduate prospects and social life. If you can't find what you're looking for, ask university staff and students as many questions as you like until you're happy.

Full listings of all British university open days can be found in *Open Days 2009* (published by UCAS), and on the UCAS website (www.ucas.com/students/beforeyouapply/opendays). You can also check with www.opendays.com, which contains general advice as well as listings. Since dates may be announced late and may be subject to change, you should also contact institutions nearer the time you plan to visit to ensure that they will be proceeding as planned.

## Remembering your priorities

Once you've made your near-final choices, take a moment to come back and look through any notes you made while you were reading this chapter. Do the courses and universities you've chosen meet your overall aims? Do they tick some or most of your personal checklist items? You may need to compromise on a few points here and there, but try not to lose sight of your most important goals, hopes and wishes during the complicated decisions process. After all, whoever you are, you want to enjoy the next few years as much as possible and create the brightest possible future for yourself.

# Chapter 2

# The academic hit lists

There are many factors you can look at if you're wondering how academically 'good' a university is, though you may find that some of these factors are more useful to you than others. You might be interested in some or all of the following:

▶ National Student Survey results – what recent students thought of the quality of their courses (see page 22)

▶ quality assurance and institutional audit reports – what academic experts think of the teaching, etc. (see page 29)

▶ course entry standards, or the average actual UCAS points gained by first-year undergraduates (see page 29)

▶ student to staff ratios (see page 31)

▶ amount of academic spending per student (see page 33)

▶ drop-out rates (see page 37)

▶ the percentage of students who graduate with a first or a 2.i (see page 40)

▶ the quality of research undertaken at the university (see page 42)

It's best to look at a few different factors to get a more rounded overview, as no single set of figures can tell you the whole story. While it's very interesting to look at how each university performs as a whole, what's likely to make the main difference to you, on the academic side of things at least, is what's being said about potential *courses*. This chapter also contains information to help you evaluate departments, subject areas and courses.

# The cream of the university crop

The most commonly consulted indicators of course and teaching quality come from the students themselves, which can be very detailed, informative and helpful, but they do also have a few limitations that you need to be aware of.

## Overall student satisfaction with course quality

Student satisfaction levels are measured by the annual National Student Survey, and the main figure the survey produces shows how happy students are with the overall quality of their courses. Answers to each year's survey are also broken down into six subcategories, including teaching; assessment and feedback; academic support; organisation and management; learning resources; and personal development.

Figures are sometimes missing from the National Student Survey. This can happen if a university doesn't participate in the survey, or if too few of the students on a course complete the survey. However, most universities participated in the survey last year, even some that had not done so previously, and the 2008 figures represent the largest number of student respondents since the National Student Survey began. This is good news, as you're more probably going to be able to find the information you need in most cases, and it's more likely to be a representative sample of what the students are really saying.

However, there have been some criticisms of the survey. For example, it represents what first-degree undergraduates think of their course quality – but some experts believe that, since they've only studied in one place, they don't have the experience to know how their degree compares with other courses at different universities.

There have also been allegations that students in some departments have been pressured by staff into inflating their scores, in order to push the department up the various commercial/newspaper league tables.

In spite of this, the National Student Survey can still give you a good idea of what final-year students think, and it's well worth your time and consideration. The main question in the survey is about students' satisfaction with the overall quality of their course, so let's see what they said about their universities.

**Table 5 Overall student satisfaction with the quality of courses at each main UK university**

| Rank | Institution | % of students satisfied with course quality | | | |
|------|-------------|------|------|------|------|
| | | 2008 | 2007 | 2006 | 2005 |
| 1 | University of St Andrews | 93 | 94 | 92 | — |
| 2 | University of Cambridge | 93 | — | — | — |
| 3 | University of Oxford | 92 | 92 | — | — |
| 4 | University of East Anglia | 92 | 89 | 89 | 88 |
| 5 | University of Leicester | 92 | 90 | 89 | 89 |
| 6 | University of Exeter | 91 | 91 | 85 | 86 |
| 7 | University of Aberdeen | 91 | 88 | — | — |
| 8 | Loughborough University | 91 | 89 | 88 | 88 |
| 9 | Aberystwyth University | 90 | 90 | 90 | 87 |
| 10 | University of Kent | 90 | 88 | 86 | 86 |
| 11 | University of Sheffield | 89 | 87 | 84 | 86 |
| 12 | Aston University | 89 | 87 | 84 | 83 |
| 13 | Lancaster University | 89 | 89 | 86 | 89 |
| 14 | University of Hull | 89 | 89 | 88 | 88 |
| 15 | University of Durham | 89 | 87 | 89 | 87 |
| 16 | University of Reading | 89 | 88 | 87 | 86 |
| 17 | University of Portsmouth | 88 | 86 | 79 | 76 |
| 18 | Keele University | 88 | 85 | 85 | 85 |
| 19 | University College London | 88 | 87 | — | 85 |
| 20 | University of Essex | 88 | 83 | 81 | 83 |
| 21 | University of Bath | 88 | 85 | 83 | 85 |
| 22 | University of Warwick | 88 | 85 | — | — |
| 23 | Swansea University | 87 | 88 | 86 | 88 |
| 24 | Cardiff University | 87 | 87 | 85 | 87 |
| 25 | University of Chichester | 87 | 87 | 84 | 80 |
| 26 | University of Southampton | 87 | 88 | 86 | 85 |
| 27 | University of Glasgow | 86 | 87 | 84 | — |
| 28 | University of Winchester | 86 | 82 | 82 | 83 |
| 29 | Queen's University Belfast | 86 | 83 | 84 | 85 |
| 30 | University of York | 86 | 84 | 84 | 86 |
| 31 | Bangor University | 86 | 84 | 86 | 85 |
| 32 | Oxford Brookes University | 86 | 84 | 84 | 83 |
| 33 | University of Sussex | 86 | 78 | 76 | 80 |

*(Continued)*

**Table 5 (Continued)**

| Rank | Institution | % of students satisfied with course quality | | | |
|------|-------------|------|------|------|------|
| 34 | University of Newcastle | **86** | 82 | 81 | 83 |
| 35 | University of Leeds | **86** | 82 | 81 | 81 |
| 36 | University of Stirling | **86** | — | — | — |
| 37 | Glasgow Caledonian University | **85** | 83 | — | — |
| 38 | University of Birmingham | **85** | 84 | — | 84 |
| 39 | University of Worcester | **85** | 85 | 85 | 85 |
| 40 | Imperial College | **85** | 86 | 87 | 81 |
| 41 | University of Dundee | **85** | 89 | — | — |
| 42 | Lampeter (University of Wales) | **85** | 83 | 86 | 83 |
| 43 | School of Oriental and African Studies | **85** | 84 | 80 | 84 |
| 44 | University of Nottingham | **85** | 85 | 85 | 85 |
| 45 | University of Strathclyde | **85** | 86 | — | — |
| 46 | King's College London | **85** | 86 | 87 | 84 |
| 47 | Royal Holloway, University of London | **85** | 84 | — | 88 |
| 48 | Heriot-Watt University | **85** | 86 | — | — |
| 49 | University of West of England, Bristol | **84** | 83 | 78 | 79 |
| 50 | University of Liverpool | **84** | 86 | 85 | 82 |
| 51 | Queen Mary, University of London | **84** | 86 | 83 | 83 |
| 52 | Bath Spa University | **84** | 83 | 79 | 86 |
| 53 | University of Plymouth | **84** | 82 | 81 | 79 |
| 54 | Northumbria University | **83** | 78 | 79 | 80 |
| 55 | University of Bristol | **83** | 83 | 86 | 85 |
| 56 | Canterbury Christ Church University | **83** | 84 | 84 | 81 |
| 57 | University of Sunderland | **83** | 78 | 76 | 74 |
| 58 | University of Teesside | **83** | 79 | 80 | 80 |
| 59 | Edge Hill University | **83** | 82 | 79 | 84 |
| 60 | De Montfort University | **83** | 80 | 70 | 74 |
| 61 | Nottingham Trent University | **83** | 77 | 75 | 78 |
| 62 | University of Northampton | **83** | 80 | 81 | 78 |
| 63 | University of Edinburgh | **83** | 82 | 83 | — |
| 64 | Kingston University | **82** | 79 | 78 | 75 |

**Table 5 (Continued)**

| Rank | Institution | % of students satisfied with course quality | | | |
|------|-------------|------|------|------|------|
| 65 | University of Lincoln | 82 | 77 | 68 | 76 |
| 66 | Goldsmiths College | 82 | 80 | 83 | 82 |
| 67 | University of Surrey | 82 | 82 | 75 | 81 |
| 68 | University College Plymouth | 82 | 87 | 88 | 89 |
| 69 | University of Central Lancashire | 81 | 81 | 78 | 78 |
| 70 | University of Manchester | 81 | 81 | — | 81 |
| 71 | University of Greenwich | 81 | 71 | 70 | 73 |
| 72 | Staffordshire University | 81 | 82 | 79 | 76 |
| 73 | University of Wales Institute, Cardiff | 81 | 76 | 77 | 75 |
| 74 | Liverpool Hope University | 81 | 82 | 78 | 83 |
| 75 | University of Ulster | 81 | 81 | 81 | 82 |
| 76 | Sheffield Hallam University | 81 | 80 | 75 | 77 |
| 77 | University of Brighton | 81 | 77 | 78 | 76 |
| 78 | Bournemouth University | 80 | 76 | 72 | 74 |
| 79 | City University, London | 80 | 79 | 79 | — |
| 80 | University of Chester | 80 | 80 | 84 | 84 |
| 81 | York St John University | 80 | 77 | 74 | 79 |
| 82 | Roehampton University | 80 | 81 | 83 | 80 |
| 83 | University of Bedfordshire | 79 | 77 | 75 | — |
| 84 | University of Salford | 79 | 76 | 76 | 76 |
| 85 | University of Gloucestershire | 79 | 77 | 79 | 81 |
| 86 | Liverpool John Moores University | 79 | 78 | — | 80 |
| 87 | Coventry University | 78 | 81 | 81 | 81 |
| 88 | University of Bradford | 78 | 80 | 82 | 82 |
| 89 | University of Cumbria | 78 | 73 | 72 | 75 |
| 90 | University of Glamorgan | 78 | 81 | 82 | 80 |
| 91 | London School of Economics | 77 | 81 | — | 81 |
| 92 | University of Hertfordshire | 77 | 77 | 77 | 76 |
| 93 | Brunel University | 77 | 75 | 74 | 72 |
| 94 | Swansea Metropolitan University | 77 | 76 | 81 | 76 |
| 95 | University of Bolton | 77 | 81 | 81 | 79 |

*(Continued)*

**Table 5 (Continued)**

| Rank | Institution | % of students satisfied with course quality | | | |
|------|-------------|------|------|------|------|
| 96 | University of Derby | **76** | 74 | 77 | 74 |
| 97 | North East Wales Institute | **76** | 73 | 73 | 70 |
| 98 | University of Wolverhampton | **76** | 75 | 72 | 75 |
| 99 | University of Wales, Newport | **76** | 73 | 78 | 80 |
| 100 | University of Huddersfield | **76** | 75 | 80 | 83 |
| 101 | Middlesex University | **75** | 72 | 72 | 68 |
| 102 | London South Bank University | **75** | 80 | — | — |
| 103 | Manchester Metropolitan University | **75** | 78 | 74 | 76 |
| 104 | Thames Valley University | **75** | 73 | 67 | — |
| 105 | Birmingham City University | **74** | 74 | 76 | 72 |
| 106 | University of Westminster | **73** | 74 | 74 | 74 |
| 107 | University of East London | **73** | 76 | — | — |
| 108 | London Metropolitan University | **72** | 70 | — | 67 |
| 109 | Leeds Metropolitan University | **70** | 68 | 72 | 75 |
| 110 | Buckinghamshire New University | **68** | 68 | 73 | 71 |
| 111 | Southampton Solent University | **68** | 76 | 72 | — |
| 112 | Anglia Ruskin University | **66** | 74 | 75 | 78 |
| 113 | University of the Arts, London | **63** | 64 | — | 63 |

*Source: HEFCE (www.hefce.ac.uk/learning/nss/data/2008/NSS_08.xls)*

**Notes:**
1. Percentages are for respondents who 'definitely' or 'mostly' agreed with question 22 of the National Student Survey, 'Overall, I am satisfied with the quality of my course'.
2. Where a result is not shown, either the institution did not take part in the survey in that year, or their results were below the 50% response rate, or fewer than 23 students responded.
3. Comparisons between years should be made with caution because the profile of the respondents will differ and this has not been adjusted for.
4. Universities that mainly teach part-time students and specialist institutions offering only a narrow range of subjects have been excluded from this list.

If you already have a subject in mind, a low overall student course satisfaction ranking for a whole university should not necessarily put you off. The overall student satisfaction figure can give you a rough guide to the general course quality at any given university, but it really comes into its own when you're comparing specific subjects at different institutions. After all, you don't apply only to the university, you apply for a place on a specific course at that university, so as an

individual applicant this should mean more to you This can be done easily using the Unistats website (www.unistats.com). To help you narrow down your choices even further there are answers to another 21 questions on teaching quality for most subjects at most universities, allowing you to make a range of comparisons and get the wider picture.

While this guide mostly concentrates on full-time courses of undergraduate study at the main UK universities, if you're considering attending an independent or specialist institution then Tables 6 and 7 may be useful to you.

**Table 6 Overall student satisfaction with the quality of courses at top 25 specialist institutions, university colleges, further education colleges and independent universities**

| Rank | Name of Institution | % of students satisfied with course quality | | | |
|------|---------------------|------|------|------|------|
| | | **2008** | 2007 | 2006 | 2005 |
| 1 | North Warwickshire and Hinckley College | **97** | — | — | — |
| 2 | City College, Birmingham | **97** | — | — | — |
| 3 | Uxbridge College | **96** | — | — | — |
| 4 | University of Buckingham | **96** | 93 | 94 | — |
| 5 | Grantham College | **96** | — | — | — |
| 6 | Royal Academy of Music | **94** | 90 | 81 | 95 |
| 7 | Open University | **94** | 95 | 95 | 95 |
| 8 | Courtauld Institute of Art | **93** | 74 | 81 | 100 |
| 9 | Herefordshire College of Technology | **92** | — | | |
| 10 | Birkbeck College | **92** | 92 | 91 | 90 |
| 11 | Bishop Grosseteste University College | **92** | 87 | 89 | 88 |
| 12 | Knowsley Community College | **92** | — | — | — |
| 13 | Central Sussex College | **91** | — | — | — |
| 14 | Harper Adams University College | **90** | 91 | 86 | 90 |
| 15 | St George's Hospital Medical School | **90** | 87 | 80 | 86 |
| 16 | Institute of Education | **90** | 80 | — | 83 |
| 17 | Wyggeston and Queen Elizabeth I College | **90** | — | — | — |
| 18 | Ealing Hammersmith and West London College | **89** | — | — | — |
| 19 | St Mary's University College | **89** | 91 | 89 | 85 |

*(Continued)*

**Table 6 (Continued)**

| Rank | Institution | % of students satisfied with course quality | | | |
|------|-------------|------|------|------|------|
| 20 | Xaverian College | **88** | — | — | — |
| 21 | Heythrop College | **88** | — | — | — |
| 22 | South Nottingham College | **88** | — | — | — |
| 23 | School of Pharmacy | **88** | 86 | 86 | 83 |
| 24 | East Berkshire College | **88** | — | — | — |
| 25 | Trinity St David's (Carmarthen) | **87** | 83 | 78 | 77 |

Source: HEFCE (www.hefce.ac.uk/learning/nss/data/2008/NSS_08.xls)

**Notes:**
1. Percentages are for respondents who 'definitely' or 'mostly' agreed with question 22 of The National Student Survey, 'Overall, I am satisfied with the quality of my course'.
2. Where a result is not shown, either the institution did not take part in the survey in that year, or their results were below the 50% response rate, or fewer than 23 students responded.
3. Comparisons between years should be made with caution because the profile of the respondents will differ and this has not been adjusted for.
4. The main universities offering mostly full-time undergraduate degrees in a wide range of subjects have been excluded from this list.

For completeness, the 15 institutions with the lowest ratings for students' overall course satisfaction are listed in Table 7.

**Table 7 Overall student satisfaction with the quality of courses at bottom 15 specialist institutions, university colleges, further education colleges and independent universities 2008**

| Rank | Institution | % of students satisfied with course quality |
|------|-------------|------|
| 1 | Easton College | 30 |
| 2 | South Kent College | 46 |
| 3 | Milton Keynes College | 52 |
| 4 | Redcar and Cleveland College | 52 |
| 5 | Askham Bryan College | 53 |
| 6 | Pershore Group of Colleges | 54 |
| 7 | Northumberland College | 57 |
| 8 | South Thames College | 59 |
| 9 | South East Essex College of A&T | 60 |
| 10 | Moulton College | 61 |
| 11 | Bicton College of Agriculture | 62 |
| 12 | City and Islington College | 63 |
| 13 | Amersham and Wycombe College | 63 |
| 14 | Weymouth College | 63 |
| 15 | Northampton College | 63 |

Source: HEFCE (www.hefce.ac.uk/learning/nss/data/2008/NSS_08.xls)

## The Quality Assurance Framework (QAF)

You've seen what the students think about academic quality, but what do the education experts have to say? The QAF is designed to secure the quality of teaching and the standard of awards in higher education institutions, to check you're being taught properly and to make sure the university hasn't made it too easy or too difficult to get a degree. It includes:

▶ publication of teaching quality information through the Unistats website (www. unistats.com), which includes the National Student Survey and the Destinations of Leavers from Higher Education survey

▶ institutional audit (all universities receive one every six years).

Institutional audits are carried out by the Quality Assurance Agency (QAA) and are performed by an external team of academics who review the institution's quality and standards. After each audit, the QAA publishes a report on the audit team's findings, which you can find on their website, www.qaa.ac.uk. While it's not possible to create a ranking from their data, if you're seriously considering applying to a particular university then it's probably worth at least reading the summaries contained in the relevant report.

## Entry standards

These are the average UCAS tariff points of first-degree entrants to a subject area, or to a whole university. They don't represent the offers that the university makes to the students, they're what the entrants actually score in their pre-university courses, mainly their A levels or Highers. Some universities attract an intake of students who have already done well academically; others do not.

### How are entry standards useful?

From an individual point of view, they can give you an approximate idea of the academic ability of your peers if you get into a university, or on to a specific course. Think about how you'd feel if you were a student with high grades on a course with lower entry standards. Would you feel challenged enough? If you had lower grades, would you struggle on the course compared to other students, or even stand much chance of being accepted in the first place?

From an employer's point of view, they suggest that the new students as a whole have a certain level of intellect or academic ability – with 'brighter' students being seen as better. It's not something to ignore, but it's not the whole story either. Doing well at A level, or in equivalent exams, does not automatically guarantee that you will do well in your degree studies. The transition to higher education, with less of the educational 'spoon feeding' that you get at school, can affect some students more than others and it's hard to tell who will thrive best in the university environment. In addition, if a degree course is not particularly well taught or supported, it will not bring out the best from its undergraduates. It's best to read university entry standards alongside course satisfaction and teaching standards, and levels of awards that are given at graduation.

Tables 8 and 9 will provide you with a guide to the highest and lowest entry standards at the main UK universities. If you're already thinking about studying a particular subject you can also use the www.unistats.com website to compare average entry standards for particular subjects at different universities. The website shows you the full range of UCAS tariff points scored, and also highlights the most common score.

**Table 8 Top 20 average UCAS tariff scores on entry to university**

| Rank | University | Tariff scores |
|------|-----------|---------------|
| 1 | University of Cambridge | 538.5 |
| 2 | University of Oxford | 523.9 |
| 3 | Imperial College London | 489.4 |
| 4 | London School of Economics | 483.0 |
| 5 | University of St Andrews | 467.9 |
| 6 | University of Warwick | 463.0 |
| 7 | Durham University | 459.0 |
| 8 | University College London | 452.1 |
| 9 | University of Bristol | 447.2 |
| 10 | University of Edinburgh | 447.0 |
| 11 | University of Bath | 440.4 |
| 12 | University of York | 434.0 |
| 13 | King's College London | 414.7 |
| 14 | University of Manchester | 412.5 |
| 15 | University of Glasgow | 412.4 |
| 16 | University of Nottingham | 408.0 |
| 17 | University of Southampton | 406.6 |
| 18 | University of Sheffield | 406.0 |
| 19 | Newcastle University | 405.2 |
| 20 | University of Birmingham | 403.3 |

Source: www.thecompleteuniversityguide.co.uk

**Table 9 Bottom 20 average UCAS tariff scores on entry to university**

| Rank | University | Tariff scores |
|------|-----------|---------------|
| 1 | London South Bank University | 178.6 |
| 2 | University of East London | 191.2 |
| 3 | Middlesex University | 194.3 |
| 4 | Thames Valley University | 196.5 |
| 5 | University of Wolverhampton | 203.6 |
| 6 | Buckinghamshire New University | 210.4 |
| 7 | Southampton Solent University | 211.0 |
| 8 | University of Greenwich | 211.7 |
| 9 | Glyndŵr University | 212.3 |
| 10 | University of Bolton | 213.3 |
| 11 | University of Bedfordshire | 215.1 |
| 12 | University of Sunderland | 225.9 |
| 13 | University of Wales Newport | 228.6 |
| 14 | University of Derby | 231.4 |
| 15 | Staffordshire University | 231.7 |
| 16 | University of Northampton | 233.2 |
| 17 | University of Chichester | 233.5 |
| 18 | University of Worcester | 235.7 |
| 19 | Kingston University | 236.2 |
| 20 | Canterbury Christ Church University | 237.8 |

Source: www.thecompleteuniversityguide.co.uk

## Student to staff ratios

At first glance, having fewer students per member of staff can look very appealing. It might suggest that you'll get more individual academic attention when you're studying, or that members of staff will perhaps be less overworked. Low student to staff ratios do roughly correlate with other positive academic indicators, but they're certainly not something that should be considered an exact science.

For example, it's no guarantee that the staff will be well motivated or better at teaching simply because there are rather a lot of them in one university or department. Neither is there any guarantee that they'll be more available to help if you have difficulties with your studies. At the other end of the spectrum, there may well be some staff who are overworked or demoralised in places where the student to staff ratios are especially high, and low staffing levels can be part of a wider pattern of under-funding or other problems within a university. With this in mind, it's worth looking briefly at the universities that have the most and the fewest students per member of staff.

**Table 10 Top 34 universities for student:staff ratios**

| Rank | University | Student:staff ratio |
|------|------------|---------------------|
| 1 | University College London | 9 |
| 2 | Imperial College London | 10 |
| 3 | SOAS | 11 |
| =4 | University of Oxford | 12 |
| =4 | University of Cambridge | 12 |
| =4 | King's College London | 12 |
| =7 | London School of Economics | 13 |
| =7 | University of St Andrews | 13 |
| =7 | University of Edinburgh | 13 |
| =7 | University of York | 13 |
| =7 | University of Lancaster | 13 |
| =7 | University of Glasgow | 13 |
| =7 | University of Manchester | 13 |
| =7 | University of Liverpool | 13 |
| =7 | Queen Mary, University of London | 13 |
| =16 | University of Warwick | 14 |
| =16 | University of Dundee | 14 |
| =16 | University of Nottingham | 14 |
| =16 | University of Aberdeen | 14 |
| =16 | Cardiff University | 14 |
| =16 | University of Essex | 14 |
| =22 | University of Leicester | 15 |
| =22 | Durham University | 15 |
| =22 | University of Leeds | 15 |
| =22 | University of Birmingham | 15 |
| =22 | University of Bristol | 15 |
| =22 | University of Stirling | 15 |
| =22 | University of Sussex | 15 |
| =22 | Royal Holloway, University of London | 15 |
| =22 | University of Sheffield | 15 |
| =22 | Newcastle University | 15 |
| =22 | Queen's University Belfast | 15 |
| =22 | University of Bradford | 15 |
| =22 | Swansea University | 15 |

Source: The Guardian University Guide 2009

**Table 11 Bottom 20 universities for student:staff ratios**

| Rank | University | Student:staff ratio |
|---|---|---|
| =1 | Lampeter (University of Wales) | 25 |
| =1 | London South Bank University | 25 |
| =3 | Leeds Metropolitan University | 24 |
| =3 | University of Lincoln | 24 |
| =5 | Leeds Trinity and All Saints | 23 |
| =5 | University of Greenwich | 23 |
| =7 | St Mary's University College, Twickenham | 22 |
| =7 | Marjon (St Mark and St John) | 22 |
| =7 | Edge Hill University | 22 |
| =7 | York St John University | 22 |
| =7 | Middlesex University | 22 |
| =12 | University of the Arts, London | 21 |
| =12 | Northumbria University, Newcastle | 21 |
| =12 | Thames Valley University | 21 |
| =12 | University of Bedfordshire | 21 |
| =12 | Swansea Metropolitan University | 21 |
| =12 | Roehampton University | 21 |
| =12 | Southampton Solent University | 21 |
| =12 | University of East London | 21 |
| =12 | University of Bolton | 21 |

Source: The Guardian University Guide 2009

# University academic spending – library and IT

Libraries and information technology form a major part of academic services spending, and these services can absolutely make or break your studies. The availability of books, journals, study places, hardware and software will certainly impact upon you if they are lacking, but if the resources are allocated generously and wisely then they can significantly enhance your learning experience.

**Table 12 Highest library and IT spending per student**

| Rank | University | £ per student |
|------|-----------|---------------|
| 1 | University of Cambridge | 385 |
| 2 | Imperial College London | 317 |
| Top 3 | University of Oxford[1] | Exact figure unknown |
| 4 | University College London | 259 |
| 5 | London School of Economics | 251 |
| 6 | University of Liverpool | 244 |
| 7 | University of Glasgow | 221 |
| 8 | University of St Andrews | 208 |
| 9 | University of Manchester[2] | 199 |
| =10 | University of Leicester | 197 |
| =10 | University of York | 197 |
| 12 | Newcastle University | 194 |
| 13 | SOAS | 191 |
| 14 | King's College London | 190 |
| 15 | University of Leeds | 189 |
| 16 | University of Warwick | 181 |
| 17 | University of Bristol | 180 |
| =18 | Aberdeen University | 178 |
| =18 | University of Edinburgh | 178 |
| 20 | University of Sussex | 177 |
| =21 | University of Surrey | 176 |
| =21 | University of Wales Swansea | 176 |
| 23 | Durham University | 168 |
| 24 | Cardiff University | 164 |
| =25 | University of Bath[2] | 161 |
| =25 | Queen's University Belfast | 161 |
| 27 | University of Nottingham | 159 |
| 28 | University of Birmingham | 149 |
| =29 | Aberystwyth University | 147 |
| =29 | Lancaster University | 147 |

*Source: Guide to UK Universities 2010/SCONUL*

**Notes:**
1. The University of Oxford has a unique way of presenting the finances of its colleges, and it is not directly comparable with the other data.
2. The universities of Manchester and Bath both house national computing facilities, which may partly skew the results in their favour. The same goes for universities with libraries that operate at national level.

**Table 13 Lowest library and IT spending per student**

| Rank | University | £ per student |
|------|------------|---------------|
| 1 | Glyndŵr University | 45 |
| 2 | Thames Valley University | 46 |
| =3 | Arts London | 49 |
| =3 | University of Wales Newport | 49 |
| 5 | Bath Spa University | 53 |
| 6 | Middlesex University | 54 |
| 7 | University of Worcester | 57 |
| =8 | Canterbury CC University | 59 |
| =8 | Leeds Metropolitan University | 59 |
| 10 | University for Creative Arts | 60 |
| 11 | Birmingham City University | 61 |
| =12 | University of Greenwich | 62 |
| =12 | Lampeter (University of Wales) | 62 |
| 14 | Goldsmiths, London | 65 |
| 15 | University of Plymouth | 67 |
| =16 | Bedfordshire University | 68 |
| =16 | University of East London | 68 |
| =16 | University of Northampton | 68 |
| =19 | University of Chester | 70 |
| =19 | University of Central Lancashire | 70 |

*Source: Guide to UK Universities 2010/SCONUL*

**?** Did you know?

*Many television presenters have scientific academic backgrounds. David Attenborough studied natural sciences at Clare College, Cambridge, David Bellamy trained as a botanist at Durham University, and Chris Packham studied biological sciences at the University of Southampton.*

## Continuation rates

On average, around 14% of students drop out of their courses without finishing them, and there are different ways of measuring drop-out rates. The 'continuation rate' is a measure of student retention. It is the proportion of an institution's intake that is still enrolled in higher education in the second year of their course, i.e. the percentage who continue at university after their first year. The reasons for non-continuation are complex, and there's rarely one single factor involved. Reasons given are likely to be a mix of personal, institution and course related, and financial. The most commonly cited reason is that 'the course is not what I expected/wanted', but there are many others, for example:

*Personal:*

▶ homesickness
▶ lack of self-management skills for independent living
▶ lack of integration/social aspirations not being met
▶ taking up a more attractive opportunity
▶ lack of commitment to the course
▶ general lack of preparedness.

*Academic/institution:*

▶ dissatisfaction with course/institution
▶ lack of self-management skills for independent study
▶ poor academic progress
▶ finding the course content too difficult
▶ locality was not what was required.

*Financial:*

▶ change in personal/family circumstances
▶ expected money does not arrive
▶ unrealistic expectations for living expenses
▶ lack of money management skills.

There are great differences between universities in the rate at which students continue to a second year of study, as you'll be able to see from Table 14. As non-continuation is so complex, the exact reasons for this are hard to pinpoint. Some universities have populations of students that contain fewer of the vulnerable groups (mature students, students from lower socio-economic backgrounds) and more of the least-vulnerable groups (students with very high entry standards), thus keeping their non-continuation rates low. Many universities also have a raft of measures in place to stop students from dropping out, such as welfare and support provision for students who are experiencing emotional or financial difficulties, and help with life skills, study skills or changing courses.

**Table 14 Non-continuation rates among first-year undergraduates**

| Rank | University | Non-continuation rate: % of students |
|---|---|---|
| =1 | University of Cambridge | 1 |
| =1 | University of Oxford | 1 |
| 3 | University of St Andrews | 2 |
| =4 | University of Bath | 3 |
| =4 | Durham University | 3 |
| =4 | Imperial College London | 3 |
| =4 | University of Nottingham | 3 |
| =4 | University of Sheffield | 3 |
| =9 | University of the Arts, London | 4 |
| =9 | Aston University | 4 |
| =9 | University of Bristol | 4 |
| =9 | University of Exeter | 4 |
| =9 | Loughborough University | 4 |
| =9 | Newcastle University | 4 |
| =9 | University of Southampton | 4 |
| =9 | University of Warwick | 4 |
| =9 | University of York | 4 |
| =18 | University of Birmingham | 5 |
| =18 | Cardiff University | 5 |
| =18 | University of Chichester | 5 |
| =18 | University of Edinburgh | 5 |
| =18 | King's College London | 5 |
| =18 | University of Lancaster | 5 |
| =18 | University of Liverpool | 5 |
| =18 | London School of Economics | 5 |
| =18 | University of Manchester | 5 |
| =18 | University of Reading | 5 |
| =18 | Royal Holloway, University of London | 5 |
| =18 | University College London | 5 |
| =30 | Aberystwyth University | 6 |
| =30 | Bath Spa University | 6 |
| =30 | University of Hull | 6 |

*(Continued)*

37

**Table 14 (Continued)**

| Rank | University | Non-continuation rate: % of students |
|---|---|---|
| =30 | University of Leeds | 6 |
| =30 | University of Leicester | 6 |
| =30 | University of Sunderland | 6 |
| =36 | Bournemouth University | 7 |
| =36 | University of East Anglia | 7 |
| =36 | University of Glasgow | 7 |
| =36 | University of Gloucestershire | 7 |
| =36 | University of Greenwich | 7 |
| =36 | University of Kent | 7 |
| =36 | University of Lincoln | 7 |
| =36 | Nottingham Trent University | 7 |
| =36 | University of Portsmouth | 7 |
| =36 | University of Stirling | 7 |
| =36 | University of Surrey | 7 |
| =36 | Swansea University | 7 |
| =48 | University of Abertay Dundee | 8 |
| =48 | Bangor University | 8 |
| =48 | University of Brighton | 8 |
| =48 | University of Essex | 8 |
| =48 | University of Plymouth | 8 |
| =48 | Queen's University Belfast | 8 |
| =48 | Sheffield Hallam University | 8 |
| =48 | SOAS | 8 |
| =48 | University of Sussex | 8 |
| =48 | York St John University | 8 |
| =58 | University of the West of England, Bristol | 9 |
| =58 | Brunel University | 9 |
| =58 | Goldsmiths College | 9 |
| =58 | Heriot-Watt University | 9 |
| =58 | University of Hertfordshire | 9 |
| =58 | Keele University | 9 |
| =58 | Kingston University | 9 |
| =58 | Lampeter (University of Wales) | 9 |
| =58 | Leeds Metropolitan University | 9 |

**Table 14 (Continued)**

| Rank | University | Non-continuation rate: % of students |
|---|---|---|
| =58 | Northumbria University, Newcastle | 9 |
| =58 | Oxford Brookes University | 9 |
| =58 | Queen Mary, University of London | 9 |
| =58 | Robert Gordon University | 9 |
| =58 | University of Winchester | 9 |
| =72 | University of Aberdeen | 10 |
| =72 | Buckinghamshire New University | 10 |
| =72 | Canterbury Christ Church University | 10 |
| =72 | University for the Creative Arts | 10 |
| =72 | University of Cumbria | 10 |
| =72 | De Montfort University | 10 |
| =72 | University of Dundee | 10 |
| =72 | University of Huddersfield | 10 |
| =72 | University of Worcester | 10 |
| =81 | University of Bradford | 11 |
| =81 | University of Chester | 11 |
| =81 | City University | 11 |
| =81 | Coventry University | 11 |
| =81 | Liverpool John Moores University | 11 |
| =81 | Manchester Metropolitan University | 11 |
| =81 | Staffordshire University | 11 |
| =81 | University of Strathclyde | 11 |
| =81 | University of Teesside | 11 |
| =90 | Anglia Ruskin University | 12 |
| =90 | Birmingham City University | 12 |
| =90 | Liverpool Hope University | 12 |
| =90 | University of Wales, Newport | 12 |
| =90 | University of Northampton | 12 |
| =90 | University of Wales Institute, Cardiff | 12 |
| =90 | University of Wolverhampton | 12 |
| =97 | University of Bedfordshire | 13 |
| =97 | University of East London | 13 |
| =97 | Edge Hill University | 13 |

*(Continued)*

**Table 14 (Continued)**

| Rank | University | Non-continuation rate: % of students |
|---|---|---|
| =97 | Glasgow Caledonian University | 13 |
| =97 | London South Bank University | 13 |
| =97 | Middlesex University | 13 |
| =97 | Roehampton University | 13 |
| =97 | Southampton Solent University | 13 |
| =97 | University of Westminster | 13 |
| =106 | University of Derby | 14 |
| =106 | London Metropolitan University | 14 |
| =106 | Queen Margaret University, Edinburgh | 14 |
| =106 | University of Salford | 14 |
| =106 | Swansea Metropolitan University | 14 |
| =106 | University of Central Lancashire | 14 |
| =112 | Thames Valley University | 15 |
| =112 | University of Ulster | 15 |
| 114 | Glyndŵr University | 16 |
| 115 | West of Scotland University | 17 |
| =116 | University of Glamorgan | 18 |
| =116 | Edinburgh Napier University | 18 |
| 118 | University of Bolton | 22 |

Source: Guide to UK Universities 2010 by Klaus Boehm and Jenny Lees-Spalding

## Good honours – percentage of firsts and upper seconds

Of the students who obtained a classified degree in the academic year 2007–2008, 61% were awarded 'good' honours, i.e. they were awarded either Firsts or Upper Second Class Honours. First Class Honours made up only 13% of the total of all classified degrees. In an increasingly depressed and competitive labour market, a good honours degree can really help a graduate's employment prospects, and a good degree is a sound investment of time, effort and cold, hard cash.

Many universities have a higher than average proportion of students gaining good honours, and you may well find this attractive. Of course, this is mainly a mixture of two things: first, it could genuinely be a sign of fantastic teaching and academic support; second, it could simply represent the fact that the university has a higher than average intake of super-bright and hard-working students. There are various external and internal checks and balances in place to make sure that universities aren't just making their marking schemes too easy.

**Table 15 Top 30 universities for students awarded high honours 2008**

| Rank | University | Total % of students awarded firsts and upper seconds | % of students awarded firsts | % of students awarded upper seconds |
|------|-----------|------|------|------|
| 1 | University of Oxford | 84.3 | 25.4 | 58.9 |
| 2 | University of St Andrews | 78.5 | 19.1 | 59.4 |
| 3 | University of Sussex | 78.0 | 16.5 | 61.6 |
| 4 | University of Durham | 77.5 | 17.7 | 59.9 |
| 5 | University of Exeter | 77.3 | 19.2 | 58.0 |
| 6 | University of Warwick | 76.0 | 22.1 | 53.9 |
| 7 | London School of Economics | 75.6 | 21.9 | 53.7 |
| 8 | University of Reading | 75.6 | 17.7 | 57.8 |
| 9 | University of Bath | 73.7 | 23.2 | 50.5 |
| 10 | SOAS | 73.6 | 14.0 | 59.5 |
| 11 | University of Cambridge | 72.5 | 20.8 | 51.7 |
| 12 | University of Bristol | 72.4 | 18.1 | 54.3 |
| 13 | University of York | 72.1 | 21.2 | 50.9 |
| 14 | University College London | 70.7 | 21.0 | 49.7 |
| 15 | University of Lancaster | 69.6 | 14.0 | 55.6 |
| 16 | University of Sheffield | 69.3 | 13.6 | 55.8 |
| 17 | University of Nottingham | 69.2 | 15.5 | 53.7 |
| 18 | University of Leeds | 68.8 | 14.8 | 54.1 |
| 19 | Loughborough University | 67.6 | 14.8 | 52.7 |
| 20 | Bath Spa University | 67.4 | 10.1 | 57.3 |
| 21 | University of East Anglia | 67.0 | 12.3 | 54.7 |
| 22 | University of Edinburgh | 66.2 | 18.2 | 48.0 |
| 23 | Goldsmiths College | 65.0 | 11.9 | 53.1 |
| 24 | University of Manchester | 64.8 | 14.1 | 50.6 |
| 25 | University of Newcastle | 64.7 | 13.1 | 51.6 |
| 26 | Brunel University | 64.6 | 13.0 | 51.6 |
| 27 | University of Surrey | 64.4 | 16.7 | 47.7 |
| 28 | Queen's University Belfast | 64.1 | 15.2 | 48.9 |
| 29 | University of Birmingham | 63.4 | 13.6 | 49.8 |
| 30 | University of London | 63.2 | 16.5 | 46.8 |

*Source: HESA, Students in Higher Education 2007/2008*

**Table 16 Bottom 15 universities for students awarded high honours 2008**

| Rank | University | Total % of students awarded firsts and upper seconds | % of students awarded firsts | % of students awarded upper seconds |
|------|------------|---------------------------|---------------------|---------------------|
| 1 | University of West of Scotland | 13.6 | 2.3 | 11.3 |
| 2 | University of Abertay Dundee | 30.2 | 5.0 | 25.2 |
| 3 | Edinburgh Napier University | 30.3 | 7.3 | 23.0 |
| 4 | Robert Gordon University | 34.2 | 9.4 | 24.8 |
| 5 | University of Dundee | 37.1 | 9.7 | 27.3 |
| 6 | Glasgow Caledonian University | 38.2 | 7.5 | 30.7 |
| 7 | Queen Margaret University, Edinburgh | 38.8 | 9.9 | 28.9 |
| 8 | University of Stirling | 39.6 | 6.0 | 33.6 |
| 9 | University of Bradford | 42.5 | 9.3 | 33.2 |
| 10 | University of Greenwich | 44.2 | 10.1 | 34.1 |
| 11 | University of East London | 44.3 | 9.0 | 35.3 |
| 12 | University of Hertfordshire | 44.4 | 9.4 | 35.0 |
| 13 | Heriot-Watt University | 44.5 | 10.7 | 33.8 |
| 14 | University of Wolverhampton | 44.7 | 5.2 | 39.5 |
| 15 | Liverpool John Moores University | 45.3 | 7.6 | 37.8 |

Source: HESA, Students in Higher Education 2007/2008

## Graduate prospects

Once you have been awarded your degree, you'll almost certainly be hoping that it will help you to get ahead in your chosen career after graduating. All the main university league tables look at graduate prospects, usually based on the numbers of students from each university who go on to graduate jobs (rather than general jobs) or who begin a course of postgraduate study. These prospects, including graduate salaries, are discussed in Chapter 6.

## Research standards – the Research Assessment Exercise (RAE)

University guides aimed at potential undergraduates often discuss research standards, although this information may be more relevant to students who are considering taking a postgraduate qualification. World-class research can bring an element of prestige and extra financial support with it, and some of this may well trickle down to infuse the undergraduate courses; but world-class research doesn't necessarily translate into excellent course design, and world-class researchers don't automatically make the best teachers. In addition, you might be interested in the kind of course that does not have academic research at its heart. If research quality does interest you, you'll probably want to look at the outcomes of the Research Assessment Exercise.

The Research Assessment Exercise (RAE) is carried out every few years on behalf of the UK higher education funding councils to evaluate the quality of research undertaken by British higher education institutions. The last RAE was carried out in 2008, and returned a profile, rather than a single quality score, for each unit. It used a four-point quality scale, as follows:

▶ 4* – quality that is world leading in terms of originality, significance and rigour
▶ 3* – quality that is internationally excellent in terms of originality, significance and rigour but which nonetheless falls short of the highest standards of excellence
▶ 2* – quality that is recognised internationally in terms of originality, significance and rigour
▶ 1* – quality that is recognised nationally in terms of originality, significance and rigour
▶ unclassified – quality that falls below the standard of nationally recognised work.

Various publications have used different methodologies to produce league tables of institutions based on the 2008 RAE results. While the RAE has produced its own subject-level overview reports, the information that was collected is not actually designed to be used at institution level to create research ratings for entire universities. As you're going to be applying for a course in a particular subject area, you're better off looking at the RAE data as it stands. All the 2008 results can be viewed online at http://submissions.rae.ac.uk/results/.

## *Which Uni?*'s academic 'league tables' – just for fun

Which universities made it into the 'top 20' lists the most times for the variables above? As a reminder, that list includes:

▶ overall student satisfaction with course
▶ average UCAS tariff points gained before entry to the first year
▶ student to staff ratio
▶ spending on library and IT
▶ continuation rates
▶ good honours awards.

This is just for fun and general interest: it's not based upon any scientific principles, so don't make any important decisions based solely upon Table 17.

**Table 17 Universities with the most 'top 20' mentions**

| Rank | University | Mentions in the 'top 20' tables in this section |
|------|-----------|:---:|
| =1 | University of Cambridge | 6 |
| =1 | University of Oxford | 6 |
| =1 | University of St Andrews | 6 |
| =1 | University College London | 6 |
| =5 | London School of Economics | 5 |
| =5 | University of Warwick | 5 |
| =5 | University of York | 5 |
| =8 | University of Bristol | 4 |
| =8 | Durham University | 4 |
| =8 | University of Edinburgh | 4 |
| =8 | Imperial College London | 4 |
| =8 | King's College London | 4 |
| =8 | Lancaster University | 4 |
| =8 | University of Manchester | 4 |
| =8 | University of Nottingham | 4 |
| =8 | University of Sheffield | 4 |
| =17 | University of Aberdeen | 3 |
| =17 | University of Bath | 3 |
| =17 | University of Exeter | 3 |
| =17 | University of Glasgow | 3 |
| =17 | University of Liverpool | 3 |
| =17 | Loughborough University | 3 |
| =17 | Newcastle University | 3 |
| =17 | University of Reading | 3 |
| =17 | SOAS | 3 |
| =26 | Aston University | 2 |
| =26 | Cardiff University | 2 |
| =26 | University of Essex | 2 |
| =26 | University of Leeds | 2 |
| =26 | University of Leicester | 2 |
| =26 | University of Southampton | 2 |
| =26 | University of Sussex | 2 |

*Source: Compiled from previous results in this chapter*

**Note:** Do not use this table to make any important decisions.

While we're playing around with the results tables, it's interesting to see which universities have turned up most frequently in the 'bottom 15' in the tables. Again, this is just for fun: don't take it too seriously, as it hasn't been arranged around a scientific model for analysis.

**Table 18 Universities with the most 'bottom 15' mentions**

| Rank | University | Mentions in the 'bottom 15' tables in this section |
|------|------------|---------------------------------------------------|
| =1 | University of East London | 5 |
| =1 | Middlesex University | 5 |
| =1 | Thames Valley University | 5 |
| =4 | London South Bank | 4 |
| =4 | University of Greenwich | 4 |
| =4 | Southampton Solent University | 4 |
| =7 | Arts London | 3 |
| =7 | Bolton University | 3 |
| =7 | Glyndŵr University | 3 |
| =7 | Leeds Metropolitan University | 3 |
| =7 | University of Wales Newport | 3 |
| =12 | Bedfordshire University | 2 |
| =12 | Birmingham City University | 2 |
| =12 | Bucks New University | 2 |
| =12 | University of Derby | 2 |
| =12 | Edge Hill University | 2 |
| =12 | Glasgow Caledonian University | 2 |
| =12 | Lampeter (University of Wales) | 2 |
| =12 | London Metropolitan | 2 |
| =12 | Edinburgh Napier University | 2 |
| =12 | Queen Margaret University | 2 |
| =12 | Roehampton University | 2 |
| =12 | Swansea Metropolitan | 2 |
| =12 | University of West of Scotland | 2 |
| =12 | University of Westminster | 2 |
| =12 | University of Wolverhampton | 2 |

*Source: Compiled from previous results in this chapter*

**Note:** Do not use this table to make any important decisions.

# Cracking courses

From an academic point of view, it's best to spend a lot more time looking at possible subjects and courses than at overall university profiles. As we've already seen, lack of research into course style and content can put you in the wrong place on the wrong course with an increased risk of dropping out. Get it right and you'll be on a course you really enjoy and you're more likely to be successful in your studies.

## Tracking down a cracking course

Many publications and people have their own distinct idea of what the 'best' courses are at different universities. 'Best' could mean almost anything: courses that have high teaching standards, lots of resources, high graduate employment, an intake of bright students with high grades, an output of graduates with top-class degrees, etc. While all these indications can indeed point to a course that many students will aspire to study, they don't on their own tell you much about how a particular course will suit you as an individual. You'll still have to look carefully into the following:

▶ the exact course content and format

▶ teaching style

▶ department location

▶ general university environment.

As there's no national curriculum for degrees, the content and format of courses with the same or similar names can vary wildly from one institution to another. This information is impossible to rank because there is so much variation, so you'll have to scour prospectuses, course guides and departmental websites to work out what you might be letting yourself in for, and whether you'll like it or not. This research should also give you a better idea of the teaching style and department location. As for the general university environment, use some of the many resources from Chapter 1 of this book, and try to get along to an open day to see for yourself.

## Top subjects/courses in ranking guides

Looking at different courses at the subject level can be quite an eye opener. You'll soon notice that many of the universities that rarely top the general lists and rankings tables still have some internationally recognised star subjects, often in specialised fields. For example, drama schools and separate medical schools tend to be left out of university tables as they're so narrow in terms of subjects taught and intake, but they often excel when it comes to course standards.

The next section lists the top 10 universities teaching each subject, according to *The Guardian University Guide 2009*. Each league table has its own way of deciding which course is the best, and the *Guardian* starts by grouping certain subjects together. The variables they then consider are:

► student satisfaction with teaching

► student satisfaction with assessment

► spend per student

► student to staff ratio

► job prospects

► average entry tariff.

The *Guardian* also includes its own 'value added' rating, which equates roughly to how well university courses help students to improve themselves though study. For example, if the average student on a course enters with a relatively low UCAS entry tariff and leaves with a first or a 2.i, the course will be given a higher 'value added' score.

This is a subjective ranking based upon what the *Guardian* thinks is most important – and you may disagree with its opinions – but it's interesting to see which courses they rate highly. Just remember that you need to carry out your own research as well, in line with your specific needs and preferences.

**Table 19 The *Guardian*'s top 10 universities teaching each subject**
**Agriculture and Forestry**

| Ranking | *Guardian* choice | Ranking | *Guardian* choice |
|---------|-------------------|---------|-------------------|
| 1 | Reading | 6 | Newcastle |
| 2 | Nottingham | 7 | Royal Agricultural College |
| 3 | Central Lancashire | 8 | Aberystwyth |
| 4 | Queen's University Belfast | 9 | Lincoln |
| 5 | Harper Adams UC | 10 | Nottingham Trent |

**Anatomy and Physiology**

| Ranking | *Guardian* choice | Ranking | *Guardian* choice |
|---------|-------------------|---------|-------------------|
| 1 | Oxford | 6 | UCL |
| 2 | Cardiff | 7 | Manchester |
| 3 | Liverpool | 8 | Queen's University Belfast |
| 4 | Plymouth | 9 | Bristol |
| 5 | Aston | 10 | Bradford |

*(Continued)*

## Anthropology

| Ranking | Guardian choice | Ranking | Guardian choice |
|---|---|---|---|
| 1 | Oxford | 6 | Kent |
| 2 | UCL | 7 | Edinburgh |
| 3 | LSE | 8 | St Andrews |
| 4 | SOAS | 9 | Queen's University Belfast |
| 5 | Cambridge | 10 | Nottingham Trent |

## Archaeology

| Ranking | Guardian choice | Ranking | Guardian choice |
|---|---|---|---|
| 1 | UCL | 6 | York |
| 2 | Cambridge | 7 | Queen's University Belfast |
| 3 | Oxford | 8 | Reading |
| 4 | Durham | 9 | Leicester |
| 5 | Glasgow | 10 | Southampton |

## Architecture

| Ranking | Guardian choice | Ranking | Guardian choice |
|---|---|---|---|
| 1 | Cambridge | 6 | Nottingham |
| 2 | UCL | 7 | Edinburgh |
| 3 | Cardiff | 8 | Liverpool |
| 4 | Bath | 9 | Manchester School of Architecture |
| 5 | Newcastle | 10 | Sheffield |

## Art and Design

| Ranking | Guardian choice | Ranking | Guardian choice |
|---|---|---|---|
| 1 | UCL | 6 | Loughborough |
| 2 | Brunel | 7 | Newcastle |
| 3 | Dartington College | 8 | Plymouth |
| 4 | York | 9 | Lancaster |
| 5 | Edinburgh | 10 | Goldsmiths |

## Biosciences

| Ranking | Guardian choice | Ranking | Guardian choice |
|---|---|---|---|
| 1 | Cambridge | 6 | Surrey |
| 2 | Oxford | 7 | St Andrews |
| 3 | Leicester | 8 | Bristol |
| 4 | Imperial College | 9 | Ulster |
| 5 | York | 10 | Warwick |

## Building and Town and Country Planning

| Ranking | *Guardian* choice | Ranking | *Guardian* choice |
|---|---|---|---|
| 1 | UCL | 6 | Glasgow Caledonian |
| 2 | Loughborough | 7 | Liverpool |
| 3 | Salford | 8 | Reading |
| 4 | Cardiff | 9 | Nottingham |
| 5 | Gloucestershire | 10 | Dundee |

## Business and Management Studies

| Ranking | *Guardian* choice | Ranking | *Guardian* choice |
|---|---|---|---|
| 1 | Oxford | 6 | Strathclyde |
| 2 | Warwick | 7 | St Andrews |
| 3 | City University | 8 | Bath |
| 4 | Exeter | 9 | Manchester |
| 5 | Lancaster | 10 | Glasgow |

## Chemical Engineering

| Ranking | *Guardian* choice | Ranking | *Guardian* choice |
|---|---|---|---|
| 1 | Cambridge | 6 | Birmingham |
| 2 | Newcastle | 7 | Nottingham |
| 3 | Manchester | 8 | Leeds |
| 4 | Imperial College | 9 | Loughborough |
| 5 | Edinburgh | 10 | Sheffield |

## Chemistry

| Ranking | *Guardian* choice | Ranking | *Guardian* choice |
|---|---|---|---|
| 1 | St Andrews | 6 | Liverpool |
| 2 | Imperial College | 7 | Queen's University Belfast |
| 3 | Oxford | 8 | Sheffield |
| 4 | Sussex | 9 | Southampton |
| 5 | York | 10 | Warwick |

## Civil Engineering

| Ranking | *Guardian* choice | Ranking | *Guardian* choice |
|---|---|---|---|
| 1 | Imperial College | 6 | Edinburgh |
| 2 | Manchester | 7 | Bristol |
| 3 | Dundee | 8 | Loughborough |
| 4 | Sheffield | 9 | Queen's University Belfast |
| 5 | Nottingham | 10 | Southampton |

*(Continued)*

### Classics

| Ranking | Guardian choice | Ranking | Guardian choice |
|---|---|---|---|
| 1 | Oxford | 6 | UCL |
| 2 | Cambridge | 7 | Durham |
| 3 | Warwick | 8 | Bristol |
| 4 | St Andrews | =9 | Exeter |
| 5 | Edinburgh | =9 | King's College London |

### Computer Sciences and IT

| Ranking | Guardian choice | Ranking | Guardian choice |
|---|---|---|---|
| 1 | Oxford | 6 | Cambridge |
| 2 | Imperial College | 7 | Glasgow |
| 3 | Southampton | 8 | Lancaster |
| 4 | Edinburgh | 9 | Sheffield |
| 5 | York | 10 | Newcastle |

### Dentistry

| Ranking | Guardian choice | Ranking | Guardian choice |
|---|---|---|---|
| 1 | Dundee | 6 | Glasgow |
| 2 | Leeds | 7 | King's College London |
| 3 | Queen's University Belfast | 8 | Manchester |
| 4 | Sheffield | 9 | Newcastle |
| 5 | Cardiff | 10 | Birmingham |

### Drama and Dance

| Ranking | Guardian choice | Ranking | Guardian choice |
|---|---|---|---|
| 1 | Liverpool Institute for Performing Arts | =5 | Birmingham City |
| 2 | Conservatoire for Dance and Drama | 7 | Rose Bruford College |
| 3 | Warwick | 8 | UEA |
| 4 | Trinity Laban | 9 | Loughborough |
| =5 | Bristol | 10 | Royal Holloway |

### Earth and Marine Sciences

| Ranking | Guardian choice | Ranking | Guardian choice |
|---|---|---|---|
| 1 | UCL | 6 | UEA |
| 2 | Liverpool | 7 | York |
| 3 | Manchester | 8 | Leicester |
| 4 | Royal Holloway | 9 | Edinburgh |
| 5 | Imperial College | 10 | Leeds |

**Economics**

| Ranking | *Guardian* choice | Ranking | *Guardian* choice |
|---|---|---|---|
| 1 | Oxford | 6 | UCL |
| 2 | Cambridge | 7 | Durham |
| 3 | LSE | 8 | St Andrews |
| 4 | Birmingham | 9 | Lancaster |
| 5 | Warwick | 10 | SOAS |

**Educational studies**

| Ranking | *Guardian* choice | Ranking | *Guardian* choice |
|---|---|---|---|
| 1 | Cambridge | 6 | Edinburgh |
| 2 | Warwick | 7 | Exeter |
| 3 | Aberdeen | 8 | St Mary's UC, Belfast |
| 4 | Kingston | 9 | Reading |
| 5 | Dundee | 10 | Stirling |

**Electrical and Electronic Engineering**

| Ranking | *Guardian* choice | Ranking | *Guardian* choice |
|---|---|---|---|
| 1 | Imperial College | 6 | Manchester |
| 2 | Edinburgh | 7 | Birmingham |
| 3 | Glasgow | 8 | Essex |
| 4 | Leeds | 9 | UCL |
| 5 | Queen's University Belfast | 10 | Sheffield |

**English**

| Ranking | *Guardian* choice | Ranking | *Guardian* choice |
|---|---|---|---|
| 1 | Oxford | 6 | Durham |
| 2 | Cambridge | 7 | Dundee |
| 3 | UCL | 8 | Queen Mary |
| 4 | Warwick | 9 | Exeter |
| 5 | St Andrews | 10 | Edinburgh |

**General Engineering**

| Ranking | *Guardian* choice | Ranking | *Guardian* choice |
|---|---|---|---|
| 1 | Cambridge | 6 | Brunel |
| 2 | Imperial College | 7 | Warwick |
| 3 | Oxford | 8 | Hull |
| 4 | Leicester | 9 | Exeter |
| 5 | Bournemouth | 10 | Durham |

*(Continued)*

**Geography and Environmental Sciences**

| Ranking | *Guardian* choice | Ranking | *Guardian* choice |
|---|---|---|---|
| 1 | Cambridge | 6 | Durham |
| 2 | Oxford | 7 | Royal Holloway |
| 3 | Edinburgh | 8 | UEA |
| 4 | Bristol | 9 | Leicester |
| 5 | UCL | 10 | St Andrews |

**History and History of Art**

| Ranking | *Guardian* choice | Ranking | *Guardian* choice |
|---|---|---|---|
| 1 | Oxford | 6 | Durham |
| 2 | Courtauld Institute | 7 | UCL |
| 3 | Cambridge | 8 | St Andrews |
| 4 | King's College London | 9 | LSE |
| 5 | Warwick | 10 | Queen Mary |

**Law**

| Ranking | *Guardian* choice | Ranking | *Guardian* choice |
|---|---|---|---|
| 1 | Oxford | 6 | Warwick |
| 2 | Cambridge | 7 | Birmingham |
| 3 | LSE | 8 | Edinburgh |
| 4 | King's College London | 9 | Durham |
| 5 | UCL | 10 | SOAS |

**Materials Engineering**

| Ranking | *Guardian* choice | Ranking | *Guardian* choice |
|---|---|---|---|
| 1 | Oxford | 6 | Exeter |
| 2 | Manchester | 7 | Birmingham |
| 3 | Bath | 8 | Sheffield |
| 4 | Imperial College | 9 | Loughborough |
| 5 | Leeds | 10 | Queen Mary |

**Mathematics**

| Ranking | *Guardian* choice | Ranking | *Guardian* choice |
|---|---|---|---|
| 1 | Oxford | 6 | Warwick |
| 2 | Cambridge | 7 | Imperial College |
| 3 | Lancaster | 8 | Leicester |
| 4 | Portsmouth | 9 | Sheffield Hallam |
| 5 | Durham | 10 | Birmingham |

## Mechanical Engineering

| Ranking | *Guardian* choice | Ranking | *Guardian* choice |
|---------|-------------------|---------|-------------------|
| 1 | Teesside | 6 | Nottingham |
| 2 | Imperial College | 7 | Bristol |
| 3 | Southampton | 8 | Newcastle |
| 4 | Loughborough | 9 | Queen's University Belfast |
| 5 | Edinburgh | 10 | Robert Gordon |

## Media Studies and Communications and Librarianship

| Ranking | *Guardian* choice | Ranking | *Guardian* choice |
|---------|-------------------|---------|-------------------|
| 1 | Southampton | 6 | Cardiff |
| 2 | Birmingham | 7 | Surrey |
| 3 | Newcastle | 8 | Bournemouth |
| 4 | Warwick | 9 | Royal Holloway |
| 5 | Leeds | 10 | Sheffield |

## Medicine

| Ranking | *Guardian* choice | Ranking | *Guardian* choice |
|---------|-------------------|---------|-------------------|
| 1 | Dundee | 6 | Imperial College |
| 2 | Cambridge | 7 | Leicester |
| 3 | Oxford | 8 | King's College London |
| 4 | Edinburgh | 9 | Newcastle |
| 5 | UCL | 10 | Leeds |

## Modern Languages

| Ranking | *Guardian* choice | Ranking | *Guardian* choice |
|---------|-------------------|---------|-------------------|
| 1 | Oxford | 6 | SOAS |
| 2 | Cambridge | 7 | UCL |
| 3 | Southampton | 8 | Warwick |
| 4 | St Andrews | 9 | Queen Mary |
| 5 | Bath | 10 | Birmingham |

## Music

| Ranking | *Guardian* choice | Ranking | *Guardian* choice |
|---------|-------------------|---------|-------------------|
| 1 | Royal Scottish Academy of Music and Drama | 6 | Plymouth |
| 2 | Oxford | 7 | Trinity Laban |
| 3 | Royal Academy of Music | 8 | Nottingham |
| 4 | King's College London | 9 | Cambridge |
| 5 | Royal College of Music | 10 | Manchester |

*(Continued)*

**Nursing**

| Ranking | *Guardian* choice | Ranking | *Guardian* choice |
|---------|-------------------|---------|-------------------|
| 1 | Edinburgh | 6 | Southampton |
| 2 | St George's Medical School | 7 | Leeds |
| 3 | UEA | 8 | Thames Valley |
| 4 | Marjon | 9 | Bradford |
| 5 | Nottingham | 10 | Kent |

**Pharmacology and Pharmacy**

| Ranking | *Guardian* choice | Ranking | *Guardian* choice |
|---------|-------------------|---------|-------------------|
| 1 | UCL | 6 | Queen's University Belfast |
| 2 | Leeds | 7 | Liverpool |
| 3 | Cardiff | 8 | Bath |
| 4 | Strathclyde | 9 | School of Pharmacy |
| 5 | Nottingham | 10 | Bristol |

**Philosophy**

| Ranking | *Guardian* choice | Ranking | *Guardian* choice |
|---------|-------------------|---------|-------------------|
| 1 | Oxford | 6 | Aberdeen |
| 2 | Cambridge | 7 | LSE |
| 3 | St Andrews | 8 | Anglia Ruskin |
| 4 | UCL | 9 | Durham |
| 5 | Warwick | 10 | Edinburgh |

**Physics**

| Ranking | *Guardian* choice | Ranking | *Guardian* choice |
|---------|-------------------|---------|-------------------|
| 1 | Oxford | 7 | UCL |
| 2 | Imperial College | 8 | Manchester |
| 3 | Leeds | 9 | Lancaster |
| 4 | Liverpool | =10 | Glasgow |
| 5 | Heriot-Watt | =10 | Strathclyde |
| 6 | Edinburgh | | |

**Politics**

| Ranking | *Guardian* choice | Ranking | *Guardian* choice |
|---------|-------------------|---------|-------------------|
| 1 | Oxford | 6 | King's College London |
| 2 | LSE | 7 | Durham |
| 3 | St Andrews | 8 | Birmingham |
| 4 | Cambridge | 9 | Edinburgh |
| 5 | Warwick | 10 | SOAS |

## Psychology

| Ranking | Guardian choice | Ranking | Guardian choice |
|---|---|---|---|
| 1 | Oxford | 6 | York |
| 2 | UCL | 7 | Bristol |
| 3 | St Andrews | 8 | Kent |
| 4 | Exeter | 9 | Bath |
| 5 | Glasgow | 10 | Birmingham |

## Religious Studies and Theology

| Ranking | Guardian choice | Ranking | Guardian choice |
|---|---|---|---|
| 1 | Oxford | 6 | Aberdeen |
| 2 | St Andrews | 7 | Glasgow |
| 3 | Cambridge | 8 | Durham |
| 4 | Edinburgh | 9 | King's College London |
| 5 | SOAS | 10 | Heythrop College |

## Social Policy and Administration

| Ranking | Guardian choice | Ranking | Guardian choice |
|---|---|---|---|
| 1 | Bristol | 6 | Leeds |
| 2 | LSE | 7 | Cardiff |
| 3 | York | 8 | Bath |
| 4 | Nottingham | 9 | Loughborough |
| 5 | Birmingham | 10 | Nottingham Trent |

## Social Work

| Ranking | Guardian choice | Ranking | Guardian choice |
|---|---|---|---|
| 1 | Strathclyde | 6 | Manchester |
| 2 | Oxford Brookes | 7 | Anglia Ruskin |
| 3 | Sheffield | 8 | Portsmouth |
| 4 | York | 9 | Southampton |
| 5 | Kent | 10 | Leeds |

## Sociology

| Ranking | Guardian choice | Ranking | Guardian choice |
|---|---|---|---|
| 1 | Oxford | 6 | Edinburgh |
| 2 | Cambridge | 7 | Manchester |
| 3 | Warwick | 8 | LSE |
| 4 | Birmingham | 9 | Durham |
| 5 | Surrey | 10 | Exeter |

*(Continued)*

**Sports and Exercise Science**

| Ranking | Guardian choice | Ranking | Guardian choice |
|---------|-----------------|---------|-----------------|
| 1 | Bath | 6 | Birmingham |
| 2 | Loughborough | 7 | Edinburgh |
| 3 | Exeter | 8 | Heriot-Watt |
| 4 | Bournemouth | 9 | Ulster |
| 5 | Essex | 10 | Bangor |

**Tourism and Leisure Management**

| Ranking | Guardian choice | Ranking | Guardian choice |
|---------|-----------------|---------|-----------------|
| 1 | Bournemouth | 6 | Sunderland |
| 2 | Surrey | 7 | Edinburgh Napier |
| 3 | Brighton | 8 | Gloucestershire |
| 4 | Plymouth | 9 | Ulster |
| 5 | Oxford Brookes | 10 | Central Lancashire |

**Veterinary science***

| Ranking | Guardian choice | Ranking | Guardian choice |
|---------|-----------------|---------|-----------------|
| 1 | Cambridge | 4 | Glasgow |
| 2 | Edinburgh | 5 | Royal Veterinary College |
| 3 | Liverpool | 6 | Bristol |

Source: The Guardian University Guide 2009

*Fewer than 10 universities offer this course.

# Oxford and Cambridge

While Oxbridge colleges may have a reputation for being elitist, don't let that put you off trying for a place at one of them if you're likely to get the grades. Applications to study at Oxford and Cambridge are now made via UCAS, but the process can be more complicated than applications to other institutions. Check application deadlines and entry requirements very carefully, and find out whether you also need to submit extra written material or sit an admissions test. If this stage goes well, you have the choice of applying directly to a specific college or making an open application to the whole university. Some people think you stand a better chance of getting in if you apply to a specific college, so try to research the colleges as thoroughly as time allows, and ideally aim to visit a few on a university open day.

To find out more about Oxford colleges and applications, check the university's website (www.ox.ac.uk), and consider the alternative prospectus from their Student Union at www.ousu.org/prospective-students. For Cambridge information go to www.cam.ac.uk, and their very up-to-date student's-eye view, www.cusu.cam. ac.uk/prospective/prospectus/. There are some useful college profiles in the *Guide to UK Universities 2010* by Klaus Boehm and Jenny-Lees Spalding, and in *The Times Good University Guide*. For a complete overview try reading *Getting Into Oxford & Cambridge 2010 Entry* by Sarah Alakija.

For Cambridge applicants only, you will need to submit a Supplementary Application Questionnaire soon after making your UCAS application. If your application gets you shortlisted, expect to be called for at least one interview. Unlike other universities, if you don't get into your college of choice, you may still be offered a place at one of the university's other colleges.

The most famous Oxbridge ranking guides are the Norrington Table for Oxford and the Tompkins Table for Cambridge. The only type of data involved is the undergraduate degree class awards for the year, so be prepared to carry out a range of other supporting research of your own. The Norrington Table is based upon a simple calculation, but the Tompkins data undergo some weighting and manipulation before the final score is produced.

## Oxford college rankings – the Norrington Table

Table 20 lists the degree classifications awarded to undergraduate students at each Oxford college for the academic year 2007–2008. It also displays an assigned 'Norrington score' for each college. The Norrington score, developed by Sir Arthur Norrington, former President of Trinity, in the 1960s, provides a way of measuring the performance of students at each college in finals. The score is calculated by attaching a score of five to a first-class degree, three to a 2.i degree, two to a 2.ii degree and one to a third-class degree. The total score is expressed as a percentage of the maximum possible score (i.e. five times the number of degrees awarded), which allows a ranking of colleges. However, since the number of degrees awarded per college is small, the rankings should be treated with caution.

**?** ## Did you know?

*The University of Cambridge is thought to have been founded in the early thirteenth century by scholars from the University of Oxford who left there after a dispute.*

**Table 20 Norrington Table for Oxford undergraduate degrees 2007–2008**

| Rank | College | Norrington score (%) | Class of undergraduate degree award | | | | | Total |
|---|---|---|---|---|---|---|---|---|
| | | | 1st | 2.i | 2.ii | 3rd | Other | |
| 1 | Merton | 77.17 | 43 | 44 | 3 | 2 | | 92 |
| 2 | St John's | 76.19 | 46 | 52 | 7 | | | 105 |
| 3 | Balliol | 75.14 | 48 | 54 | 6 | 3 | | 111 |
| 4 | Magdalen | 74.11 | 45 | 59 | 5 | 3 | | 112 |
| 5 | Christ Church | 72.99 | 42 | 69 | 4 | 2 | | 117 |
| 6 | New | 71.54 | 39 | 77 | 7 | | | 123 |
| 7 | Queen's | 71.11 | 32 | 61 | 4 | 1 | 1 | 99 |
| 8 | Jesus | 70.64 | 33 | 70 | 5 | | 1 | 109 |
| 9 | St Hugh's | 70.00 | 32 | 69 | 9 | | | 110 |
| 10 | Lincoln | 69.88 | 24 | 51 | 4 | 2 | | 81 |
| 11 | Corpus Christi | 69.71 | 21 | 40 | 5 | 2 | | 68 |
| 12 | St Anne's | 69.17 | 34 | 74 | 11 | 1 | | 120 |
| 13 | Keble | 68.91 | 26 | 68 | 7 | | | 101 |
| 14 | Oriel | 68.86 | 24 | 55 | 9 | | | 88 |
| 15 | Trinity | 68.64 | 25 | 47 | 4 | 4 | 1 | 81 |
| 16 | Wadham | 68.43 | 38 | 89 | 10 | 2 | 1 | 140 |
| 17 | Hertford | 68.14 | 30 | 79 | 7 | 1 | 1 | 118 |
| 18 | University | 67.96 | 31 | 64 | 8 | 4 | 1 | 108 |
| 19 | Exeter | 67.74 | 24 | 60 | 7 | 1 | 1 | 93 |
| 20 | St Peter's | 67.22 | 26 | 69 | 13 | | | 108 |
| 21 | Brasenose | 67.00 | 22 | 70 | 7 | 1 | | 100 |
| 22 | St Edmund Hall | 66.61 | 25 | 75 | 6 | 1 | 2 | 109 |
| 23 | Mansfield | 66.29 | 14 | 50 | 6 | | | 70 |
| 24 | Harris Manchester | 66.15 | 5 | 19 | 2 | | | 26 |
| 25 | Pembroke | 66.13 | 24 | 73 | 14 | | | 111 |
| 26 | St Catherine's | 65.97 | 24 | 92 | 6 | 1 | | 124 |
| 27 | Worcester | 65.87 | 21 | 78 | 10 | | | 109 |
| 28 | Somerville | 65.57 | 18 | 72 | 5 | 2 | | 97 |
| 29 | St Hilda's | 65.13 | 21 | 79 | 13 | | | 113 |
| 30 | Lady Margaret Hall | 63.47 | 22 | 81 | 13 | 5 | | 121 |

*Source: University of Oxford*

# Cambridge college rankings – the Tompkins Table

The Tompkins Table is an annual ranking that lists the colleges of the University of Cambridge in order of their undergraduate students' performances in that year's examinations. Created in 1981 by an undergraduate mathematics student, Peter Tompkins, the table covers all exams for which grades are allocated (not just final-year exams). The table awards five points for a first-class degree, three points for a 2.i, two points for a 2.ii, one point for a third and no points for someone only granted an allowance towards an Ordinary Degree. The scores in each subject are then weighted to a common average, to avoid the bias towards colleges with higher proportions of students entered for subjects that receive higher average grades, and the result is expressed as a percentage of the total number of points available. It should be noted that the rankings are not officially endorsed by the university.

**Table 21 Tompkins Table for Cambridge undergraduate degrees 2008**

| Rank | College | Tompkins score (%) | % of first-class degrees |
|------|---------|--------------------|--------------------------|
| 1 | Selwyn | 68.47 | 29.9 |
| 2 | Emmanuel | 68.30 | 30.6 |
| 3 | Trinity | 68.27 | 31.4 |
| 4 | Gonville and Caius | 67.33 | 27.9 |
| 5 | Magdalene | 65.97 | 24.5 |
| 6 | Churchill | 65.72 | 27.1 |
| 7 | Jesus | 65.60 | 25.2 |
| 8 | Christ's | 65.27 | 25.7 |
| 9 | Corpus Christi | 65.24 | 24.1 |
| 10 | Pembroke | 64.96 | 24.5 |
| 11 | St Catharine's | 64.63 | 23.5 |
| 12 | Downing | 64.47 | 22.8 |
| 13 | Clare | 64.44 | 22.5 |
| 14 | Sidney Sussex | 64.21 | 20.9 |
| 15 | Trinity Hall | 63.76 | 19.3 |
| 16 | Queens' | 63.58 | 22.3 |
| 17 | Robinson | 63.32 | 20.6 |
| 18 | Peterhouse | 63.21 | 22.9 |
| 19 | King's | 63.07 | 22.5 |
| 20 | St John's | 62.48 | 20.5 |
| 21 | Fitzwilliam | 61.08 | 18.2 |

*(Continued)*

**Table 21 (Continued)**

| Rank | College | Tompkins score (%) | % of first-class degrees |
|------|---------|--------------------|--------------------------|
| 22 | Girton | 60.84 | 15.3 |
| 23 | Murray Edwards | 60.02 | 13.9 |
| 24 | Newnham | 59.96 | 13.3 |
| 25 | Homerton | 58.62 | 13 |
| 26 | Hughes Hall | 56.36 | 20.8 |
| 27 | Wolfson | 55.13 | 7.4 |
| 28 | Lucy Cavendish | 52.60 | 8.7 |
| 29 | St Edmund's | 51.55 | 11.2 |

*Source: The Independent*

# Chapter 3

# Money matters

Money is becoming more of an issue for students with each passing year, although it hasn't put them off applying to enter higher education. Tuition fees may rise still further, the cost of living has substantially increased, and parents have less spare cash with which to help out. This all adds up to a greater debt load for students, and less of a safety net.

Fortunately there is some good news too.

► As graduates tend to earn significantly higher salaries over the course of their working lives, getting a degree should eventually more than offset the debt you incur while you're studying (see Chapter 6).

► Some students this year may also find themselves immediately better off than students were a few years ago, since more non-repayable bursaries are being given out, especially to those from households with lower incomes (more about this on page 71 in this chapter).

## The basics of student finance

Financial issues influence the university choices of many students, whether they're living with their parents while they study, fitting degrees around full-time jobs, studying subjects with better employment prospects, or picking courses with generous bursaries attached to them.

To keep your finances in good shape, follow these six simple steps while you're choosing where to study.

1. Find out how much it costs to study and live at your chosen institutions (see page 62 for tuition fees, page 80 for rent costs and page 72 for the general cost of student living)
2. Work out what money you might have coming in, such as part-time wages, in your favourite towns or cities (see page 86), and any parental contributions.

## Good to know – serious debt help

There's a charity service called the Student Debtline (0800 328 1813) that can help you tackle serious problems and hopefully prevent any further damage to your credit rating. The Student Debtline is run by the Consumer Credit Counselling Service (CCCS) who charge no fees and will give you good advice and moral support.

3.  Find out about everything you could possibly be entitled to at your chosen universities, such as full or part grants, bursaries, scholarships, and allowances (more about this on page 65)

4.  Arrange to borrow cheaply. The cheapest borrowing is via the low-cost Student Loans system, which offers loans that cover tuition fees, and loans that partly cover subsistence (see page 70). You should also look into free student overdrafts. Avoid credit cards and store cards.

5.  Make a rough weekly, monthly or termly budget. The main categories for student expenditure in different regions and cities are listed in this chapter on pages 75 to 79, so you can use them as a basis for working out how much you might expect to spend and when.

6.  Call up student unions for more information. Also, don't be scared to ask for help when you get there. Many universities have designated counselling staff trained to help students with money woes (see page 115 for those that offer the most student support), and the National Union of Students has a lot of helpful advice, and campaigns against student hardship.

# The cost of studying

The cost of studying comes in two main parts: university tuition fees, and maintenance money to support yourself with while you're studying.

## Tuition fees in England

In England, almost all universities charge the full amount they can (currently £3,225) for tuition fees, with only two exceptions:

1.  University of Greenwich (£2,835)
2.  Leeds Metropolitan University (£2,000).

Both of these figures may be subject to change in the next few months.

If you're short of cash, should you cut costs by picking a university that charges lower tuition fees? Perhaps not. If you're from a household in a lower income bracket, there's every chance that a different university could offer you some financial help with your expenses, which could more than make up for the money you'd save if you opted for the institution that asks for lower tuition fees. Failing that, picking an institution in an area of the country with a lower cost of living than, say, Leeds or Greenwich could also leave you better off (see later in this chapter for more about the cost of living). The situation is more complex than it may first appear, so it pays to follow the whole six-point list above to keep your costs down and your income up.

## Tuition fees in Scotland, Wales and Northern Ireland

The cost of tuition fees is slightly different in the rest of the UK. Welsh home students who decide to study in Wales will effectively pay fees of £1,285, since they'll receive a fee grant of £1,940 p.a. to offset part of the expense. This also applies to non-UK European Union students. Students originally resident in Wales who decide to study outside Wales are not entitled to claim a fee grant, and will have to pay whatever fees the university requires.

Scottish students studying in Scotland do not pay fees, and neither do non-UK European Union students. Scottish students attending universities in England, Wales and Northern Ireland will have to pay that country's standard fees. If you are from outside Scotland and you want to study there, expect to be asked for a yearly tuition fee of £1,820. While this may seem relatively cheap and could attract you to study there, remember that many undergraduate degree courses in Scotland last for four years, not three.

## Help with tuition fees

What help can you get towards paying your tuition fees? While the government does not expect parents to contribute to tuition fees, in practice many parents do help out. Otherwise, your best bet is usually to apply for a low-interest Fees Loan, which is administered by the Student Loans Company, and most UK-resident students who apply will be loaned the full amount. It's worth noting that even students from lower-income families do not qualify for any help with university fees, although they may get help with their living expenses.

## Good to know – borrowing from the Student Loans Co.

The money the Student Loans Co. lends you does not gather much interest, so the debt does not snowball out of control over a long period of time, and it is linked to inflation; so in real terms, what you borrow has the same 'spending power' as the amount you eventually pay back.

# Funds for maintenance costs

## Paying for everyday living costs

After you've arranged payment for your tuition fees, you're going to have to find the funds to pay for your everyday living costs, or maintenance. You may be given some money, and you may have to borrow some money.

Money that may be given to you:

▶ maintenance grants (and other government money)

▶ university bursaries

▶ parental contributions

▶ Access to Learning Funds (or similar funds)

▶ your earnings from part-time jobs, holiday jobs, or paid work placements

▶ other – sponsorships, scholarships, awards, etc.

Money you can borrow but will have to pay back:

▶ Student Maintenance Loan

▶ interest-free student overdraft

▶ Access to Learning Funds (can also be given as a short-term loan).

## Maintenance grants in England

Students may be entitled to non-repayable maintenance grants of up to £2,906, depending on family income. The awards are made on a sliding scale, so some students will have partial grants and others will have full grants. This year maintenance grants are going to be made to students with a combined family income of less than £50,000 if their family lives in England, with lower family incomes in the rest of the UK. Roughly 30% of students are expected to gain the full grant, and a further 30% or so will gain a part-grant of some kind. English students need to apply to Student Finance England, see www.direct.gov.uk/ studentfinance or call 0845 300 50 90 to find out more about the process.

## Maintenance grants outside England

▶ In Northern Ireland the basic grant can be up to £3,406, and it is also non-repayable and means-tested (see www.delni.gov.uk for full details).

▶ Whatever part of the UK they choose to study in, Welsh students from lower-income families can apply for a Higher Education Assembly Grant of up to £2,906 to help with their maintenance (see www.studentfinancewales.co.uk).

▶ In Scotland, the Young Students' Bursary may be paid instead of part of the student loan, which supposedly reduces the amount of loan you need to take out. It's paid on a sliding scale, with the highest amount set at £2,640 a year if your household income is £19,310 or less p.a., and goes down to zero for household income over £34,195 a year (see www.student-support-saas.gov.uk).

Students meeting specific requirements, such as lone parents, care givers and disabled students, can also apply to the government to obtain non-repayable Special Support Grants worth up to £2,906.

## University bursaries

Universities make non-repayable bursaries available to all or some of their students, often focusing on those from lower-income families, and last year 42% of students across all universities and colleges received some form of bursary or scholarship. This year, an estimated total of 400,000 students will benefit to some extent. In 2007/2008 universities and colleges paid around £192m to over 205,000 first and second year students from lower-income groups. More than 70% of this £192m was spent on the poorest students, classed as those with a household income of less than £17,910, representing a population of almost 133,000 students.

# How much bursary money might you get?

According to Sir Martin Harris, Director of the Office for Fair Access (OFFA), a student starting in 2009 and receiving the maximum state maintenance grant can expect to receive a bursary of, on average, between £900 and £1,000 a year. He also says this: 'Some universities and colleges give bursaries to all their students, regardless of income, so, whoever you are, it's worth finding out what you're entitled to.'

# Bursaries 'to do' list

▶ Make a point of asking your favourite universities what's potentially on offer for the year you hope to begin your studies.

▶ Have a good look at http:// bursarymap.direct.gov.uk.

University bursaries can be another helpful source of income, but you must remember that if you don't ask, you may not automatically get any money to which you might be entitled. According to OFFA, to the best of their knowledge all eligible students who applied for a bursary through the correct channels have received one.

The money for university bursaries comes from a variety of sources, but there is an increasing trend for universities to take some of the money they make from charging top-up/tuition fees, and give it back to students (often from lower-income backgrounds) as bursaries. On average, institutions charging the full fee spent 21.5% of their additional fee income during 2007/2008 on bursary and scholarship expenditure for lower-income students. Table 22 shows how much of this money different universities offered as bursaries in 2007, the complete year for which figures were collected by OFFA.

**Table 22 Percentage of top-up fee income spent on bursaries/scholarships for low-income students**

| University | % of top-up fee income given as bursaries |
|---|---|
| Anglia Ruskin University | 36.6 |
| Aston University | 21.1 |
| University of Bath | 19.0 |
| Bath Spa University | 23.7 |
| University of Bedfordshire | 40.7 |
| University of Birmingham | 20.6 |
| Birmingham City University | 14.5 |
| University of Bolton | 18.7 |
| Bournemouth University | 28.5 |
| University of Bradford | 22.9 |
| University of Brighton | 23.1 |
| University of Bristol | 16.5 |

**Table 22 (Continued)**

| University | % of top-up fee income given as bursaries |
|---|---|
| Brunel University | 14.6 |
| Buckinghamshire New University | 40.2 |
| University of Cambridge | 24.0 |
| Canterbury Christ Church University | 21.5 |
| University of Central Lancashire | 34.5 |
| University of Chester | 20.8 |
| University of Chichester | 20.7 |
| City University, London | 17.9 |
| Coventry University | 19.9 |
| University of Cumbria | 29.6 |
| De Montfort University | 21.3 |
| University of Derby | 26.4 |
| University of Durham | 28.1 |
| University of East Anglia | 18.8 |
| University of East London | 22.0 |
| Edge Hill University | 35.3 |
| University of Essex | 12.0 |
| University of Exeter | 20.6 |
| University of Gloucestershire | 13.0 |
| Goldsmiths, University of London | 21.2 |
| University of Greenwich | 8.1 |
| University of Hertfordshire | 31.0 |
| University of Huddersfield | 24.8 |
| University of Hull | 24.3 |
| Imperial College London | 31.9 |
| Keele University | 11.5 |
| University of Kent | 18.3 |
| King's College London | 19.3 |
| Kingston University | 16.2 |
| Lancaster University | 18.2 |
| University of Leeds | 15.7 |
| Leeds Metropolitan University | 0.6 |
| University of Leicester | 18.8 |
| University of Lincoln | 25.4 |

*(Continued)*

**Table 22 (Continued)**

| University | % of top-up fee income given as bursaries |
|---|---|
| University of Liverpool | 25.9 |
| Liverpool Hope University | 43.5 |
| Liverpool John Moores University | 26.9 |
| University of the Arts London | 10.6 |
| London School of Economics | 24.3 |
| London Metropolitan University | 25.7 |
| London South Bank University | 18.0 |
| Loughborough University | 14.9 |
| University of Manchester | 28.5 |
| Manchester Metropolitan University | 21.9 |
| Middlesex University | 7.0 |
| Newcastle University | 14.6 |
| University of Northampton | 24.8 |
| University of Northumbria | 19.5 |
| University of Nottingham | 19.2 |
| Nottingham Trent University | 20.2 |
| School of Oriental and African Studies | 15.9 |
| University of Oxford | 33.4 |
| Oxford Brookes University | 31.6 |
| University of Plymouth | 15.9 |
| University of Portsmouth | 17.8 |
| Queen Mary, London | 29.8 |
| University of Reading | 26.0 |
| Roehampton University | 14.3 |
| Royal Holloway, London | 23.6 |
| University of Sheffield | 13.3 |
| Sheffield Hallam University | 24.2 |
| University of Southampton | 14.0 |
| Southampton Solent University | 24.2 |
| Staffordshire University | 38.3 |
| University of Sunderland | 31.4 |
| University of Surrey | 17.4 |
| University of Sussex | 14.1 |
| University of Teesside | 35.9 |

**Table 22 (Continued)**

| University | % of top-up fee income given as bursaries |
| --- | --- |
| Thames Valley University | 32.4 |
| University College London | 24.6 |
| University of Warwick | 27.1 |
| University of West of England | 24.4 |
| University of Westminster | 22.9 |
| University of Winchester | 23.9 |
| University of Wolverhampton | 23.0 |
| University of Worcester | 18.7 |
| University of York | 19.5 |
| York St John University | 33.0 |

*Source: OFFA report, 'Access agreement monitoring – Outcomes for 2007–08'*

**Notes:** *This report only deals with OFFA-countable bursaries and scholarships (those for incomes up to £48,330 or in other under-represented groups), and this data does not show how many beneficiaries received bursaries and scholarships at each institution.*

## Parental contributions

According to NatWest student banking, parents are contributing record amounts of maintenance cash to help their offspring gain a university education. Over 60% of students currently receive some kind of financial support from their parents, whether it's regular cash or the occasional one-off payment. Parents are not expected to help students out with more money than the government suggests, but many of them are more generous.

## Access to Learning Funds

These funds are administered by universities in England, and the rules for giving them out vary between institutions. In Wales similar payments are made through the Financial Contingency Funds (FCFs) scheme, Scotland provides help through Hardship Funds, and Northern Ireland through Support Funds. The funds can be given out as a gift, or as a repayable loan, and the amount of money given depends on the applicant's circumstances, and on how much money there is in the university pot. You have to apply via your university to get these funds once you have started studying there.

## Sponsorships

Most sponsorships are usually applied for around the same time you apply for courses. They are usually offered by commercial employers or professional bodies

# Resources for scholarships research

▶ For a comprehensive overview of what's available, read *University Scholarships, Awards and Bursaries* by Brian Heap, published by Trotman.

▶ You may also like to contact the Educational Grants Advisory Service, www.egas-online.org.

▶ Try looking at www.scholarship-search.org.uk.

(most commonly in the fields of engineering and finance), institutions such as the British Army, or by the universities themselves. You can obtain them by applying to the employers themselves, or via the university, depending upon the requirements.

You are required to sign a contract which is legally binding, so read the small print carefully – there may be requirements to work for the sponsor during holidays or after graduation, or penalties such as the withdrawal of funds or job offers if you fail too many exams.

## Scholarships and other awards

It can be quite hard to track down scholarship money, which usually comes from universities or charitable trusts. To gain a scholarship you may have to meet very specific entry requirements, such as having exceptional talent in music or sport, to have been born in a particular church parish, and so on. Some funds disbursed in this way may amount to only a few pounds, others may be larger sums of money or 'gifts in kind', such as equipment. Expect to put in quite a lot of effort, and don't count too much on getting any results.

## Student maintenance loans

These are commonly called 'student loans' and they're low-interest loans administered by the Student Loans Company and subsidised by the UK government. The low interest means that they're a cheap way to borrow, and you're not required to start paying them back until the April after you graduate, and then only if you're earning more than £15,000 per year. The amount that students are paying back at the moment is 9% of any salary above the basic £15,000 income, and the money is taken out of their wages.

Student maintenance loans are part-tested on two things: the amount of maintenance grant you receive, and your parental/household income. If you receive a full or partial grant you will get less loan, the idea being that you will not need to borrow so much if you have that non-repayable cash coming in (even if that's not always how it works out in real life). If your family or spouse has a household income over £50,000, you may also receive less loan, on the grounds that your parents/partner will be expected to make up the shortfall by providing you with a financial contribution.

For the coming academic year, 2009/2010, the maximum amount first-year students can expect to receive from the standard student maintenance loan is:

- ▶ £3,838 if they are living at home
- ▶ £4,950 if they are living away from home at a university outside London
- ▶ £6,928 if they are living away from home at a London college or university.

You can phone the Student Loans Company free helpline on 0845 607 7577 or visit their website, www.slc.co.uk, if there's anything you don't understand, or if you have any problems applying for or receiving loan money.

## Student overdrafts

An interest-free student overdraft on your current account can be a lifeline if you've exhausted other sources of money. To get one, you need to apply for a student account with a bank or building society, and agree the amount of interest-free overdraft that comes with it. Some commercial financial websites such as www.moneyfacts.co.uk allow you to compare the different student accounts, including the amount of free overdraft that's available during each year of study.

## Useful books to help you track down that extra cash

That's a very brief overview of the world of student finance, but if you'd like to learn more about loans, fees, bursaries and suchlike there are a couple of useful books available: *Guide to Student Money 2010* by Gwenda Thomas, published by Trotman, which contains unique survey data and comprehensive information for

## Taming an out-of-hand overdraft

- ▶ If you're likely to go over the agreed limit, don't try to pretend it isn't happening and ignore it, as you'll almost certainly be hit with bank charges and penalties that will add to your debts at a time when you're least able to repay what you owe.

- ▶ Contact the bank as soon as possible and arrange a new limit, which will probably mean that the bank charges you interest on the amount you've borrowed that's beyond their interest-free limit.

students living in all parts of the UK; and *The Complete University Guide to Student Finance* by Bernard Kingston.

# The cost of living

After paying your fees, you'll need to pay for your general cost of living while you're at university. Having some idea of what to expect can help you plan ahead, and hopefully avoid major problems. Let's start by looking at the absolute minimum amount you'll need for survival at different universities.

**Table 23 Cheapest university basic cost of living (according to student union)**

| Rank | University | £ per year |
|------|-----------|-----------|
| 1 | University of Dundee | 4,500 |
| 2 | Glyndŵr University | 4,680 |
| 3 | Canterbury Christ Church University | 4,860 |
| 4 | University of Wolverhampton | 4,950 |
| =5 | Aberystwyth University | 5,000 |
| =5 | University of Ulster | 5,000 |
| =5 | Keele University | 5,000 |
| =5 | University of Stirling | 5,000 |
| =5 | University of Teesside | 5,000 |
| =5 | University of Chichester | 5,000 |
| =5 | Swansea Metropolitan | 5,000 |
| =5 | University of Northampton | 5,000 |
| 13 | Abertay Dundee University | 5,250 |
| 14 | Aberdeen University | 5,280 |
| 15 | Edge Hill University | 5,300 |
| 16 | Edinburgh Napier University | 5,310 |
| 17 | University of Leicester | 5,400 |
| =18 | University of Liverpool | 5,500 |
| =18 | University of Wales Swansea | 5,500 |
| =18 | Queen's University Belfast | 5,500 |
| =18 | University of Strathclyde | 5,500 |
| =18 | Aston University | 5,500 |
| =18 | University of Hull | 5,500 |
| =18 | University of Huddersfield | 5,500 |
| =18 | York St John University | 5,500 |
| =18 | Bedfordshire University | 5,500 |

Source: Guide to UK Universities 2010 by Klaus Boehm and Jenny Lees-Spalding

**Table 24 Most expensive university basic cost of living (according to student union)**

| Rank | University | £ per year |
|------|------------|-----------|
| 1 | University of St Andrews | 12,000 |
| 2 | Imperial College London | 10,500 |
| =3 | London School of Economics | 10,000 |
| =3 | SOAS | 10,000 |
| 5 | London Metropolitan | 9,000 |
| 6 | King's College London | 8,610 |
| 7 | Glasgow Caledonian University | 8,500 |
| 8 | London South Bank | 8,320 |
| 9 | University College London | 8,140 |
| 10 | Oxford Brookes University | 8,060 |
| =11 | University of Warwick | 8,000 |
| =11 | Queen Mary, London | 8,000 |
| =11 | University of West of England | 8,000 |
| =11 | Middlesex University | 8,000 |
| =11 | University of Wales Newport | 8,000 |
| 16 | University of Birmingham | 7,950 |
| =17 | Manchester Metropolitan University | 7,800 |
| =17 | University of Lincoln | 7,800 |
| =19 | University of Leeds | 7,500 |
| =19 | City University, London | 7,500 |
| 21 | University of Manchester | 7,480 |
| 22 | University of Westminster | 7,420 |
| 23 | University of York | 7,400 |
| 24 | University of Winchester | 7,350 |
| 25 | Bournemouth University | 7,300 |

*Source: Guide to UK Universities 2010 by Klaus Boehm and Jenny Lees-Spalding*

Now, this is the absolute minimum amount for survival, stripped back to the bare bones, and includes only:

► the cheapest rent
► the most basic food
► very few books and course materials
► no money for clothes and socialising.

Very few of us can live a lifestyle like this for any period. Your time at university is about so much more than turning up to lectures, completing assignments and sitting exams: the whole experience counts, including all the extra-curricular activities. It would be almost criminal to go to a new place and not try at least a few of the new experiences on offer.

Similarly, we are all social animals, even the shyest among us, and it is unrealistic to expect students to have no social life at all. Yes, you'll probably have to spend a few skint nights in watching the telly or old DVDs in weeks or months when the cash flow's particularly tight, but you do have to get out and have some fun and see your friends every now and again.

**TIP**

**General money-saving tips**
► *cut your transport costs by walking, cycling, or using student discount cards*
► *claim all benefits and allowances for prescription charges, dental care, etc.*
► *tell the local council you're exempt from paying council tax*
► *shop around for gas, electricity, telephone and broadband deals – try online price comparison services*
► *if you are sent an estimated bill, read the meter yourself*
► *don't leave TVs, Sky boxes, DVD players, stereos, or computers on standby.*

## How much does the average student really spend?

What does this all add up to if you're having a reasonable, but not excessive, university lifestyle? Look at Table 25 for the latest survey by the National Union of Students (NUS) for the academic year of 2008/2009.

If you compare this total average figure with the usual amount that students can gain in grants and bursaries, plus what they can borrow cheaply with Student Loans and free overdrafts, you'll see that for most students there will be a significant shortfall. Some lucky students will have well-off, generous parents who are able to

**Table 25 NUS survey results for student expenses 2008/2009**

| Spending category (average per 39-week academic year) | London | Rest of the UK |
| --- | --- | --- |
| Accommodation | £3,906 | £2,928 |
| Food and household spending | £2,141 | £1,748 |
| Total spend, including rent, books, travel, clothing, food and leisure | £15,769 | £13,626 |

# True levels of student debt

Speaking of debt levels, it's hard to find reliable official figures for how much UK students owe as a whole, since they're not all borrowing from the same places. Some take out student loans, others take out bank loans or pay for things with credit cards, and others may have informal borrowing arrangements with their parents or other lenders. The best you can hope for is a rough estimate from surveys, such as the annual surveys carried out by www.push.co.uk at each university, and displayed in the profiles on their website.

help them out with their financial situation, but those receiving the full quota of loans and maintenance grants could be left with a shortfall next year of between £7,012 and £7,768 compared to the NUS suggested amount. Following the six-step plan at the start of this chapter should help to minimise this and keep your debts under control.

## Weekly spending patterns

In addition to the annual basic cost of living, you can also look at weekly costs to help break the annual amount down into a more manageable figure to work with when you're planning your spending. If you're thinking about studying in

**Table 26 Expenses in England**

| Expense | Cost per week | Expense | Cost per week |
|---|---|---|---|
| Rent | £67.67* | Long trips | £11.37 |
| Alcohol | £28.29 | Daily travel | £10.86 |
| Supermarket | £20.79 | Phone/mobile | £9.65 |
| Clothes | £16.75 | Books/materials | £8.70 |
| Going out | £15.96 | Laundry | £9.36 |
| Eating out | £15.18 | Photocopying, etc. | £3.80 |
| Utility bills | £13.77 | | |

Source: Guide to Student Money 2010 by Gwenda Thomas
*Excludes London and Oxbridge rents

a particular region of the UK, it can be helpful to get a rough idea of how the average student's actual spending breaks down in that area.

The figures shown here are taken from survey results in *Guide to Student Money 2010* by kind permission of its author, Gwenda Thomas. As you can see, some places are more expensive than others, and if you're thinking about studying there, then it's useful to know what to expect.

**Table 27 Expenses in Northern Ireland**

| Expense | Cost per week | Expense | Cost per week |
|---------|---------------|---------|---------------|
| Rent | £58.27 | Long trips | £14.54 |
| Alcohol | £28.89 | Daily travel | £12.99 |
| Supermarket | £22.12 | Phone/mobile | £10.94 |
| Clothes | £20.11 | Books/materials | £10.05 |
| Going out | £17.24 | Laundry | £4.05 |
| Eating out | £20.08 | Photocopying, etc. | £4.17 |
| Utility bills | £10.44 | | |

Source: Guide to Student Money 2010 by Gwenda Thomas

**Table 28 Expenses in Scotland**

| Expense | Cost per week | Expense | Cost per week |
|---------|---------------|---------|---------------|
| Rent | £72.00 | Long trips | £12.05 |
| Alcohol | £25.47 | Daily travel | £9.00 |
| Supermarket | £24.29 | Phone/mobile | £5.96 |
| Clothes | £14.96 | Books/materials | £10.68 |
| Going out | £15.29 | Laundry | £3.99 |
| Eating out | £15.34 | Photocopying, etc. | £3.86 |
| Utility bills | £13.41 | | |

Source: Guide to Student Money 2010 by Gwenda Thomas

**Table 29 Expenses in Wales**

| Expense | Cost per week | Expense | Cost per week |
|---------|---------------|---------|---------------|
| Rent | £64.29 | Long trips | £13.70 |
| Alcohol | £30.58 | Daily travel | £9.20 |
| Supermarket | £22.31 | Phone/mobile | £11.42 |
| Clothes | £16.46 | Books/materials | £8.79 |
| Going out | £16.70 | Laundry | £4.49 |
| Eating out | £12.96 | Photocopying, etc. | £4.62 |
| Utility bills | £12.63 | | |

Source: Guide to Student Money 2010 by Gwenda Thomas

**Table 30 Expenses in London**

| Expense | Cost per week | Expense | Cost per week |
|---|---|---|---|
| Rent | £90.24 | Long trips | £12.11 |
| Alcohol | £27.93 | Daily travel | £16.35 |
| Supermarket | £25.16 | Phone/mobile | £11.76 |
| Clothes | £16.63 | Books/materials | £10.32 |
| Going out | £20.45 | Laundry | £6.84 |
| Eating out | £21.03 | Photocopying, etc. | £5.37 |
| Utility bills | £18.95 | | |

Source: Guide to Student Money 2010 by Gwenda Thomas

**Table 31 Expenses in Oxbridge**

| Expense | Cost per week | Expense | Cost per week |
|---|---|---|---|
| Rent | £89.17 | Long trips | £10.52 |
| Alcohol | £23.65 | Daily travel | £8.70 |
| Supermarket | £22.32 | Phone/mobile | £8.40 |
| Clothes | £16.42 | Books/materials | £8.10 |
| Going out | £14.18 | Laundry | £3.28 |
| Eating out | £19.13 | Photocopying, etc. | £3.65 |
| Utility bills | £13.68 | | |

Source: Guide to Student Money 2010 by Gwenda Thomas

# Budgeting 'to-do' list

▶ Work out how much money you have available for the week, and allocate some to each category.

▶ Keep a close eye on what you're spending – you can try keeping a spending diary to help you to get a better idea of where the money's going.

▶ Sticking to a budget can be hard, but remember that clawing your way back out from under a mountain of extra debt can be far harder.

The NatWest Student Living Index 2008 provides estimates of weekly outlay, showing weekly levels of spending for 26 different university towns. Table 32 should give most UK students an approximate idea of how much they should allow for their overall weekly personal budget. The NatWest research estimated that, in total, British students spent over £10.8bn in housing and living costs over the 2008/2009 academic year, an increase of half a billion pounds on the total cost of living in 2007 (£10.3bn).

**Table 32 Total weekly student spending in main university towns 2008**

| Rank | University town or city | Weekly average spending (£) |
|------|-------------------------|------------------------------|
| 1 | London | 311 |
| 2 | Oxford | 290 |
| 3 | Leicester | 289 |
| 4 | Exeter | 286 |
| 5 | Brighton | 274 |
| 6 | Lancaster | 269 |
| 7 | Aberdeen | 268 |
| 8 | Glasgow | 264 |
| 9 | Belfast | 262 |
| 10 | Cardiff | 261 |
| 11 | Birmingham | 260 |
| 12 | Nottingham | 256 |
| 13 | Portsmouth | 255 |
| 14 | Newcastle | 254 |
| 15 | Bristol | 253 |
| 16 | Liverpool | 249 |
| 17 | Manchester | 244 |
| 18 | Edinburgh | 243 |
| 19 | Southampton | 241 |
| 20 | Leeds | 240 |
| 21 | Swansea | 240 |
| 22 | Cambridge | 240 |
| 23 | Dundee | 218 |
| 24 | Sheffield | 217 |
| 25 | Plymouth | 216 |
| 26 | York | 212 |

*Source: NatWest Student Living Index 2008*
**Notes:** average local weekly student expenditure on living and accommodation costs calculated by total of spending on rent, supermarket food shopping, books and course materials, going out, alcohol, cigarettes, buying clothes, laundry, transport costs, utility bills, telephone bills, eating out, buying CDs, DVDs and videos, photocopying and library costs.

It's worth reminding yourself that the student unions' recommended minimums for the cost of living while at university are guides to the absolute basics needed for survival. The NatWest index represents what students actually spend, rather than what they need, so it includes a lot of 'discretionary' spending on things that don't count as the basics.

The list on the next page can be a handy to use when you're drawing up a weekly or monthly budget for yourself, as it's really easy to forget certain categories here and there, and then the forgotten costs can creep up on you unexpectedly. While it's hard to get a reduction on your rent, this list does show you some other areas

# A student's main expenses (most expensive at top of list)

1. Rent.

2. Alcohol (all consumed at home and while out).

3. Supermarket food shopping.

4. Buying clothes.

5. Going out (cinema/clubs/gigs).

6. Eating out (inc. café, restaurant, canteen food, etc.).

7. Cigarettes.

8. Utility bills.

9. Transport costs for longer trips.

10. Day-to-day travel (including taxis).

11. Telephone/mobile phone bill.

12. Books and course materials.

13. Buying CDs, DVDs and videos.

14. Laundry/dry cleaning.

15. Photocopying/library costs, fines, etc.

*Source: The NatWest Student Living Index 2008*

where you can be a bit more clever with your spending and cut your costs, such as supermarket food shopping, clothes buying and alcohol intake (see also the Tips section on page 85).

The NatWest survey suggested that, on average, UK students are paying around £73 per week for their rent (if they're living outside London). In London, the average student rents were approximately £90 per week, and while students have the option of living further away from the centre of the capital they are then hit with expensive travel costs that sometimes wipe out much of the savings. There was also a surprise in the survey: the average student weekly rent in Oxford was estimated to be around £92 per week. Lancaster was one of the cheapest rental areas, coming in at approximately £58 per week. (See Table 33 for the average university and private local rents at each institution.)

# Total student spend

The NatWest Student Living Index research estimated that, out of the 2008 total student spend, approximately:

► £3.9 billion was spent on rent

► £1.2 billion on supermarket food shopping

► £864 million on going out

► £489 million on books and course materials

► £773 million on cigarettes.

**TIP**

**Keeping in touch for less**
- ▶ *although the cost per unit is higher, a pay-as-you-go mobile is the easiest way to keep your total bill manageable (unless you're very disciplined with your mobile phone usage)*
- ▶ *if your chatterbox mate keeps you on the phone for hours, send them a text message instead*
- ▶ *use free university email, social networking sites and messenger software to keep in touch with friends and relations.*

## Accommodation prices at individual universities

Table 33 provides an approximate guide to the cost of accommodation at UK universities. The prices quoted here are only a guideline, and private rents in particular can vary quite a lot. Not every university provides catered accommodation nowadays, so these figures are not available for each institution, although most universities provide at least some self-catering places.

Some universities charge a flat fee for accommodation, while others have a wide price range: this is usually because the university in question owns a wide variety of different types of places to rent. These can include shared or private rooms in halls, rooms with shared bathrooms or with en suite bathrooms, places in commercially owned and run halls, university-owned houses, and even university-owned bedsits or one-person flats. If you'd like to know more about housing at any institution, start by contacting their accommodation office for details of availability and an up-to-date price list.

**Table 33 Range of local and university-owned accommodation costs by university**

| University | Catered university accommodation (£/week) | Self-catering university accommodation (£/week) | Local private rents (£/week) |
|---|---|---|---|
| Aberdeen University | 116–137 | 72–103 | 72–90 |
| Abertay Dundee University | | 70–101 | 50+ |
| Aberystwyth University | 84–96 | 69–90 | 69–90 |
| Anglia Ruskin University | | 62–123 | 42–105 |
| Arts London | | 76–167 | 70–120 |
| Aston University | 89–125 | 65–101 | 45–70 |
| Bangor University | | 63–98 | 55* |

*(Continued)*

**Table 33 (Continued)**

| University | Catered university accommodation (£/week) | Self-catering university accommodation (£/week) | Local private rents (£/week) |
|---|---|---|---|
| University of Bath | | 75–115 | 65–90 |
| Bath Spa University | | 58–92 | 65–75 |
| Bedfordshire University | | 69–81 | 60–80 |
| University of Birmingham | 115–142 | 78–115 | 65+ |
| Birmingham City University | | 74–96 | 65+ |
| Bolton University | | 62 | 40+ |
| Bournemouth University | | 75–91 | 65–85 |
| University of Bradford | | 65–86 | 45–84 |
| University of Brighton | 66–100 | 66–110 | 75–95 |
| University of Bristol | 92–136 | 73–116 | 70–100 |
| Brunel University | | 82–100 | 85–90 |
| Bucks New University | | 76–88 | 50–75 |
| University of Cambridge | | 70–100 | |
| Canterbury CC University | 113–118 | 65–96 | |
| Cardiff University | 70–80 | 56–82 | 55–60 |
| University of Central Lancs | | 79–81 | 50–80 |
| University of Chester | 63–126 | 53–84 | 55–95 |
| University of Chichester | | 74–104 | 62–70 |
| City University, London | | 97–108 | 95–150 |
| Coventry University | 94 | 60–128 | |
| University for Creative Arts | | 49–105 | 65–85 |
| University of Cumbria | 100 | 70+ | 45–60 |
| De Montfort University | | 70–90 | 60–70 |
| University of Derby | | 60–87 | 65–70 |
| University of Dundee | | 67–99 | 50+ |
| Durham University | 150 | 92–96 | 43–75 |
| University of East Anglia | | 58–93 | 50–60 |
| University of East London | | 92–128 | |
| Edge Hill University | 82 | 51–66 | 60–70 |
| University of Edinburgh | 111–173 | 56–98 | |
| Edinburgh Napier University | | | 70–80 |
| University of Essex | | 61–99 | 55–80 |

*(Continued)*

**Table 33 (Continued)**

| University | Catered university accommodation (£/week) | Self-catering university accommodation (£/week) | Local private rents (£/week) |
|---|---|---|---|
| University of Exeter | 98–156 | 65–104 | 55–100 |
| University of Glamorgan | | 64–78 | 50* |
| University of Glasgow | 107–111 | 66–99 | 60–70 |
| Glasgow Caledonian University | | 72–82 | 70+ |
| University of Gloucestershire | | 69–102 | 55–65 |
| Glyndŵr University | | 60–72 | 50–57 |
| Goldsmiths, London | | 85–114 | 80–110 |
| University of Greenwich | | 78–151 | 75–105 |
| Heriot-Watt University | 95–104 | 57–82 | 83–75 |
| University of Hertfordshire | | 62–97 | 65–75 |
| University of Huddersfield | | 66–86 | 55* |
| University of Hull | 84–123 | 56–110 | 37* |
| Imperial College London | | 55–142 | 105+ |
| Keele University | | 61–95 | 50–60 |
| University of Kent | | 83–140 | 70–110 |
| King's College London | 108–119 | 67–175 | 60–95 |
| Kingston University | | 88–110 | 80–90 |
| Lampeter (University of Wales) | | 60–75 | 40–45 |
| Lancaster University | | 66–125 | 55* |
| University of Leeds | 90–136 | 63–124 | 60–75 |
| Leeds Metropolitan University | | 63–103 | 60+ |
| University of Leicester | 93–138 | 67–83 | 40–50 |
| University of Lincoln | 112 | 84 | |
| University of Liverpool | | 69 | 46–85 |
| Liverpool Hope University | 75–89 | 67 | 60* |
| Liverpool John Moores | | 72–86 | 59–69 |
| London Metropolitan | | | 80–150 |
| London School of Economics | 130–180 | 89–210 | 80–120 |
| London South Bank University | | 87–106 | 85–95 |
| Loughborough University | 109–134 | 60–124 | 60–75 |
| University of Manchester | 82–118 | 63–108 | 55–70 |

**Table 33 (Continued)**

| University | Catered university accommodation (£/week) | Self-catering university accommodation (£/week) | Local private rents (£/week) |
|---|---|---|---|
| Manchester Metropolitan University | 87–89 | 70–130 | 40–150 |
| Middlesex University | | 70–97 | 75–90 |
| Newcastle University | 93–108 | 66–91 | 64* |
| University of Northampton | | 38–80 | 50–55 |
| University of Northumbria | 89–99 | 72–112 | 46–80 |
| University of Nottingham | | | 55–80 |
| Nottingham Trent University | | 68–118 | 55–80 |
| University of Oxford | | | 60–105 |
| Oxford Brookes University | 110–129 | 75–120 | 60–105 |
| University of Plymouth | | 74–114 | 55–90 |
| University of Portsmouth | 89–114 | 75–102 | 62–65 |
| Queen Margaret University | | 91–96 | 70* |
| Queen Mary, London | 91–106 | 64–114 | 85–100 |
| Queen's University Belfast | | 61–86 | 52* |
| University of Reading | 114–153 | 65–104 | 70–105 |
| Robert Gordon University | | 66–86 | 55–70 |
| Roehampton University | 120 | 88–106 | 82–86 |
| Royal Holloway | 101–145 | 81–120 | 65–90 |
| University of St Andrews | 99–146 | 53–116 | 77+ |
| University of Salford | | 56–90 | 50–65 |
| University of Sheffield | 98–122 | 70–110 | 55–70 |
| Sheffield Hallam University | 90 | 50–120 | 50–70 |
| SOAS | 96–145 | 120 | |
| University of Southampton | 102–146 | 66–109 | 60–65 |
| Southampton Solent University | | 74–97 | 55–65 |
| Staffordshire University | 80–113 | 52–85 | 35–65 |
| University of Stirling | | 60–88 | 42–65 |
| University of Strathclyde | 84 | 66–88 | |
| University of Sunderland | | 52–70 | 58* |
| University of Surrey | | 57–99 | 80–85 |

*(Continued)*

**Table 33 (Continued)**

| University | Catered university accommodation (£/week) | Self-catering university accommodation (£/week) | Local private rents (£/week) |
|---|---|---|---|
| University of Sussex | | 71–110 | 85+ |
| Swansea Metropolitan | | 50–66 | 45–58 |
| University of Teesside | | 43–70 | 35–50 |
| Thames Valley University | | 89–159 | 70–165 |
| University of Ulster | | 45–95 | 52* |
| University College London | | 83–157 | 100–110 |
| University of Wales Institute Cardiff | 104–106 | 73–82 | 50–65 |
| University of Wales Newport | | 60–81 | 60* |
| University of Wales Swansea | 94–110 | 62–94 | 55–65 |
| University of Warwick | | 70–115 | 55+ |
| University of West of England | | 87–122 | 60–130 |
| University of West of Scotland | | 55–63 | 40–60 |
| University of Westminster | | 68–153 | 80–140 |
| University of Winchester | 108 | 70–90 | |
| University of Wolverhampton | | 60–90 | 40–50 |
| University of Worcester | | 65–95 | 50–60 |
| University of York | | | 60* |
| York St John University | 104 | 65–86 | 62* |

Source: Guide to UK Universities 2010 by Klaus Boehm and Jenny Lees-Spalding
*Average

## The price of alcohol

After rent, the second greatest non-academic expenditure for most students is on alcohol. Table 34 shows the average price of a pint in different areas of the UK to give you some idea of what to allow for when you're planning a night out on the town.

**Table 34 The local booze ranking**

| UK region | Average price of a pint of lager |
|---|---|
| North West | £2.50 |
| Wales | £2.52 |
| East Midlands | £2.61 |
| Yorkshire | £2.62 |
| West Midlands | £2.64 |
| Scotland | £2.65 |
| South West | £2.75 |
| North | £2.81 |
| Northern Ireland | £2.85 |
| Eastern England | £2.94 |
| South East | £2.95 |
| London | £3.01 |

*Source: CAMRA's Annual Prices Survey 2009, www.camra.org.uk*

**TIP**

**For cheaper grocery bills**
► *plan weekly menus and food shopping, and write a shopping list before you hit the shops*
► *buy food and drink in bulk with friends, and cook together if you can*
► *drink beer or cider at home, rather than more expensive spirits and cocktails*
► *buy from the budget supermarkets (Aldi, Lidl, Netto), or stick to bargain ranges from the bigger supermarkets*
► *make meals at home based on cheap, filling foods like pasta, rice, potatoes, beans or bread*
► *go for BOGOFs (buy one get one free) on toiletries and household goods (but only if they're things you already like and know you'll use).*

# Part-time jobs at university

Many students take on part-time jobs to help make ends meet. Part-time and vacation work can be good experience and bring in some much-needed funds, but it can also interfere with your studies if you are working long hours and finding yourself exhausted afterwards.

Nearly half (42%) of undergraduates were in part-time term employment during 2008, and they earned a combined total of more than £2bn, according to NatWest. Their research reveals that the number of students in part-time employment during the academic terms rose sharply last year, with an extra 25,000 more undergraduates taking on jobs – an increase the size of Oxford University. The national average for working part time is 14 hours per week, although Portsmouth-based students work the most (about 18.5 hours) and Exeter-based students the least (about 9.9 hours).

**Table 35 Undergraduates with part-time jobs, by town or city**

| Rank | University town or city | % of students with part-time job | Average hours worked weekly | Average weekly earnings (£) |
|---|---|---|---|---|
| 1 | Belfast | 64 | 15 | 102 |
| 2 | Dundee | 61 | 17 | 98 |
| 3 | Aberdeen | 58 | 17 | 99 |
| 4 | London | 58 | 15 | 103 |
| 5 | Lancaster | 56 | 12 | 88 |
| 6 | Bristol | 52 | 14 | 107 |
| 7 | Liverpool | 52 | 17 | 101 |
| 8 | Glasgow | 51 | 15 | 88 |
| 9 | Leicester | 49 | 14 | 88 |
| 10 | Cardiff | 44 | 14 | 85 |
| 11 | Plymouth | 43 | 18 | 115 |
| 12 | Portsmouth | 43 | 18.5 | 110 |
| 13 | Southampton | 41 | 11 | 59 |
| 14 | Edinburgh | 40 | 12 | 76 |
| 15 | York | 40 | 12 | 65 |
| 16 | Manchester | 40 | 12 | 64 |
| 17 | Sheffield | 39 | 14 | 75 |
| 18 | Nottingham | 39 | 14 | 85 |
| 19 | Newcastle | 38 | 14 | 92 |
| 20 | Brighton | 36 | 12 | 120 |
| 21 | Birmingham | 35 | 10 | 72 |
| 22 | Leeds | 30 | 15 | 99 |
| 23 | Exeter | 30 | 9.9 | 67 |
| 24 | Oxford | 28 | 14 | 87 |
| 25 | Swansea | 23 | 15 | 64 |
| 26 | Cambridge | 19 | 15 | 110 |

*Source: NatWest Student Living Index 2008*

The NatWest Student Living Index 2008 is a report on university cost of living which analyses weekly expenditure data for rent and living items, and sets this against weekly earnings figures from part-time work.

As you can see from Table 35, Cambridge, Swansea and Oxford have the lowest percentage of student part-time workers, and Belfast and Dundee have the highest percentage. Students at Oxford and Cambridge are usually actively discouraged from taking on part-time paid work by their colleges.

**Get paid at least the minimum wage**
*If you're thinking about taking on a part-time student job or doing holiday work, remember that you should never be paid less than the minimum wage. At the moment that's a 'development' rate of £4.77 per hour if you're aged between 18 and 21, and £5.73 if you're aged 22 and over (see www.hmrc.gov.uk/nmw for the full details).*

In the 2008 NatWest Student Living Index survey, the student interviewees said that they earned about £6.50 per hour, but looking at the whole picture it's clear that there's quite a wide variation in rates of pay. The best hourly rates of pay in the 2008 survey were found in Brighton, followed by Bristol, Lancaster and Cambridge, whereas the lowest hourly rates of pay were found in Swansea (below the minimum wage in many cases), followed by Manchester, Sheffield, York and Southampton.

# Chapter 4

# Finding the right place and people

The general atmosphere at a university, and the non-academic side of life, can vary widely between institutions. Each is unique, and with a little searching you'll be able to find the one that suits you the best. This chapter looks at:

▶ campuses

▶ surroundings

▶ the different people who make up the student body

▶ accommodation

▶ the range of student support available.

The social and entertainment side of university life is covered in Chapter 5, but meanwhile let's look at some of the variables so that you can choose the right location and people for you – remember, you could be spending years at university, so considering these elements will help ensure that you feel happy and fit in.

There's a lot to consider when you're researching the lifestyle at any university. The campus itself may be important to you. For example, you might want to study somewhere old and established, or newer and more modern. You might want to be surrounded by classical or strikingly modern architecture, or the view might not bother you much at all. The setting could be important too: would you prefer to be slap bang in the middle of a city or town, in the outskirts of a city, or in an out-of-town or rural setting? Perhaps you'd like everything on one convenient site, or would you rather have multiple sites to explore? See pages 90–99 to find out more about different types of campus.

The total number of students at any university might also influence your decision, as this can affect the general atmosphere. Would you like to study somewhere with crowds of students around you, or would you rather go somewhere much more small and intimate? Turn to page 97 for more about university sizes.

After considering the overall number of students at a university, you might also be interested in the mix of different types of student. You could look at: numbers of male or female students, part-time students, mature students, overseas students; ethnic diversity; students from different socio-economic groups; local students; students with disabilities; and so on. This information is found on pages 99–114.

# What kind of campus?

Each university has its own special flavour and there's something to suit almost everyone. A university's style is influenced by its age and history, the area or areas it's situated in, the number of students it serves, its buildings and grounds and the number of sites that it spans.

## Old or new?

Some students love to study at the oldest, most established universities. They enjoy the history, the reputation and, more often than not, the beautiful architecture. Older universities are often much better funded than the newer ones, which sometimes (but not always) translates into better amenities and information provision. They may have a good general academic reputation, or be centres of excellence for certain subjects, and have amassed an incredible body of knowledge and research.

However, they may also have lots of outdated rules and regulations, or be a bit stuck in their ways on certain issues. You might find that quaint and amusing, or you might find it restrictive or irritating – it depends upon your personality and outlook on life. If you're thinking about applying to an older university there will be plenty of information about it available to sift through, to help you make a balanced decision.

**Table 36 Britain's oldest universities**

| Rank | University | Year founded |
|------|------------|--------------|
| 1 | University of Oxford | 12th century |
| 2 | University of Cambridge | 13th century |
| 3 | University of St Andrews | 1413 |
| 4 | University of Glasgow | 1451 |
| 5 | Aberdeen University | 1495 |
| 6 | University of Edinburgh | 1582 |

*Source: University websites*

At the other end of the scale, you might prefer one of Britain's youngest universities. They don't have a fuddy-duddy image, they might be centres of excellence, and some of them might be trying extra hard to prove themselves. One thing that's worth noting is that some of the institutions below didn't suddenly pop into existence on the dates given – they may have been created from university mergers (step forward the University of Manchester), they might have recently changed their names (like the University of Lincoln), or they could be the descendants of much older institutes, teaching colleges and church schools that have recently been awarded university status (such as Canterbury Christ Church).

On the downside, the newer universities may have a variety of teething troubles, be struggling to co-ordinate their efforts over four or five different campuses, or lack funding. They may be too new to have gained a reputation yet, including with the best employers. Again, it's important to take your research further than the basic guidebooks as there's a lot to consider.

**Table 37 The UK's newest universities**

| Rank | University | Year gained university status |
|------|------------|-------------------------------|
| =1 | University for the Creative Arts | 2008 |
| =1 | Swansea Metropolitan University | 2008 |
| =1 | Glyndŵr University | 2008 |
| =4 | Queen Margaret University | 2007 |
| =4 | Bucks New University | 2007 |
| =4 | University of the West of Scotland | 2007 |
| =7 | Edge Hill University | 2006 |
| =7 | York St John University | 2006 |
| =9 | Bath Spa University | 2005 |
| =9 | Bolton University | 2005 |
| =9 | Canterbury Christ Church University | 2005 |
| =9 | University of Chester | 2005 |
| =9 | University of Chichester | 2005 |
| =9 | Liverpool Hope University | 2005 |
| =9 | University of Northampton | 2005 |
| =9 | Southampton Solent University | 2005 |
| =9 | University of Winchester | 2005 |
| =9 | University of Worcester | 2005 |
| =19 | University of the Arts, London | 2004 |
| =19 | University of Manchester | 2004 |
| =19 | Roehampton University | 2004 |
| =19 | University of Wales Institute Cardiff | 2004 |
| 23 | University of Wales Newport | 2003 |
| =24 | University of Gloucestershire | 2001 |
| =24 | University of Lincoln | 2001 |

*Source: University websites*

## One campus or many colleges?

The list of 'one-stop shops' below shows all the universities where every department and teaching centre is housed on one main campus. It therefore excludes several universities that have a main site plus smaller separate sites for medical schools, conservatoires and so on. Is a one-site university right for you? If everything's concentrated in one area, it's easy to walk between buildings to different lectures, bump into friends, and drop in to the students' union afterwards to relax and socialise. There might be a closely knit community where everyone knows everyone. On the other hand, it can mean that students stay in one place and miss out on the opportunities in and around the nearest town or city. Also, if you're all in one place and everyone knows everyone, rumours and gossip spread quickly, so you don't have many secrets.

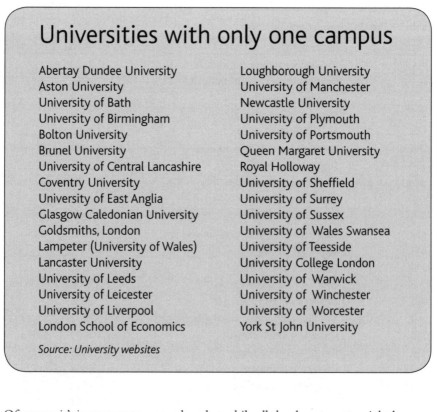

# Universities with only one campus

Abertay Dundee University
Aston University
University of Bath
University of Birmingham
Bolton University
Brunel University
University of Central Lancashire
Coventry University
University of East Anglia
Glasgow Caledonian University
Goldsmiths, London
Lampeter (University of Wales)
Lancaster University
University of Leeds
University of Leicester
University of Liverpool
London School of Economics

Loughborough University
University of Manchester
Newcastle University
University of Plymouth
University of Portsmouth
Queen Margaret University
Royal Holloway
University of Sheffield
University of Surrey
University of Sussex
University of Wales Swansea
University of Teesside
University College London
University of Warwick
University of Winchester
University of Worcester
York St John University

*Source: University websites*

Of course, it's important to remember that while all the departments might be concentrated in one place, that doesn't necessarily mean that your accommodation is guaranteed to be near campus. For more information about accommodation, see page 121.

# Most constituent colleges or teaching sites

1. University of Oxford (38 independent colleges).

2. University of Cambridge (31 colleges, including two for postgraduates).

3. University of London (19 colleges).

4. Arts London (six colleges over 17 sites).

5. Birmingham City University (eight sites).

*Source: University websites*

## ? Did you know?

*The three greenest, most sustainable and ethical universities in the UK are the University of Gloucestershire, the University of Plymouth, and the University of the West of England, according to People & Planet.*

If a single-campus university is not something that appeals to you, perhaps you'd prefer to look in the other direction, at collegiate universities, or institutions that are spread over several different main sites. Where there are several colleges you can have collaboration or rivalry, and sometimes rivalry spurs people on to get the best exam or sports results. It can also be a refreshing change to travel from site to site and meet lots of new people, although it's less pleasant it you're on foot in the winter or rushing to a distant building to get there in time for an appointment.

## Where you're coming from

The location of the university in relation to its nearest town or city can strongly influence the atmosphere. If you're on a main campus right in the city or town centre, the delights of the local entertainment are laid out on the doorstep. This can make it easier to have a rich and varied social life, keep up with your favourite interests, and get to all the major transport links. It can also mean that students don't stick around the university to socialise, it can be distracting or noisy at times when you need to sleep or study, and the temptation to spend too much money is always close by. The location lists in this chapter are for the main campuses of each university (universities with more than one main campus have been omitted to avoid confusion).

# Main campus location

**City centre universities**
Aberdeen University
Abertay Dundee University
Aston University
Bangor University
Bolton University
University of Brighton
Coventry University
Durham University
University of Cambridge
University of Central Lancashire
University of Edinburgh
Glasgow Caledonian University
University of Glasgow
Leeds Metropolitan University
University of Liverpool

Liverpool John Moores
Newcastle University
University of Northumbria
Nottingham Trent University
University of Oxford
University of Plymouth
University of Portsmouth
Robert Gordon University
Sheffield Hallam University
Southampton Solent
University
University of Strathclyde
University of Sunderland
Swansea Metropolitan
University of Wolverhampton

**Town centre universities**
Bedfordshire University
University for Creative Arts
University of Greenwich
University of Huddersfield

Kingston University
Lampeter (University of Wales)
University of St Andrews

**Universities within Greater London**
Arts London
City University, London
University of East London
Goldsmiths, London
Imperial College London
King's College London
London Metropolitan
London School of Economics

London South Bank
Middlesex University
Queen Mary, London
Roehampton University
SOAS
Thames Valley University
University College London
University of Westminster

*Source: University websites*

A university with a main campus on the edge of town can have a number of benefits. You're close enough to the town or city to use the amenities easily; students might spend more time in the union building because it's convenient; you can get out into the countryside quicker if that's something you love; and the outskirts of a town tend to have cheaper private accommodation. On the other hand, you might find a 25-minute uphill walk back from the city centre annoying after a while.

# Campuses on the outskirts

**City outskirts**

University of Birmingham
University of Bradford
University of Bristol
Canterbury Christ Church University
Cardiff University
University of Chester
University of Chichester
De Montfort University
University of Derby
University of Dundee
University of Exeter
University of Kent
University of Leeds

University of Leicester
Liverpool Hope University
University of Manchester
Manchester Met University
University of Northampton
University of Nottingham
Oxford Brookes University
Queen Margaret University
Queen's University Belfast
University of Sheffield
University of Ulster
University of Winchester
York St John University

**Town outskirts**

Brunel University
Bucks New University
Glyndŵr University
Loughborough University

Royal Holloway
University of Surrey
University of Wales Swansea
University of Teesside

*Source: University websites*

Universities that are based a couple of miles or more out of a town or city often have close-knit communities of students, and attractive green and leafy campuses – ideal if you love the countryside. The downsides are that some people might find the atmosphere slightly static or claustrophobic, it's harder to get into the town or to major transport links, and if there's very little entertainment on offer the place can become a bit of a dead zone at weekends.

## Beautiful buildings or surroundings

A select number of universities are regularly described as having attractive or beautiful campuses. This can be due to their impressive architecture, their surrounding grounds, or a mixture of the two. Older listed buildings tend to put a university on the 'attractive' list, but it doesn't necessarily mean that you should only consider the oldest universities in the UK, since some of the newer institutions are housed in classic mansions or even on world heritage sites (such as Greenwich). Some students also say that they love the radical modern architecture at certain universities, although this often sparks some quite fierce debate. If a

## Out of town campuses

University of Bath
Bath Spa University
Birmingham City University
University of Cumbria
University of East Anglia
Edge Hill University
Edinburgh Napier University
University of Essex
University of Glamorgan
University of Hertfordshire
University of Hull
Keele University

Lancaster University
University of Reading
University of Salford
University of Stirling
University of Southampton
University of Sussex
University of Wales Newport
University of Warwick
University of the West of
England
University of Worcester
University of York

*Source: University websites*

pretty or striking environment is very important to you, look at the pictures on
university websites and in prospectuses, and make personal visits to make your own
mind up. After all, beauty is in the eye of the beholder.

## Attractive campuses

University of Birmingham
University of Bristol
University of Cambridge
Durham University
University of East Anglia
University of Edinburgh
University of Essex
University of Exeter
University of Glasgow
University of Greenwich
Imperial College London
Keele University
King's College London

London School of Economics
Queen Mary, London
Queen's University Belfast
University of Nottingham
University of Oxford
University of Reading
Royal Holloway
St Andrews University
University of Southampton
University of Stirling
University of Sussex
University College London
University of Warwick

*Source: Student surveys*

## Size matters – number of students

The size of a university and the number of undergraduates can hugely influence your enjoyment, depending on what you like best. The super-sized universities offer an incredible range of diversity, and if you have an unusual interest or hobby there's a good chance that you'll be able to find similar people who like the same things. On the other hand, you might feel lost in the crowd, or so overwhelmed by the number of people that you don't know where to begin. The smallest universities are places where you bump into the same people over and over again, which can be a good or a bad thing, and they may have fewer clubs, societies and general facilities. If both these options sound too extreme then you might be happier looking for something in the middle range, size-wise.

Let's start by finding out where you can find the biggest universities, looking at both the total number of higher education students, and the total number of undergraduates. As you can see, the two universities with the highest total number of higher education students are both in the same town, Manchester.

**Table 38 Top 20 biggest universities (most higher education students)**

| Rank | Most total (undergraduates + postgraduates) | | Most undergraduate students | |
|------|------------------------------|--------|------------------------------|--------|
| | University | Number | University | Number |
| 1 | University of Manchester | 37,360 | Manchester Metropolitan University | 27,635 |
| 2 | Manchester Metropolitan University | 32,965 | University of Central Lancashire | 27,325 |
| 3 | University of Leeds | 32,250 | University of Manchester | 26,845 |
| 4 | University of Nottingham | 31,830 | University of Plymouth | 25,715 |
| 5 | University of the West of England | 31,700 | University of the West of England | 25,420 |
| 6 | University of Central Lancashire | 31,245 | University of Nottingham | 23,865 |
| 7 | Sheffield Hallam University | 31,090 | University of Leeds | 23,845 |
| 8 | University of Northumbria | 29,995 | Sheffield Hallam University | 23,535 |
| 9 | University of Plymouth | 29,375 | Leeds Metropolitan University | 23,310 |
| 10 | University of Warwick | 28,445 | University of Northumbria | 23,245 |
| 11 | University of Birmingham | 28,240 | University of Teesside | 22,425 |

*(Continued)*

**Table 38 (Continued)**

| Rank | Most total (undergraduates + postgraduates) | | Most undergraduate students | |
|---|---|---|---|---|
| 12 | London Metropolitan University | 27,975 | London Metropolitan University | 20,920 |
| 13 | Leeds Metropolitan University | 27,215 | Liverpool John Moores University | 19,980 |
| 14 | Cardiff University | 26,585 | Cardiff University | 19,820 |
| 15 | University of Teesside | 25,405 | Birmingham City University | 19,760 |
| 16 | University of Sheffield | 24,560 | University of Warwick | 19,750 |
| 17 | University of Greenwich | 24,505 | University of Greenwich | 19,105 |
| 18 | Liverpool John Moores University | 24,445 | University of Glamorgan | 19,060 |
| 19 | Kingston University | 23,985 | University of Ulster | 19,045 |
| 20 | University of Oxford | 23,985 | Kingston University | 18,910 |

Source: HESA, Students in Higher Education Institutions 2007/2008

Not everyone wants to go to a gigantic university, and many students are happier with smaller and more manageable institutions. It may be easier to get to know everyone, and to stand out from the crowd if things are going well – you might like the idea of being a big fish in a small pond.

**Table 39 Top 20 smallest universities (fewest higher education students)**

| Rank | Least total (undergraduates + postgraduates) | | Total undergraduate students | |
|---|---|---|---|---|
| | University | Number | University | Number |
| 1 | University of Abertay Dundee | 4,140 | SOAS | 2,775 |
| 2 | SOAS | 4,730 | University of Abertay Dundee | 3,555 |
| 3 | University of Chichester | 4,805 | University of Chichester | 3,795 |
| 4 | University of Winchester | 5,235 | London School of Economics | 3,920 |
| 5 | Queen Margaret University | 5,330 | Queen Margaret University | 4,120 |
| 6 | University for the Creative Arts | 5,430 | University of Winchester | 4,330 |
| 7 | Swansea Metropolitan University | 5,595 | Swansea Metropolitan University | 4,520 |

**Table 39 (Continued)**

| Rank | Least total (undergraduates + postgraduates) | | Total undergraduate students | |
|------|------|------|------|------|
| 8 | York St John University | 6,205 | Bath Spa University | 4,880 |
| 9 | Liverpool Hope University | 7,060 | University for the Creative Arts | 5,155 |
| 10 | Glyndŵr University | 7,265 | Goldsmiths College | 5,280 |
| 11 | Bath Spa University | 7,470 | York St John University | 5,370 |
| 12 | Goldsmiths College | 7,495 | Heriot-Watt University | 5,395 |
| 13 | University of Worcester | 7,765 | Liverpool Hope University | 5,665 |
| 14 | University of Bolton | 7,845 | University of Worcester | 6,175 |
| 15 | Lampeter (University of Wales) | 7,885 | University of Bolton | 6,380 |
| 16 | University of St Andrews | 8,175 | Roehampton University | 6,435 |
| 17 | Roehampton University | 8,235 | Royal Holloway, London | 6,560 |
| 18 | Royal Holloway, London | 8,385 | Glyndŵr University | 6,625 |
| 19 | University of Gloucestershire | 8,515 | University of St Andrews | 6,655 |
| 20 | London School of Economics | 9,105 | University of Gloucestershire | 6,700 |

*Source: HESA, Students in Higher Education Institutions 2007/2008*

# Meet the students

A higher education institution would be nothing without its students, and the mix of different people adds something unique to the atmosphere of every university. Going to university is a once in a lifetime chance to meet different people from all over the world (and from parts of the UK you don't know much about), and experience new ideas, opinions and cultures. As a whole universities tend to be very accepting places, and all should have non-discrimination policies in place.

## Male:female ratios

Women currently make up around 57% of the entire UK higher education population, although some universities are especially popular with female undergraduates (see Tables 40 and 41). Subjects that have particularly high numbers of female full-time first degree undergraduate students include subjects allied to medicine (81%), veterinary science (76%), education (76%) and languages (67%). If you'd like to study in a woman-friendly environment, or you'd simply prefer to be surrounded by women, consider one of the following universities.

**Table 40 Universities with the most female undergraduates**

| Rank | University | % females | Female:male ratio | Total females | Total males |
|------|-----------|-----------|-------------------|---------------|-------------|
| 1 | Queen Margaret University, Edinburgh | 78.3 | 3.6 | 3,225 | 895 |
| 2 | Roehampton University | 76.4 | 3.2 | 4,915 | 1,515 |
| 3 | Edge Hill University | 76.2 | 3.2 | 9,760 | 3,045 |
| 4 | Liverpool Hope University | 72.4 | 2.6 | 4,100 | 1,570 |
| 5 | University of Cumbria | 72.2 | 2.6 | 7,130 | 2,745 |
| 6 | University of Winchester | 71.7 | 2.5 | 3,105 | 1,225 |
| 7 | University of the Arts, London | 71.7 | 2.5 | 9,135 | 3,615 |
| 8 | University of Worcester | 71.6 | 2.5 | 4,420 | 1,755 |
| 9 | University of Chester | 70.6 | 2.4 | 7,440 | 3,100 |
| 10 | Canterbury Christ Church University | 70.3 | 2.3 | 8,320 | 3,510 |
| 11 | University of Bedfordshire | 69.0 | 2.2 | 8,420 | 3,785 |
| 12 | Bath Spa University | 67.9 | 2.1 | 3,315 | 1,565 |
| 13 | York St John University | 67.9 | 2.1 | 3,645 | 1,725 |
| 14 | Anglia Ruskin University | 66.5 | 1.9 | 11,100 | 5,600 |
| 15 | University of Northampton | 65.8 | 1.9 | 6,455 | 3,350 |
| 16 | University for the Creative Arts | 65.6 | 1.9 | 3,380 | 1,780 |
| 17 | Robert Gordon University | 65.5 | 1.9 | 5,740 | 3,025 |
| 18 | Goldsmiths College | 65.4 | 1.8 | 3,455 | 1,825 |
| 19 | University of Chichester | 65.4 | 1.8 | 2,480 | 1,320 |
| 20 | University of Dundee | 64.5 | 1.8 | 7,140 | 3,930 |

Source: HESA, Students in Higher Education Institutions 2007/2008

Conversely, a few universities have a higher intake of male students, and this is partly linked to centres of excellence that specialise in some of the more male-dominated degree subjects. Courses with higher numbers of male students include engineering and technology (86%), computer science (80%) and architecture, building and planning (69%). As you can see from Table 41, there are now only 10 UK universities where the males outnumber the females. If you want to be surrounded by males, they're the places to choose.

**Table 41 Universities with the most male undergraduates**

| Rank | University | % males | Male:female ratio | Total males | Total females |
|---|---|---|---|---|---|
| 1 | Imperial College London | 65.0 | 1.9 | 5,545 | 2,990 |
| 2 | Loughborough University | 62.5 | 1.7 | 7,165 | 4,300 |
| 3 | Southampton Solent University | 58.9 | 1.4 | 5,965 | 4,165 |
| 4 | Heriot-Watt University | 57.8 | 1.7 | 3,115 | 2,275 |
| 5 | University of Bath | 56.0 | 1.7 | 5,075 | 4,000 |
| 6 | University of Portsmouth | 52.9 | 1.1 | 8,430 | 7,540 |
| 7 | Aston University | 51.1 | 1.0 | 3,655 | 3,500 |
| 8 | Swansea Metropolitan University | 51.0 | 1.0 | 2,305 | 2,215 |
| 9 | Coventry University | 50.7 | 1.0 | 8,530 | 8,305 |
| 10 | Brunel University | 50.4 | 1.0 | 5,240 | 5,165 |
| 11 | University of Oxford | 49.8 | 1.0 | 7,995 | 8,065 |
| 12 | London School of Economics | 49.7 | 1.0 | 1,950 | 1,970 |
| 13 | Glyndŵr University | 49.6 | 1.0 | 3,285 | 3,340 |
| 14 | Newcastle University | 49.2 | 1.0 | 7,080 | 7,305 |
| 15 | Kingston University | 49.2 | 1.0 | 9,295 | 9,615 |
| 16 | Leeds Metropolitan University | 48.7 | 1.0 | 11,360 | 11,950 |
| 17 | University of Bolton | 48.4 | 0.9 | 3,095 | 3,290 |
| 18 | University of Abertay Dundee | 48.2 | 0.9 | 1,715 | 1,840 |
| 19 | University of Durham | 48.2 | 0.9 | 5,615 | 6,025 |
| 20 | University College London | 48.1 | 0.9 | 5,730 | 6,190 |

*Source: HESA, Students in Higher Education Institutions 2007/2008*

## Mature students

All students aged 21 years or over are automatically classed as mature students, and they currently make up around 21% of UK-domiciled students on full-time first degree courses. If you're thinking about going to university as a mature student, you might like to consider some of the following institutions that support large

**Mature students' reading list**
*If you're returning to study after a long gap, you might find that a few of your study skills are a little rusty. For a confidence boost and some helpful information, you might like to try reading Returning to Education: A Practical Handbook for Adult Learners, published by How to Books, or the Mature Students' Directory, published by Trotman.*

populations of people aged 21 years old and over, or you may feel that this is less of a priority consideration for you.

Table 42 Universities with the highest percentage of mature students

| Rank | University | % mature students | Number of mature students |
|------|------------|-------------------|---------------------------|
| 1 | Glyndŵr University | 65.0 | 760 |
| 2 | London South Bank University | 62.6 | 2,865 |
| 3 | Thames Valley University | 62.1 | 2,020 |
| 4 | University of East London | 60.1 | 3,090 |
| 5 | Lampeter (University of Wales) | 53.6 | 260 |
| 6 | University of Bolton | 52.8 | 840 |
| 7 | University of Greenwich | 51.4 | 3,105 |
| 8 | Edinburgh Napier University | 51.1 | 1,905 |
| 9 | London Metropolitan University | 49.3 | 2,305 |
| 10 | University of Bedfordshire | 48.6 | 1,780 |
| 11 | University of West of Scotland | 46.9 | 1,765 |
| 12 | University of Abertay Dundee | 46.9 | 680 |
| 13 | Goldsmiths College | 44.8 | 900 |
| 14 | Anglia Ruskin University | 44.7 | 1,870 |
| 15 | University of Sunderland | 44.0 | 1,585 |
| 16 | University of Northampton | 43.9 | 1,400 |
| 17 | University of Glamorgan | 42.7 | 2,175 |
| 18 | Birmingham City University | 42.0 | 2,295 |
| 19 | University College Birmingham | 40.5 | 530 |
| 20 | Middlesex University | 40.2 | 2,060 |

Source: HESA. Students in Higher Education Institutions 2007/2008
Note: students included in table are first-year full-time undergraduates.

A few universities have a lower than average intake of mature students, and it's interesting to see which ones these are. See Table 43 for the most youthful student populations in the UK.

## Overseas students

Many students say that one of the best things about going to university is the chance to meet all kinds of different types of people from all over the world. Non-UK-domiciled students currently make up approximately 19% of the full-time higher education population, and numbers are split roughly equally between

**Table 43 Universities with the lowest percentage of mature students**

| Rank | University | % mature students | Number of mature students |
|------|------------|-------------------|---------------------------|
| 1 | London School of Economics | 2.9 | 40 |
| 2 | Loughborough University | 4.1 | 150 |
| 3 | Imperial College London | 5.0 | 115 |
| 4 | University of St Andrews | 6.5 | 100 |
| 5 | University of Bristol | 6.5 | 245 |
| 6 | University of Durham | 6.7 | 245 |
| 7 | University of Lancaster | 7.5 | 200 |
| 8 | University of Leeds | 9.0 | 620 |
| 9 | University of Warwick | 9.5 | 355 |
| 10 | University of Sheffield | 9.9 | 495 |
| 11 | University of York | 10.2 | 270 |
| 12 | Aston University | 10.4 | 220 |
| 13 | University of Exeter | 10.4 | 410 |
| 14 | University of Bath | 10.4 | 280 |
| 15 | University of Oxford | 10.5 | 365 |
| 16 | University of Edinburgh | 10.6 | 455 |
| 17 | University of Birmingham | 10.7 | 530 |
| 18 | University of Cambridge | 11.3 | 410 |
| 19 | University of Newcastle | 11.3 | 525 |
| 20 | University of Manchester | 12.2 | 1,040 |

Source: HESA, Students in Higher Education Institutions 2007/2008

**Note:** students included in table are first-year full-time undergraduates.

non-UK European Union (EU) students and students coming from outside the EU. The subjects that attract the most students from outside the UK include engineering and technology, business and administrative studies, computer science, law and mathematical sciences.

There are many reasons why certain universities are popular with overseas students, including the international reputation of universities or certain university departments, good advertising of courses, word of mouth reports about excellent support for new and continuing students, and links or campuses based outside the UK.

The following universities have the greatest cultural mix.

**Table 44 Universities with the most overseas students**

| Rank | University | % of non-UK-domiciled students |
|------|-----------|-------------------------------|
| 1 | London School of Economics | 49.6 |
| 2 | Imperial College London | 34.7 |
| 3 | University of the Arts, London | 33.4 |
| 4 | SOAS | 29.1 |
| 5 | Lampeter (University of Wales) | 27.1 |
| 6 | University of Bedfordshire | 25.5 |
| 7 | City University London | 25.5 |
| 8 | University of St Andrews | 25.1 |
| 9 | University College London | 25.0 |
| 10 | University of Bath | 22.6 |
| 11 | Edinburgh Napier University | 22.5 |
| 12 | University of Bradford | 22.1 |
| 13 | University of Warwick | 22.0 |
| 14 | University of Essex | 21.8 |
| 15 | London Metropolitan University | 20.9 |
| 16 | Thames Valley University | 20.8 |
| 17 | Heriot-Watt University | 20.5 |
| 18 | University of Central Lancashire | 19.7 |
| 19 | University of Surrey | 19.6 |
| 20 | University of Abertay Dundee | 18.6 |
| 21 | University of Nottingham | 17.8 |
| 22 | Middlesex University | 17.5 |
| 23 | University of Greenwich | 17.3 |
| 24 | University of Manchester | 16.9 |
| 25 | London South Bank University | 16.8 |
| 26 | University of Kent | 16.4 |
| 27 | King's College London | 16.4 |
| 28 | University of Sunderland | 16.4 |
| 29 | Coventry University | 16.0 |
| 30 | Oxford Brookes University | 16.0 |

*Source: HESA, Students in Higher Education Institutions 2007/2008*
**Note:** students included in table are first-year full-time undergraduates.

Some universities are less 'international' than others, for all sorts of reasons. For example, some of the newer universities have not had time to gain much of a reputation or build links with other countries. Table 45 lists some of the less cosmopolitan universities.

**Table 45 Universities with the fewest overseas students**

| Rank | University | % of non-UK-domiciled students |
|---|---|---|
| 1 | Edge Hill University | 0.6 |
| 2 | York St John University | 2.4 |
| 3 | University of Cumbria | 2.4 |
| 4 | University of Chester | 2.5 |
| 5 | University of Winchester | 2.6 |
| 6 | Bath Spa University | 2.9 |
| 7 | Sheffield Hallam University | 3.1 |
| 8 | University of Chichester | 3.8 |
| 9 | Glasgow Caledonian University | 4.1 |
| 10 | University of Wales, Newport | 4.4 |
| 11 | University of Strathclyde | 4.5 |
| 12 | Leeds Metropolitan University | 4.6 |
| 13 | Liverpool Hope University | 4.7 |
| 14 | University of Gloucestershire | 4.8 |
| 15 | De Montfort University | 5.0 |

Source: HESA, Students in Higher Education Institutions 2007/2008
**Note:** students included in table are first-year full-time undergraduates.

**?** Did you know?

*Many famous comedy duos attended university together. Matt Lucas and David Walliams of* Little Britain *fame both went to Bristol University, and David Mitchell and Robert Webb (*Peep Show, That Mitchell and Webb Look*) studied at Cambridge.*

## Ethnic diversity

It's estimated that approximately 17% of all first-year UK-domiciled higher education students were from ethnic minority groups in the academic year of 2007/2008, the most recent complete year for which statistics are available. Again, some universities have a much more diverse mixture of students than others. All institutions should have a range of non-discriminatory measures in place, and many universities also have designated support and campaigns officers based in their students' union who are devoted to promoting diversity and preventing discrimination.

**Table 46 Universities with the most ethnic minority students**

| Rank | University | % students from ethnic minority groups |
|------|------------|----------------------------------------|
| 1 | Brunel University | 56.9 |
| 2 | Queen Mary London | 56.6 |
| 3 | University of East London | 54.6 |
| 4 | Middlesex University | 54.1 |
| 5 | Aston University | 53.1 |
| 6 | London Metropolitan University | 52.4 |
| 7 | University of Westminster | 49.1 |
| 8 | Kingston University | 48.7 |
| 9 | University of Bradford | 47.6 |
| 10 | Thames Valley University | 46.7 |
| 11 | London South Bank University | 45.2 |
| 12 | City University | 41.8 |
| 13 | SOAS | 41.6 |
| 14 | London School of Economics | 41.2 |
| 15 | University of Greenwich | 40.9 |
| 16 | King's College London | 40.7 |
| 17 | University of Hertfordshire | 38.4 |
| 18 | Imperial College | 37.8 |
| 19 | Birmingham City University | 35.3 |
| 20 | Goldsmiths College | 34.8 |
| 21 | De Montfort University | 34.8 |
| 22 | Roehampton University | 31.6 |
| 23 | University of Wolverhampton | 31.5 |
| 24 | University College London | 31.4 |
| 25 | University of Bedfordshire | 28.7 |
| 26 | Buckinghamshire New University | 28.3 |
| 27 | Coventry University | 26.8 |
| 28 | Royal Holloway and Bedford | 25.8 |
| 29 | University of the Arts, London | 25.7 |
| 30 | University of Surrey | 23.0 |

*Source: HESA, Students in Higher Education Institutions 2007/2008*
**Note**: includes all UK home students in higher education and further education.

**Table 47 Universities with the fewest ethnic minority students**

| Rank | University | % students from ethnic minority groups |
|---|---|---|
| 1 | Queen's University Belfast | 1.5 |
| 2 | University of Ulster | 1.7 |
| 3 | Bangor University | 2.1 |
| 4 | University of Stirling | 2.3 |
| 5 | Aberystwyth University | 2.6 |
| 6 | University of Plymouth | 3.4 |
| 7 | York St John University | 3.4 |
| 8 | Swansea University | 3.9 |
| 9 | University of the West of Scotland | 3.9 |
| 10 | University of Chester | 4.1 |
| 11 | Glyndŵr University | 4.2 |
| 12 | University of Lancaster | 4.4 |
| 13 | Bath Spa University | 4.5 |
| 14 | University of Winchester | 4.6 |
| 15 | University of Chichester | 4.6 |
| 16 | University of St Andrews | 4.7 |
| 17 | University of Exeter | 4.7 |
| 18 | University of Strathclyde | 4.7 |
| 19 | University of Glamorgan | 4.7 |
| 20 | Swansea Metropolitan University | 4.8 |

*Source: HESA, Students in Higher Education Institutions 2007/2008*
**Note**: includes all UK home students in higher education and further education

## Students with disabilities

While the situation isn't perfect everywhere, access to higher education for students with disabilities has been slowly and surely improving over the last few years as universities comply with new directives and make their own initiatives. However, it's good to do your own research as some places are simply further ahead with this than others.

If you're a student with any disability you should contact any prospective university to discuss any of your specific or general requirements ahead of time. You can greatly benefit from contacting Skill, the National Bureau for Students with Disabilities, too. They provide advice on all aspects of student life, including welfare, work experience and volunteering, and they produce a range of guides, in addition to running an online database of university accessibility information and contacts.

Skill: National Bureau for Students with Disabilities
Unit 3, Floor 3
Radisson Court
219 Long Lane

London SE1 4PR
Main telephone and textphone: 020 7450 0620
Fax: 020 7450 0650
Email: skill@skill.org.uk
Website: www.skill.org.uk

**Table 48 Universities with the most students with disabilities**

| Rank | University | % of students with disabilities | Number of students with disabilities |
|---|---|---|---|
| 1 | University of the Arts, London | 22.4 | 6,560 |
| 2 | University for the Creative Arts | 15.2 | 1,180 |
| 3 | De Montfort University | 14.0 | 2,965 |
| 4 | Lampeter (University of Wales) | 13.1 | 1,035 |
| 5 | University of Winchester | 12.4 | 650 |
| 6 | University of Chichester | 12.0 | 575 |
| 7 | University of Sussex | 11.6 | 1,450 |
| 8 | Liverpool Hope University | 11.0 | 785 |
| 9 | Bournemouth University | 11.0 | 1,965 |
| 10 | University of Wales, Newport | 10.9 | 1,025 |
| 11 | Loughborough University | 10.9 | 1,925 |
| 12 | Oxford Brookes University | 10.2 | 1,875 |
| 13 | Bath Spa University | 10.2 | 760 |
| 14 | University of Ulster | 10.0 | 2,365 |
| 15 | Goldsmiths College | 9.9 | 750 |
| 16 | University of Plymouth | 9.8 | 2,890 |
| 17 | Birmingham City University | 9.8 | 2,325 |
| 18 | Leeds Metropolitan University | 9.8 | 4,030 |
| 19 | University of Salford | 9.5 | 1,815 |
| 20 | University of Bolton | 9.4 | 810 |
| 21 | University of Southampton | 9.3 | 2,205 |
| 22 | University of Hull | 9.3 | 1,945 |
| 23 | University of St Andrews | 9.2 | 755 |
| 24 | Buckinghamshire New University | 9.2 | 865 |
| 25 | York St John University | 9.0 | 560 |
| 26 | University of Portsmouth | 9.0 | 1,785 |
| 27 | University of Brighton | 8.9 | 1,895 |
| 28 | Queen Margaret University, Edinburgh | 8.9 | 475 |
| 29 | University of Lincoln | 8.7 | 1,400 |
| 30 | University of Reading | 8.7 | 1,255 |

*Source: HESA, Students in Higher Education Institutions 2007/2008*
**Note**: includes all undergraduate and postgraduate students.

**Table 49 Universities with the fewest students with disabilities**

| Rank | University | % of students with disabilities | Number of students with disabilities |
|---|---|---|---|
| 1 | University of Strathclyde | 3.3 | 715 |
| 2 | Imperial College London | 3.5 | 490 |
| 3 | City University | 3.7 | 785 |
| 4 | University College London | 3.8 | 805 |
| 5 | University of Westminster | 4.0 | 920 |
| 6 | University of Cambridge | 4.0 | 915 |
| 7 | Glasgow Caledonian University | 4.0 | 675 |
| 8 | University of Bath | 4.2 | 545 |
| 9 | Bangor University | 4.3 | 710 |
| 10 | King's College London | 4.3 | 905 |
| 11 | University of Northumbria | 4.4 | 1,345 |
| 12 | London School of Economics | 4.4 | 405 |
| 13 | University of Warwick | 4.6 | 1,295 |
| 14 | Queen Mary, University of London | 4.6 | 625 |
| 15 | Aston University | 4.6 | 440 |
| 16 | Queen's University Belfast | 4.7 | 1,040 |
| 17 | Heriot-Watt University | 4.7 | 475 |
| 18 | Nottingham Trent University | 4.9 | 1,175 |
| 19 | University of Oxford | 4.9 | 1,185 |
| 20 | SOAS | 5.1 | 240 |

*Source: HESA, Students in Higher Education Institutions 2007/2008*
**Note**: includes all undergraduate and postgraduate students.

## Studying close to home

Some universities are more 'local' than others, with significant numbers of students staying in their home town to study and remaining in the family home. A number of universities have a larger than average proportion of students living at home, including:

► University of Glasgow
► London Metropolitan
► London South Bank
► Middlesex University

▶   Queen's University Belfast

▶   University of Strathclyde.

The universities with fewest students living at home are Oxford and Cambridge. This is partly influenced by college rules about not living more than six miles away if you wish to study there.

The current average number of students living at home is about 20% of undergraduates, and numbers appear to be increasing over time, as the costs of gaining a higher education qualification continue to rise and living with the parents becomes a more attractive financial proposition.

You might relish the idea of staying in a particular area if you know many of your friends will be studying there too, or you might like to strike out on your own and try something new. If you do stay with your family while you are at university, it's cheaper and more comfortable. On the other hand, it may feel harder to meet new people, or your parents' rules may annoy you. If you do decide to live with your relations you'll still need to open a student account, and maybe put together a small cash fund to help you get started during your first term. On the other hand, if you're considering moving to an area with lots of local students, think about whether you'd enjoy the sense of mixing with a closer-knit local community or whether you might perhaps find it a bit cliquey, at least to begin with. The choice, as ever, is yours.

## Socio-economic groups

In the last two years the financial situation has improved for students from families that are less well off financially, as more government grants are given out and bigger bursaries are offered by various universities. However, the fact remains that many universities are still 'posher' than others, with a greater than average intake of undergraduates coming from higher socio-economic groups.

## Part-time students

The popularity of part-time study has increased recently, and many institutions cater well for students who would like to gain a degree without studying full time. Part-time courses usually allow students to hold down a full- or part-time job or keep up with other commitments, such as family responsibilities. This makes gaining a degree more affordable for many students, although studying and working at the same time requires a lot of dedication. Students have to give up much of their free time to gain a qualification, the workload can be heavy at times, and the hours involved mean that you may find that you miss out on much of the social side of university life.

**Table 50 Universities with most undergraduates from lower socio-economic groups**

| Rank | University | % from lower socio-economic groups |
|---|---|---|
| 1 | University of Wolverhampton | 52 |
| =2 | University of Bradford | 48 |
| =2 | Middlesex University | 48 |
| =2 | University of Sunderland | 48 |
| =2 | University of Teesside | 48 |
| 6 | University of Ulster | 47 |
| =7 | Birmingham City University | 46 |
| =7 | Bolton University | 46 |
| =7 | University of East London | 46 |
| =7 | Glyndŵr University | 46 |
| =7 | University of Greenwich | 46 |
| 12 | London South Bank | 45 |
| =13 | London Metropolitan | 44 |
| =13 | University of Westminster | 44 |
| =15 | Bedfordshire University | 43 |
| =15 | De Montfort University | 43 |
| =17 | University of Glamorgan | 42 |
| =17 | University of Huddersfield | 42 |
| =17 | Liverpool Hope University | 42 |
| =17 | Oxford Brookes University | 42 |
| =17 | Swansea Metropolitan | 42 |
| =22 | Liverpool John Moores University | 41 |
| =22 | University of Salford | 41 |
| =24 | City University, London | 40 |
| =24 | Edge Hill University | 40 |
| =24 | University of Hertfordshire | 40 |
| =24 | Thames Valley University | 40 |
| =28 | Coventry University | 39 |
| =28 | University of Derby | 39 |
| =28 | Lampeter (University of Wales) | 39 |
| =28 | Staffordshire University | 39 |
| =28 | University of Worcester | 39 |

Source: HESA

**Table 51 Universities with fewest undergraduates from lower socio-economic groups**

| Rank | University | % from lower socio-economic groups |
|------|-----------|-----------------------------------|
| 1 | University of Oxford | 10 |
| 2 | University of Cambridge | 12 |
| 3 | University of Kent | 13 |
| 4 | University of Bristol | 14 |
| 5 | Durham University | 15 |
| =6 | University of Edinburgh | 16 |
| =6 | University of St Andrews | 16 |
| =8 | University of Exeter | 17 |
| =8 | University of York | 17 |
| =10 | Bournemouth University | 18 |
| =10 | Imperial College London | 18 |
| =10 | London School of Economics | 18 |
| =10 | University of Warwick | 18 |
| =14 | University of Bath | 19 |
| =14 | University of Leeds | 19 |
| =14 | University College London | 19 |
| =17 | Newcastle University | 20 |
| =17 | University of Nottingham | 20 |
| =17 | SOAS | 20 |
| =17 | University of Southampton | 20 |

Source: HESA

Some employers are very supportive, especially if the subject studied is relevant to their business. If you're lucky you can be offered funding and/or time off from work. The Open University and Birkbeck College both cater specifically for the needs of part-time students, and many other universities are becoming more flexible with their modes of study.

**Table 52 Universities with most part-time undergraduates**

| Rank | University | % part-time undergraduates |
|---|---|---|
| 1 | Open University | 100.0 |
| 2 | Birkbeck College | 98.8 |
| 3 | Lampeter (University of Wales) | 84.0 |
| 4 | University of Teesside | 62.9 |
| 5 | Glyndŵr University | 62.2 |
| 6 | University of Wales, Newport | 56.2 |
| 7 | University of Sunderland | 50.0 |
| 8 | Edge Hill University | 49.9 |
| 9 | University of the West of Scotland | 49.8 |
| 10 | Thames Valley University | 48.3 |
| 11 | City University | 46.1 |
| 12 | University of Cumbria | 45.7 |
| 13 | University of Warwick | 44.4 |
| 14 | Anglia Ruskin University | 43.6 |
| 15 | Buckinghamshire New University | 42.6 |
| 16 | University of Bolton | 41.5 |
| 17 | University of Glamorgan | 41.1 |
| 18 | University of Hull | 39.9 |
| 19 | London South Bank University | 39.6 |
| 20 | London Metropolitan University | 38.6 |
| 21 | Canterbury Christ Church University | 38.1 |
| 22 | University of Westminster | 34.3 |
| 23 | Staffordshire University | 34.2 |
| 24 | University of Central Lancashire | 34.0 |
| 25 | University of Bedfordshire | 33.7 |
| 26 | Swansea Metropolitan University | 32.4 |
| 27 | University of Greenwich | 31.8 |
| 28 | Coventry University | 31.3 |
| 29 | University of Wolverhampton | 31.1 |
| 30 | University of Worcester | 31.1 |

*Source: HESA, Students in Higher Education Institutions 2007/2008*

**Table 53 Universities with fewest part-time undergraduates**

| Rank | University | % part-time undergraduates |
|------|------------|----------------------------|
| 1 | Imperial College London | 0.0 |
| 2 | Queen Mary, University of London | 0.6 |
| 3 | Newcastle University | 1.5 |
| 4 | London School of Economics | 1.5 |
| 5 | Loughborough University | 2.6 |
| 6 | SOAS | 3.1 |
| 7 | University of Durham | 3.1 |
| 8 | University of Bath | 3.6 |
| 9 | University of Edinburgh | 4.3 |
| 10 | Aston University | 4.6 |
| 11 | University for the Creative Arts | 4.7 |
| 12 | University of the Arts, London | 5.1 |
| 13 | University College London | 5.4 |
| 14 | University of Exeter | 6.0 |
| 15 | Heriot-Watt University | 6.1 |
| 16 | University of Buckingham | 6.2 |
| 17 | Brunel University | 6.4 |
| 18 | University of Bristol | 6.4 |
| 19 | Royal Holloway, University of London | 6.7 |
| 20 | University of Manchester | 7.2 |

Source: HESA, Students in Higher Education Institutions 2007/2008

# Student welfare and advice services

Although many people still labour under the false impression that all students live charmed and easy lives, this is very far from the truth in modern life. From time to time we all need a little support or help, whether it's a check-up with the doctor, someone to talk to in confidence, or advice about legal issues or money problems. Many universities make superb efforts to support and help their students and they offer a wide range of schemes and services including on-campus healthcare, a range of welfare officers, crèches and late-night telephone advice lines. Others provide fewer services, which may concern you, depending on which you are most likely to require. For example, if you have ongoing health concerns, you might prefer somewhere with full-time doctors on campus.

If you'd like to know the most up-to-date information about what student support is available at each university, contact both the main university and the students' union: each may provide different kinds of help.

**Table 54 Student welfare and support services**

| University | A | B | C | D | E | F | G | H | I | J | K | L |
|---|---|---|---|---|---|---|---|---|---|---|---|---|
| Aberdeen University | ✓ | ✓ | ✓ | ✓ | ✓ | ✓ | ✓ | ✓ | ✓ | ✓ | | ✓ |
| Abertay Dundee University | | ✓ | | | ✓ | ✓ | ✓ | ✓ | ✓ | | ✓ | ✓ |
| Aberystwyth University | ✓ | ✓ | | ✓ | ✓ | ✓ | | ✓ | ✓ | ✓ | ✓ | ✓ |
| Anglia Ruskin University | ✓ | ✓ | | ✓ | ✓ | ✓ | ✓ | ✓ | ✓ | ✓ | ✓ | ✓ |
| Arts London | ✓ | ✓ | | ✓ | ✓ | ✓ | | ✓ | ✓ | ✓ | ✓ | ✓ |
| Aston University | ✓ | ✓ | ✓ | ✓ | ✓ | ✓ | ✓ | ✓ | ✓ | ✓ | ✓ | |
| Bangor University | | ✓ | | ✓ | ✓ | ✓ | ✓ | ✓ | | ✓ | ✓ | ✓ |
| Bath Spa University | ✓ | ✓ | | ✓ | ✓ | ✓ | | ✓ | ✓ | ✓ | ✓ | |
| Bedfordshire University | ✓ | ✓ | | | ✓ | ✓ | ✓ | ✓ | ✓ | ✓ | ✓ | |
| University of Birmingham | | ✓ | | ✓ | ✓ | ✓ | ✓ | ✓ | ✓ | ✓ | ✓ | ✓ |
| Birmingham City University | ✓ | ✓ | | ✓ | ✓ | ✓ | ✓ | ✓ | ✓ | ✓ | | |
| Bolton University | | ✓ | | ✓ | ✓ | ✓ | ✓ | ✓ | | ✓ | ✓ | |
| Bournemouth University | ✓ | ✓ | ✓ | ✓ | | ✓ | ✓ | ✓ | ✓ | ✓ | ✓ | |
| University of Bradford | ✓ | ✓ | | ✓ | ✓ | ✓ | ✓ | | ✓ | ✓ | ✓ | |
| University of Brighton | ✓ | ✓ | | ✓ | ✓ | ✓ | ✓ | ✓ | ✓ | ✓ | ✓ | ✓ |
| University of Bristol | ✓ | ✓ | | ✓ | ✓ | ✓ | ✓ | ✓ | ✓ | ✓ | ✓ | ✓ |
| Brunel University | ✓ | ✓ | | ✓ | | ✓ | ✓ | ✓ | | ✓ | ✓ | ✓ |
| Bucks New University | | ✓ | | ✓ | ✓ | ✓ | | ✓ | | ✓ | | |
| Canterbury Christ Church University | | ✓ | | | | ✓ | | ✓ | ✓ | ✓ | | |
| Cardiff University | | ✓ | | ✓ | ✓ | ✓ | ✓ | ✓ | ✓ | ✓ | ✓ | ✓ |
| University of Central Lancashire | ✓ | ✓ | | ✓ | | ✓ | ✓ | ✓ | ✓ | ✓ | | |
| University of Chester | | ✓ | | ✓ | | ✓ | ✓ | ✓ | ✓ | ✓ | ✓ | |
| University of Chichester | | ✓ | | ✓ | ✓ | ✓ | ✓ | ✓ | | ✓ | ✓ | |
| City University, London | | ✓ | | ✓ | ✓ | ✓ | ✓ | ✓ | | ✓ | ✓ | ✓ |
| Coventry University | ✓ | ✓ | | ✓ | ✓ | ✓ | ✓ | ✓ | ✓ | ✓ | ✓ | |
| University for the Creative Arts | ✓ | ✓ | | ✓ | ✓ | ✓ | ✓ | ✓ | | ✓ | ✓ | |
| University of Cumbria | ✓ | ✓ | | ✓ | ✓ | ✓ | ✓ | ✓ | ✓ | ✓ | | |
| De Montfort University | ✓ | ✓ | | ✓ | ✓ | ✓ | ✓ | ✓ | | ✓ | ✓ | ✓ |

**Key:**

A = Own medical centre with full-time doctors
B = Counselling services
C = Dentist
D = Student advice and welfare centre
E = Designated student financial advisers
F = Designated disability support officer/team

G = International students' welfare officer
H = Chaplaincy/faith centre
I = On-site nursery
J = Learning support officer/team
K = Housing advice officer
L = Student nightline for out of hours help

*(Continued)*

**Table 54 (Continued)**

| University | A | B | C | D | E | F | G | H | I | J | K | L |
|---|---|---|---|---|---|---|---|---|---|---|---|---|
| University of Derby | ✓ | ✓ | | ✓ | ✓ | ✓ | ✓ | ✓ | | ✓ | ✓ | |
| University of Dundee | ✓ | ✓ | | ✓ | ✓ | ✓ | ✓ | ✓ | ✓ | ✓ | ✓ | |
| Durham University | ✓ | ✓ | | ✓ | ✓ | ✓ | ✓ | ✓ | ✓ | ✓ | ✓ | ✓ |
| University of East Anglia | ✓ | ✓ | ✓ | ✓ | ✓ | ✓ | ✓ | ✓ | ✓ | ✓ | | ✓ |
| University of East London | ✓ | ✓ | | ✓ | ✓ | ✓ | ✓ | ✓ | ✓ | ✓ | ✓ | ✓ |
| Edge Hill University | ✓ | ✓ | | ✓ | ✓ | ✓ | ✓ | | | ✓ | ✓ | ✓ |
| University of Edinburgh | ✓ | ✓ | | ✓ | | ✓ | ✓ | ✓ | ✓ | ✓ | | ✓ |
| Edinburgh Napier University | | ✓ | | ✓ | ✓ | ✓ | | ✓ | | ✓ | | ✓ |
| University of Essex | ✓ | ✓ | | ✓ | | ✓ | | ✓ | ✓ | ✓ | ✓ | ✓ |
| University of Exeter | ✓ | ✓ | | ✓ | | ✓ | ✓ | ✓ | ✓ | ✓ | | ✓ |
| University of Glamorgan | | ✓ | | ✓ | | ✓ | ✓ | ✓ | ✓ | ✓ | | ✓ |
| University of Glasgow | ✓ | ✓ | | ✓ | | ✓ | ✓ | ✓ | ✓ | ✓ | ✓ | ✓ |
| Glasgow Caledonian University | | ✓ | | ✓ | ✓ | ✓ | ✓ | ✓ | ✓ | ✓ | | ✓ |
| University of Gloucestershire | | ✓ | | ✓ | ✓ | ✓ | ✓ | ✓ | | ✓ | | |
| Glyndŵr University | ✓ | ✓ | | ✓ | | ✓ | ✓ | ✓ | ✓ | ✓ | | |
| Goldsmiths, London | | ✓ | | ✓ | ✓ | ✓ | | ✓ | ✓ | ✓ | | ✓ |
| Heriot-Watt University | ✓ | ✓ | ✓ | ✓ | | ✓ | ✓ | ✓ | ✓ | ✓ | ✓ | ✓ |
| University of Hertfordshire | ✓ | ✓ | | ✓ | | ✓ | | ✓ | ✓ | ✓ | | ✓ |
| University of Huddersfield | ✓ | ✓ | | ✓ | ✓ | ✓ | ✓ | ✓ | | ✓ | | |
| University of Hull | | ✓ | | ✓ | ✓ | ✓ | | ✓ | ✓ | ✓ | | ✓ |
| Imperial College London | ✓ | ✓ | ✓ | ✓ | | ✓ | ✓ | ✓ | ✓ | ✓ | ✓ | ✓ |
| Keele University | ✓ | ✓ | ✓ | ✓ | ✓ | ✓ | ✓ | ✓ | ✓ | ✓ | ✓ | ✓ |
| University of Kent | ✓ | ✓ | | ✓ | ✓ | ✓ | ✓ | ✓ | ✓ | ✓ | ✓ | |
| King's College London | ✓ | ✓ | ✓ | ✓ | ✓ | ✓ | ✓ | ✓ | ✓ | ✓ | ✓ | ✓ |
| Kingston University | ✓ | ✓ | | ✓ | ✓ | ✓ | | ✓ | ✓ | ✓ | ✓ | |
| Lampeter (University of Wales) | | ✓ | | ✓ | | | ✓ | ✓ | ✓ | ✓ | | ✓ |
| Lancaster University | ✓ | ✓ | ✓ | ✓ | ✓ | ✓ | ✓ | ✓ | ✓ | ✓ | | ✓ |

**Key:**

A = Own medical centre with full-time doctors
B = Counselling services
C = Dentist
D = Student advice and welfare centre
E = Designated student financial advisers
F = Designated disability support officer/team
G = International students' welfare officer
H = Chaplaincy/faith centre
I = On-site nursery
J = Learning support officer/team
K = Housing advice officer
L = Student nightline for out of hours help

**Table 54 (Continued)**

| University | A | B | C | D | E | F | G | H | I | J | K | L |
|---|---|---|---|---|---|---|---|---|---|---|---|---|
| University of Leeds | ✓ | ✓ | | ✓ | | ✓ | ✓ | ✓ | ✓ | ✓ | | ✓ |
| Leeds Metropolitan University | ✓ | ✓ | | ✓ | ✓ | ✓ | ✓ | ✓ | ✓ | ✓ | | ✓ |
| University of Leicester | ✓ | ✓ | | ✓ | ✓ | ✓ | ✓ | ✓ | | ✓ | ✓ | ✓ |
| University of Lincoln | ✓ | ✓ | | ✓ | ✓ | ✓ | ✓ | ✓ | | ✓ | | |
| University of Liverpool | ✓ | ✓ | | ✓ | ✓ | ✓ | ✓ | ✓ | ✓ | ✓ | | |
| Liverpool Hope University | | ✓ | | ✓ | ✓ | ✓ | ✓ | ✓ | | ✓ | | |
| Liverpool John Moores | | ✓ | | ✓ | ✓ | ✓ | ✓ | ✓ | | ✓ | | |
| London Metropolitan University | ✓ | ✓ | | ✓ | ✓ | ✓ | | ✓ | ✓ | ✓ | | |
| London School of Economics | ✓ | ✓ | | ✓ | | ✓ | ✓ | ✓ | ✓ | ✓ | ✓ | ✓ |
| London South Bank | | ✓ | | ✓ | | ✓ | | ✓ | ✓ | ✓ | | ✓ |
| Loughborough University | ✓ | ✓ | | ✓ | | ✓ | ✓ | ✓ | ✓ | ✓ | ✓ | |
| University of Manchester | ✓ | ✓ | | ✓ | ✓ | ✓ | ✓ | ✓ | ✓ | ✓ | ✓ | ✓ |
| Manchester Metropolitan University | ✓ | ✓ | | ✓ | | ✓ | ✓ | ✓ | ✓ | ✓ | | ✓ |
| Middlesex University | | ✓ | | ✓ | | ✓ | ✓ | ✓ | ✓ | ✓ | | ✓ |
| Newcastle University | | ✓ | | ✓ | | ✓ | ✓ | ✓ | | ✓ | | ✓ |
| University of Northampton | ✓ | ✓ | | ✓ | ✓ | ✓ | ✓ | ✓ | | ✓ | ✓ | ✓ |
| University of Northumbria | | ✓ | | ✓ | ✓ | ✓ | ✓ | ✓ | | ✓ | | ✓ |
| University of Nottingham | ✓ | ✓ | | ✓ | ✓ | ✓ | ✓ | ✓ | ✓ | ✓ | | ✓ |
| Nottingham Trent University | | ✓ | | ✓ | ✓ | ✓ | ✓ | ✓ | | ✓ | | |
| Oxford Brookes University | ✓ | ✓ | ✓ | ✓ | | ✓ | ✓ | ✓ | ✓ | ✓ | | ✓ |
| University of Plymouth | ✓ | ✓ | | ✓ | ✓ | ✓ | ✓ | ✓ | ✓ | ✓ | | ✓ |
| University of Portsmouth | ✓ | ✓ | | ✓ | ✓ | ✓ | ✓ | ✓ | ✓ | ✓ | ✓ | |
| Queen Margaret University | ✓ | ✓ | | ✓ | ✓ | ✓ | ✓ | | | ✓ | | ✓ |
| Queen Mary, University London | ✓ | ✓ | | ✓ | | ✓ | | ✓ | ✓ | ✓ | | ✓ |
| Queen's University Belfast | ✓ | ✓ | | ✓ | ✓ | ✓ | ✓ | ✓ | | ✓ | ✓ | ✓ |

**Key:**

A = Own medical centre with full-time doctors
B = Counselling services
C = Dentist
D = Student advice and welfare centre
E = Designated student financial advisers
F = Designated disability support officer/team
G = International students' welfare officer
H = Chaplaincy/faith centre
I = On-site nursery
J = Learning support officer/team
K = Housing advice officer
L = Student nightline for out of hours help

*(Continued)*

117

**Table 54 (Continued)**

| University | A | B | C | D | E | F | G | H | I | J | K | L |
|---|---|---|---|---|---|---|---|---|---|---|---|---|
| University of Reading | ✓ | ✓ | ✓ | ✓ | ✓ | ✓ | ✓ | ✓ | ✓ | ✓ | ✓ | ✓ |
| Robert Gordon University | ✓ | ✓ | | ✓ | | ✓ | ✓ | ✓ | ✓ | | | |
| Roehampton University | ✓ | ✓ | | ✓ | ✓ | ✓ | | ✓ | ✓ | ✓ | ✓ | ✓ |
| Royal Holloway | ✓ | ✓ | | ✓ | ✓ | ✓ | ✓ | ✓ | ✓ | | | ✓ |
| University of St Andrews | ✓ | ✓ | | ✓ | ✓ | ✓ | ✓ | ✓ | | ✓ | | ✓ |
| University of Salford | ✓ | ✓ | | ✓ | | ✓ | ✓ | ✓ | ✓ | ✓ | | ✓ |
| University of Sheffield | ✓ | ✓ | | ✓ | | ✓ | ✓ | ✓ | ✓ | ✓ | ✓ | ✓ |
| Sheffield Hallam University | | ✓ | | ✓ | ✓ | ✓ | ✓ | ✓ | ✓ | ✓ | | |
| SOAS | ✓ | ✓ | | ✓ | | ✓ | ✓ | ✓ | | ✓ | | ✓ |
| University of Southampton | ✓ | ✓ | | ✓ | ✓ | ✓ | | ✓ | ✓ | ✓ | | ✓ |
| Southampton Solent University | | ✓ | | ✓ | ✓ | ✓ | ✓ | ✓ | | ✓ | | ✓ |
| Staffordshire University | ✓ | ✓ | | ✓ | | ✓ | ✓ | ✓ | ✓ | ✓ | | ✓ |
| University of Stirling | ✓ | ✓ | ✓ | ✓ | ✓ | ✓ | | ✓ | | ✓ | | ✓ |
| University of Strathclyde | | ✓ | | ✓ | ✓ | ✓ | | ✓ | ✓ | ✓ | | ✓ |
| University of Sunderland | | ✓ | | ✓ | ✓ | ✓ | | ✓ | ✓ | ✓ | | ✓ |
| University of Surrey | ✓ | ✓ | | ✓ | ✓ | ✓ | ✓ | ✓ | ✓ | ✓ | | |
| University of Sussex | ✓ | ✓ | ✓ | ✓ | | ✓ | ✓ | ✓ | ✓ | ✓ | | |
| Swansea Metropolitan | | ✓ | | ✓ | ✓ | ✓ | | ✓ | | ✓ | | ✓ |
| Thames Valley University | ✓ | ✓ | | ✓ | | ✓ | | ✓ | ✓ | ✓ | | ✓ |
| University College London | ✓ | ✓ | ✓ | ✓ | | ✓ | ✓ | ✓ | ✓ | ✓ | | ✓ |
| University of Teesside | | ✓ | | ✓ | | ✓ | ✓ | ✓ | ✓ | ✓ | ✓ | |
| University of Ulster | | ✓ | | ✓ | ✓ | ✓ | ✓ | ✓ | ✓ | ✓ | | |
| University of Wales Inst Cardiff | ✓ | ✓ | | ✓ | ✓ | ✓ | ✓ | ✓ | ✓ | ✓ | | ✓ |
| University of Wales Newport | | ✓ | | ✓ | ✓ | ✓ | | ✓ | | ✓ | | ✓ |
| University of Wales Swansea | ✓ | ✓ | ✓ | ✓ | ✓ | ✓ | ✓ | ✓ | ✓ | ✓ | ✓ | ✓ |
| University of Warwick | ✓ | ✓ | | ✓ | ✓ | ✓ | ✓ | ✓ | ✓ | ✓ | ✓ | ✓ |
| University of the West of England | | ✓ | | ✓ | ✓ | ✓ | ✓ | | ✓ | | ✓ | |

**Key:**

A = Own medical centre with full-time doctors
B = Counselling services
C = Dentist
D = Student advice and welfare centre
E = Designated student financial advisers
F = Designated disability support officer/team
G = International students' welfare officer
H = Chaplaincy/faith centre
I = On-site nursery
J = Learning support officer/team
K = Housing advice officer
L = Student nightline for out of hours help

**Table 54 (Continued)**

| University | A | B | C | D | E | F | G | H | I | J | K | L |
|---|---|---|---|---|---|---|---|---|---|---|---|---|
| University of the West of Scotland |  | ✓ |  | ✓ | ✓ | ✓ | ✓ | ✓ | ✓ | ✓ |  |  |
| University of Westminster |  | ✓ |  |  | ✓ |  | ✓ | ✓ | ✓ | ✓ |  | ✓ |
| University of Winchester |  | ✓ |  |  | ✓ |  | ✓ | ✓ | ✓ | ✓ | ✓ |  |
| University of Wolverhampton |  | ✓ |  | ✓ | ✓ | ✓ | ✓ | ✓ | ✓ | ✓ |  |  |
| University of Worcester |  | ✓ |  | ✓ | ✓ | ✓ | ✓ | ✓ | ✓ | ✓ |  |  |
| University of York | ✓ | ✓ |  | ✓ | ✓ | ✓ | ✓ | ✓ | ✓ | ✓ |  | ✓ |
| York St John University | ✓ | ✓ |  | ✓ | ✓ | ✓ | ✓ | ✓ | ✓ | ✓ |  | ✓ |

*Source: Individual universities*
**Notes:** Oxford and Cambridge: contact individual colleges for information on their welfare provision. University of Greenwich has been excluded from this table as not enough information was available.

**Key:**

A = Own medical centre with full-time doctors
B = Counselling services
C = Dentist
D = Student advice and welfare centre
E = Designated student financial advisers
F = Designated disability support officer/team

G = International students' welfare officer
H = Chaplaincy/faith centre
I = On-site nursery
J = Learning support officer/team
K = Housing advice officer
L = Student nightline for out of hours help

# Environment and ethical policy

Some universities have much better environmental and ethical policies than others, and students are becoming increasingly concerned about these issues. People & Planet is the largest student network in the UK that campaigns on global issues of poverty, human rights and the environment. It has student campaigning groups in over 50 universities in the UK and its student-chosen campaigns currently focus on climate change, trade and corporate power.

If these issues are important to you when choosing a university, here are People & Planet's suggestions for a few questions to ask any universities that you're thinking about applying to.

► How is the university helping to tackle climate change – is there a plan to reduce the university's carbon emissions?

► Does the university have a policy to invest its money ethically?

► Does the university take poverty, human rights and the environment into account when it procures goods and services? Is it a 'Fairtrade university', for example?

► How seriously does the university take the environment, for example does the university have staff dedicated to environmental management?

**Table 55 People & Planet's 20 top-rated universities**

| Rank | University | P & P 'Award' |
|---|---|---|
| 1 | University of Gloucestershire | 1st |
| 2 | University of Plymouth | 1st |
| 3 | University of the West of England | 1st |
| 4 | Anglia Ruskin University | 1st |
| =5 | Loughborough University | 1st |
| =5 | University of Cambridge | 1st |
| =5 | University of Central Lancashire | 1st |
| =8 | Leeds Metropolitan University | 1st |
| =8 | University of Hertfordshire | 1st |
| =8 | University of Huddersfield | 1st |
| 11 | Queen's University Belfast | 1st |
| 12 | University of St Andrews | 1st |
| 13 | University of Glamorgan | 1st |
| =14 | University of Derby | 1st |
| =14 | University of Leeds | 1st |
| 16 | Oxford Brookes University | 1st |
| =17 | Swansea Metropolitan University | 1st |
| =17 | University of Liverpool | 1st |
| =19 | Nottingham Trent University | 2.i |
| =19 | University of Glasgow | 2.i |

Source: People & Planet University Report 2008, http://peopleandplanet.org

**Table 56 People & Planet's 20 lowest-rated universities**

| Rank | University | P & P 'Award' |
|---|---|---|
| 1 | London School of Hygiene | Fail |
| 2 | Trinity College Carmarthen | Fail |
| 3 | London Metropolitan University | Fail |
| =4 | Thames Valley University | Fail |
| =4 | Royal Veterinary College | Fail |
| =6 | Royal Academy of Music | Fail |
| =6 | Central School of Speech and Drama | Fail |
| 8 | Middlesex University | Fail |
| 9 | Northumbria University, Newcastle | Fail |
| =10 | University of Greenwich | Fail |
| =10 | Robert Gordon University | Fail |
| 12 | Imperial College London | Fail |

**Table 56 (Continued)**

| Rank | University | P & P 'Award' |
|------|-----------|---------------|
| =13 | University of Stirling | Fail |
| =13 | Liverpool Hope University | Fail |
| 15 | City University London | Fail |
| 16 | SOAS | 3rd |
| =17 | University of Lincoln | 3rd |
| =17 | London Business School | 3rd |
| =19 | University College London | 3rd |
| =19 | Edge Hill University | 3rd |

Source: People & Planet University Report 2008, http://peopleandplanet.org

The following universities failed to submit answers, or to submit complete responses to the People & Planet questionnaire, and so were not included in the table: University of Abertay Dundee, University of Bolton, Buckinghamshire New University, Goldsmiths College, University of London, North East Wales Institute of Higher Education, Royal College of Music, School of Pharmacy, Lampeter (University of Wales), University of Westminster, University of the West of Scotland. If you're thinking about attending any of these universities and are interested in the issues raised by People & Planet, you will have to contact them directly to ask them about your concerns.

# A place to lay your head – university accommodation

Getting into university is one thing, but finding a place to stay is another. Most non-local students decide that they want to stay in university-owned halls and flats during their first year, as these are usually near to campus and are an ideal place to meet lots of other students. Many even have their own bar or social rooms. However, not every university is able to offer a place to all their first-year students. The lists below should give you some idea of universities where you have a really good chance of getting accommodation, and a few places where your chances aren't so great.

More than 60 UK universities guarantee a place in university accommodation to all eligible first-years. By 'eligible' they usually mean that you're going to be studying full time, not already living nearby, not hoping to bring a spouse or children along with you, have firmly accepted a place at the university or have made the university your first choice via UCAS, and have filled in and returned all the relevant application forms before their deadline arrives.

# Availability of university accommodation

**Universities offering accommodation to ALL eligible first-year students**

| | |
|---|---|
| Aberdeen University | University of Leeds |
| Aberystwyth University | Leeds Metropolitan University |
| Aston University | University of Leicester |
| Bangor University | University of Liverpool |
| University of Bath | Liverpool Hope University |
| Bedfordshire University | Liverpool John Moores |
| University of Birmingham | London School of Economics |
| Bolton University | Loughborough University |
| Bournemouth University | University of Manchester |
| University of Bradford | Newcastle University |
| University of Bristol | Nottingham Trent University |
| University of Cambridge | University of Nottingham |
| Canterbury CC University | University of Oxford |
| Cardiff University | Queen's University Belfast |
| University of Central Lancashire | University of Reading |
| City University, London | University of St Andrews |
| University of Derby | University of Salford |
| University of Dundee | University of Sheffield |
| Durham University | Sheffield Hallam University |
| University of East Anglia | University of Southampton |
| University of Edinburgh | Staffordshire University |
| University of Essex | University of Stirling |
| University of Exeter | University of Sunderland |
| University of Glasgow | University of Surrey |
| University of Greenwich | University of Sussex |
| Heriot-Watt University | University of Teesside |
| University of Hertfordshire | Thames Valley University |
| University of Huddersfield | University of Ulster |
| University of Hull | University College London |
| Imperial College London | University of Wales Newport |
| Keele University | University of Warwick |
| University of Kent | University of the West |
| King's College London | of England |
| Lampeter (University of Wales) | University of Winchester |
| Lancaster University | University of York |

**Universities offering accommodation to 99–95% of eligible first-year students**

| | |
|---|---|
| Abertay Dundee University | De Montfort University |
| Anglia Ruskin University | Goldsmiths, London |
| Arts London | University of Northampton |
| Birmingham City University | Oxford Brookes University |
| University of Brighton | Queen Mary, London |
| Brunel University | Royal Holloway |
| Bucks New University | University of Wales Swansea |
| University of Chichester | York St John University |
| University of Cumbria | |

**Universities offering least accommodation to eligible first-year students**

| | |
|---|---|
| Glasgow Caledonian University | Robert Gordon University |
| Glyndwr University | University of West of Scotland |
| University of East London | University of Lincoln |

*Source: University websites*

To be fair to the institutions in the shortest list above, many of them have a high proportion of students who live at home nearby, so they do not all have such a great demand for university housing in the first place. However, if you're seriously thinking about moving to the area to study at one of these universities it's well worth contacting the relevant accommodation offices in advance to find out more

# 'To do' list if you want a room in university halls

► If you're considering applying to a particular university, talk to someone who attended the university recently and knows the halls and local rental situation, or chat to current students on message boards of university websites.

► Ask about the facilities, the atmosphere, and how close a hall is to the main campus.

► It's essential to find out what bills you're expected to pay on top of your rent or hall fees, and how often these bills arrive.

► Whatever the university, if you get accepted onto any course and you won't be living at home, you should get on the case and start arranging your accommodation.

about the situation. If you are accepted by that university, apply for accommodation quickly, since many places are allocated on a first-come first-served basis.

You may want or need to rent privately in your first year, and unless you're prepared to lodge or take a bedsit, you'll probably end up in a shared house because it's the cheapest option.

## 'To do' list if you are going to rent privately in your first year

▶ Ask the university's accommodation office for a list of recommended housing agencies or landlords.

▶ Travel to the area and view properties, preferably with a friend or relative for safety, or book a temporary room, then house hunt during your first few days in town.

▶ Meet the other tenants before you sign anything, or you could end up sharing with anyone, including a houseful of unsympathetic non-students.

▶ Read contracts carefully before signing, and ask a university welfare officer for advice if you don't understand anything.

For further information about rent prices in university-owned and privately rented accommodation, turn to Chapter 3, Table 33 for a university-by-university cost breakdown.

# The local environment

A lot of current students say they wish they'd known how cold or how rainy their new university town was going to be, so here's some information about the local climate. It's followed by a few notes about local crime rates and personal safety, as a little knowledge beforehand can really help you protect your home, your belongings and yourself.

# Weather

**Table 57 The warmest universities**

| Rank | University town or city | Average top annual temperature (°C) |
|------|------------------------|--------------------------------------|
| 1 | London | 14.8 |
| 2 | Cardiff | 14.3 |
| 3 | Exeter | 14.2 |
| =4 | Cambridge | 14.1 |
| =4 | Oxford | 14.1 |
| 6 | Southampton | 14.0 |
| =7 | Brighton | 13.7 |
| =7 | Portsmouth | 13.7 |
| 9 | Nottingham | 13.5 |
| =10 | Birmingham | 13.3 |
| =10 | Bristol | 13.3 |

Source: Met Office

**Table 58 The coldest universities**

| Rank | University town or city | Average low annual temperature (°C) |
|------|------------------------|--------------------------------------|
| 1 | Aberdeen | 4.6 |
| 2 | Dundee | 4.9 |
| =3 | Edinburgh | 5.1 |
| =3 | Leeds | 5.1 |
| =3 | York | 5.1 |
| 6 | Durham | 5.2 |
| 7 | Plymouth | 5.4 |
| 8 | Birmingham | 5.5 |
| 9 | Newcastle | 5.6 |
| =10 | Belfast | 5.8 |
| =10 | Nottingham | 5.8 |

Source: Met Office

**Table 59 The sunniest universities**

| Rank | University town or city | Average annual hours of sunshine |
|------|-------------------------|----------------------------------|
| 1 | Portsmouth | 1,902.9 |
| 2 | Brighton | 1,848.6 |
| 3 | Southampton | 1,750.7 |
| 4 | Exeter | 1,710.0 |
| 5 | Bristol | 1,565.0 |
| 6 | Newcastle | 1,540.4 |
| 7 | Lancaster | 1,540.3 |
| 8 | Oxford | 1,537.4 |
| 9 | Dundee | 1,523.2 |
| 10 | Cardiff | 1,518.0 |

Source: Met Office

**Table 60 The soggiest universities**

| Rank | University town or city | Average annual rainfall (mm) |
|------|-------------------------|------------------------------|
| 1 | Plymouth | 1,974.2 |
| 2 | Glasgow | 1,205.3 |
| 3 | Cardiff | 1,111.7 |
| 4 | Lancaster | 871.3 |
| 5 | Belfast | 862.4 |
| 6 | Exeter | 850.0 |
| 7 | Sheffield | 824.7 |
| 8 | Aberdeen | 816.3 |
| 9 | Manchester | 806.6 |
| 10 | Brighton | 789.7 |

Source: Met Office

## Campus crime

While most universities are fairly safe places with good security measures, you should also be aware that many thieves and other criminals deliberately target students. Student housing is not always situated in the nicest of areas or equipped with anti-burglary measures, and thieves assume that any student bedroom will contain several items of high value that are also easy to carry away, such as MP3 players and laptops. Transport such as bicycles, scooters, motorbikes and cars may also be stolen or vandalised at home or on campus, and bags can be snatched in computer centres or libraries (sometimes by fellow students).

# The most commonly claimed-for items on student insurance

1. Laptop
2. Mobile phone
3. Camera
4. MP3 player
=5. Games console
=5. Television

7. Desktop computer
=8. Watch
=8. Glasses
10. Jewellery
11. Clothes
12. Freezer food

*Source: Endsleigh Insurance*

It's highly advisable to get your belongings insured – think about the value of what you're taking with you to university, and work out roughly how much it would cost to replace everything if it was stolen or accidentally damaged.

## ? Did You Know?

*Endsleigh Insurance receives an estimated £350,000-worth of claims from students during their first month at university.*

**Table 61 Top 10 riskiest cities and towns for burglaries**

| Rank | University town or city | % above national average |
|------|------------------------|--------------------------|
| 1 | London | 55.4% |
| 2 | Nottingham | 50.5% |
| =3 | Bristol | 48.6% |
| =3 | Cambridge | 48.6% |
| 5 | Manchester | 48.2% |
| 6 | Reading | 42.7% |
| 7 | Stockport | 37.6% |
| 8 | Hull | 37.1% |
| 9 | Leeds | 32.4% |
| 10 | Oxford | 31.1% |

*Source: Endsleigh Insurance*

**Table 62 Top 10 safest cities and towns for burglaries**

| Rank | University town or city | % below national average |
|------|------------------------|--------------------------|
| 1 | Preston | −66.6% |
| 2 | Norwich | −60.1% |
| 3 | Ipswich | −57.6% |
| 4 | Guildford | −57.3% |
| 5 | Swindon | −48.3% |
| 6 | Bath | −47.0% |
| 7 | Glasgow | −45.9% |
| 8 | Aberdeen | −44.0% |
| 9 | Dundee | −43.9% |
| 10 | Chester | −36.1% |

*Source: Endsleigh Insurance*

**Table 63 Top 10 riskiest towns/cities for accidental damage**

| Rank | University town or city | % above national average |
|------|------------------------|--------------------------|
| 1 | Hove | 38.9% |
| 2 | Milton Keynes | 31.4% |
| 3 | Brighton | 26.7% |
| 4 | Newport | 25.1% |
| 5 | Cheltenham | 22.4% |
| 6 | Bournemouth | 17.9% |
| 7 | London | 11.6% |
| 8 | Ipswich | 7.5% |
| 9 | Plymouth | 5.8% |
| 10 | Derby | 5.0% |

*Source: Endsleigh Insurance*

**Table 64 Top 10 safest towns/cities for accidental damage**

| Rank | University town or city | % below national average |
|------|------------------------|--------------------------|
| 1 | Manchester | −40.3% |
| 2 | Leeds | −33.2% |
| 3 | Liverpool | −31.8% |
| 4 | York | −30.1% |
| 5 | Newcastle upon Tyne | −27.1% |
| =6 | Birmingham | −26.6% |
| =6 | Reading | −26.6% |
| 8 | Swindon | −25.3% |
| 9 | Nottingham | −22.2% |
| 10 | Stockport | −21.9% |

*Source: Endsleigh Insurance*

Your students' union and local police station will be able to provide you with advice about reducing your chances of being robbed or burgled. All students, male and female, also need to be aware of personal safety issues in general. Your university may have lots of help for you there too, including designated transport schemes to get you safely home after a night out, and the Suzy Lamplugh Trust provide a range of excellent personal safety information (www.suzylamplugh.org).

**TIP**

**Top tips from Endsleigh Insurance about preventing burglaries**

1. *Check the security of your accommodation when you arrive and raise any concerns with the landlord immediately.*
2. *Make sure you insure the total value of possessions you are taking with you.*
3. *Be careful not to draw too much attention to expensive goods by leaving them on display near a window or leaving them unattended when in a public place.*
4. *Always lock your windows and doors – even if you are popping out for five minutes.*
5. *If you are living in a hall of residence, make sure you do not let unidentified people into the building without checking who they are.*

# Chapter 5

# Free time – all the fun stuff

The chances are that you will have a dizzying wealth of opportunities for your free time at university. Well, it isn't all about the studying, is it? Nobody expects you to stay at home every evening on your own reading textbooks, after all.

Being at university is a chance to meet lots of new and interesting people, some of them rather attractive ones at that, and to have fun socialising. There are many different forms of entertainment laid on by the students' unions, and nearby towns have their amenities to offer as well. There are hundreds of clubs and societies to join, and all sorts of sports and fitness activities to try out, even if you don't see yourself as the sporty type. There really is something for everyone.

While you're having fun and following your interests you could also be adding to your CV without even realising it. Volunteering experience, club participation, and contributions to award-winning publications and performances can all serve to impress employers after graduation.

**?**
## Did you know?

*A few UK students' unions and students' associations currently own no entertainment facilities, including those at the University of Aberdeen, the University of Brighton, Edge Hill University, the University of Middlesex, and the University of Wolverhampton.*

# Relationships

After 'sleeping', students' favourite use of their free time is relaxing and socialising with friends. Let's be honest here, some of that is probably going to include some flirting, and quite a few people even meet their life partners while they're studying. So, where are all the hotties hiding? We're not suggesting you should base your university choice on the following lists, but if eye candy is a bonus, here's which institutions the users of WhatUni.com voted as having the 'best looking' and the 'least good looking' students.

**Table 65 Top universities for 'eye candy'**

| Rank | University | 'Eye candy' rating |
|------|------------|--------------------|
| =1 | Loughborough University | 8.3 |
| =1 | University of Wales Swansea | 8.3 |
| =3 | University of East Anglia | 8.2 |
| =3 | University of Leeds | 8.2 |
| =5 | University of Exeter | 7.9 |
| =5 | Newcastle University | 7.9 |
| =7 | University of Bristol | 7.8 |
| =7 | Leeds Metropolitan University | 7.8 |
| =7 | Edinburgh Napier University | 7.8 |
| =7 | University of St Andrews | 7.8 |
| =7 | University of Stirling | 7.8 |
| =12 | University of Chichester | 7.7 |
| =12 | University of Northumbria | 7.7 |
| =12 | University of Plymouth | 7.7 |
| =15 | Cardiff University | 7.6 |
| =15 | University of Central Lancashire | 7.6 |
| =15 | University of Worcester | 7.6 |
| =18 | Aberdeen University | 7.5 |
| =18 | Bournemouth University | 7.5 |
| =18 | University of Kent | 7.5 |
| =18 | University of Manchester | 7.5 |
| =18 | Nottingham Trent University | 7.5 |
| =18 | Sheffield Hallam University | 7.5 |
| =18 | University of Wales Institute Cardiff | 7.5 |

*Source: As voted by the members of www.whatuni.com*
**Note**: universities gaining fewer than ten votes have been excluded.

**Table 66 Bottom universities for 'eye candy'**

| Rank | University | Eye candy rating |
|------|------------|------------------|
| 1 | Thames Valley University | 4.7 |
| 2 | University for Creative Arts | 5.0 |
| =3 | Bedfordshire University | 5.1 |
| =3 | Imperial College London | 5.1 |
| =3 | Lampeter (University of Wales) | 5.1 |
| 6 | University of West of Scotland | 5.2 |
| 7 | Roehampton University | 5.3 |
| 8 | London Metropolitan University | 5.4 |
| =9 | Coventry University | 5.5 |
| =9 | Middlesex University | 5.5 |
| 11 | University of Wales Newport | 5.6 |
| =12 | London School of Economics | 5.7 |
| =12 | University of Westminster | 5.7 |
| =12 | University of Wolverhampton | 5.7 |
| =15 | Queen Mary, London | 5.8 |
| =15 | Staffordshire University | 5.8 |

Source: As voted by the members of www.whatuni.com
**Note**: universities with fewer than ten votes have been excluded.

While we're on the subject of relationships, many lesbian, gay and bisexual (LGB) students wait until they've gone away to university to come out. Most places of higher education have a supportive environment and an LGB officer or social group to help you feel more at home, and if you're lucky the nearest city might have an excellent gay social scene. Some LGB groups also run political campaigns and raise awareness about rights, in addition to providing general support and care, if that's something you might be interested in getting involved in.

# Best university or college for LBGTQ* students 2009

1. University of Manchester

2. Brighton University

3. University of Cambridge

4. University of Leeds

5. University of Hull

Source: As voted by readers of the Pink Paper

*Lesbian, bisexual, gay, transgender or questioning

# Best university LBG* group 2009

1. University of Manchester

2. Brighton University

3. Liverpool John Moores University

4. University of Leeds

5. University of Sheffield

*Source: As voted by readers of the Pink Paper*
*\*Lesbian, bisexual, gay*

# Get sporty or just get in shape

Students say their top two leisure activities are 'sleeping' and 'meeting friends in the union bar', but enjoying sport and fitness activities is the third most popular way of spending their leisure time. According to British Universities and Colleges Sport (BUCS), which represents 150 member institutions around the UK, over 3,800 sports teams operate on campus, with the highest participation in rugby, football and hockey. You can get involved in any activity from archery to windsurfing, including team sports, athletics, martial arts and even ultimate Frisbee, so there really is something for just about everyone. Prices are mostly kept reasonably low by subsidies and some activities are completely free.

Most sports teams and societies come with a ready-made social life attached, as well as bringing all the other benefits that you might expect from getting some exercise, which makes them even more popular. In addition, getting involved with teams or being the captain, secretary or treasurer can look excellent on a CV, helping to show that you're trustworthy and reliable, well organised, a team player, or someone with budding leadership skills. The best players at each university get the opportunity to compete at national or even international level, and it's worth noting that 58% of the Great Britain team at the Beijing Olympics 2008 had come through the higher education system.

As you can see from the list below, some universities are much sportier than others. If sport is your passion, consider spending some of your free time at a winning establishment.

## National winners

If you look at a few university sports websites you will see they often proudly mention that their teams finished high in the rankings of the National University Sports League. This competition is co-ordinated by British Universities and Colleges Sport (see www.bucs.org.uk for participating universities and colleges), and often inspires fierce rivalry between the teams, so no wonder they want to shout about it when they get high scores.

---

## Universities that regularly finish in the BUCS league top 10

| | |
|---|---|
| Loughborough University | University of Oxford |
| University of Bath | University of Wales Institute, Cardiff |
| University of Birmingham | University of Cambridge |
| Durham University | University of Exeter |
| University of Edinburgh | University of Manchester |
| University of Nottingham | Newcastle University |

*Source: Individual university sports websites*

---

### World class – Olympic sports training

The following universities have been named as 2012 Olympics Training Camp Centres, and as the Olympics draws closer, expect more universities to offer new training camp disciplines. Here, they've been ranked by the number of different Olympic sports that they're currently offering. If you fancy yourself as an international contender, or you'd simply like to take advantage of some world-class training facilities, read on.

**Table 67 Universities acting as 2012 Olympics Training Camp Centres**

| University | Sports | Individual sports |
|---|---|---|
| Loughborough University | 25 | Aquatics (Swimming, Synchronised Swimming, Water Polo), Archery, Athletics, Badminton, Basketball, Boxing, Cycling (Road), Fencing, Football, Gymnastics (Artistic, Rhythmic, Trampoline), Handball, Hockey, Judo, Table Tennis, Tae Kwon Do, Tennis, Triathlon, Volleyball (Beach, Indoor), Weightlifting, Wrestling |
| University of Bath | 25 | Aquatics (Swimming, Synchronised Swimming, Water Polo), Archery, Athletics, Badminton, Basketball, Boxing, Fencing, Football, Gymnastics (Artistic, Rhythmic, Trampoline), Handball, Hockey, Judo, Modern Pentathlon, Table Tennis, Tae Kwon Do, Tennis, Triathlon, Volleyball (Beach, Indoor), Weightlifting, Wrestling |
| Leeds Metropolitan University | 12 | Athletics, Badminton, Basketball, Fencing, Gymnastics (Artistic, Rhythmic, Trampoline), Judo, Table Tennis, Tae Kwon Do, Volleyball (Indoor), Wrestling |
| Brunel University | 12 | Archery, Athletics, Badminton, Basketball, Boxing, Fencing, Judo, Table Tennis, Tae Kwon Do, Volleyball (Indoor), Weightlifting, Wrestling |

*(Continued)*

**Table 67 (Continued)**

| University | Sports | Individual sports |
|---|---|---|
| University of Birmingham | 11 | Athletics, Badminton, Fencing, Gymnastics (Artistic, Rhythmic), Hockey, Judo, Table Tennis, Tae Kwon Do, Volleyball (Indoor), Wrestling |
| University of the West of England | 10 | Badminton, Basketball, Fencing, Hockey, Judo, Table Tennis, Tae Kwon Do, Volleyball (Beach, Indoor), Wrestling |
| University of Kent | 10 | Archery, Badminton, Basketball, Fencing, Gymnastics (Rhythmic), Modern Pentathlon, Table Tennis, Volleyball (Beach, Indoor), Weightlifting |
| University of Ulster | 9 | Archery, Badminton, Basketball, Boxing, Fencing, Gymnastics (Trampoline), Hockey, Judo, Table Tennis |
| University of Exeter | 9 | Athletics, Badminton, Basketball, Cycling (Road), Fencing, Hockey, Judo, Table Tennis, Volleyball (Indoor) |
| Manchester Metropolitan University | 8 | Archery, Badminton, Basketball, Fencing, Football, Table Tennis, Triathlon, Volleyball (Indoor) |
| University of Dundee | 7 | Archery, Boxing, Fencing, Judo, Tae Kwon Do, Weightlifting, Wrestling |
| University of East London | 7 | Basketball, Boxing, Fencing, Judo, Table Tennis, Tae Kwon Do, Wrestling |
| University of Bristol | 7 | Athletics, Badminton, Basketball, Fencing, Hockey, Table Tennis, Volleyball (Indoor) |
| Glyndŵr University | 7 | Badminton, Basketball, Fencing, Hockey, Judo, Table Tennis, Wrestling |
| University of Central Lancashire | 6 | Archery, Athletics, Cycling (Road), Football, Judo, Tae Kwon Do |
| Nottingham Trent University | 6 | Badminton, Basketball, Equestrian (Dressage, Eventing, Jumping), Fencing |
| Northumbria University | 6 | Badminton, Basketball, Fencing, Football, Table Tennis, Volleyball (Indoor) |
| Robert Gordon University | 6 | Badminton, Boxing, Judo, Table Tennis, Tae Kwon Do, Volleyball (Indoor) |
| University of Sunderland | 6 | Badminton, Basketball, Fencing, Football, Sailing, Table Tennis |
| University of Surrey | 6 | Aquatics (Swimming, Water Polo), Badminton, Basketball, Fencing, Table Tennis |
| University of Stirling | 5 | Aquatics (Swimming), Football, Judo, Tae Kwon Do, Wrestling |
| Heriot-Watt University | 5 | Fencing, Football, Judo, Tae Kwon Do, Wrestling |

**Table 67 (Continued)**

| University | Sports | Individual sports |
|---|---|---|
| Durham University | 5 | Archery, Fencing, Football, Hockey, Table Tennis |
| Coventry University | 5 | Badminton, Fencing, Table Tennis, Tae Kwon Do, Volleyball (Indoor) |
| Edge Hill University | 4 | Archery, Athletics, Cycling (Road), Football |
| Bradford University | 4 | Basketball, Judo, Volleyball (Indoor), Wrestling |
| University of Wales Inst, Cardiff | 4 | Archery, Athletics, Fencing, Tae Kwon Do |
| Queen's, Belfast | 4 | Hockey, Judo, Table Tennis, Tae Kwon Do |
| University of Chichester | 4 | Athletics, Boxing, Cycling (Road), Table Tennis |
| University of Warwick | 4 | Athletics, Fencing, Table Tennis, Volleyball (Indoor) |
| University of Worcester | 4 | Basketball, Fencing, Table Tennis, Volleyball (Indoor) |
| Swansea University | 3 | Athletics, Hockey, Triathlon |
| University of Chester | 3 | Archery, Basketball, Fencing |
| Canterbury Christ Church University | 3 | Badminton, Basketball, Fencing |
| University of Wolverhampton | 3 | Basketball, Judo, Tae Kwon Do |
| University of Cambridge | 3 | Archery, Athletics, Fencing |
| University of Lincoln | 3 | Equestrian (Dressage, Eventing, Jumping) |
| University of Wales, Newport | 2 | Basketball, Cycling (Road) |
| University of Oxford | 2 | Athletics, Hockey |
| University of Essex | 2 | Basketball, Football |
| Imperial College London | 2 | Fencing, Football |
| University of Westminster | 2 | Hockey, Fencing |
| University of Reading | 2 | Basketball, Fencing |
| London Metropolitan University | 2 | Basketball, Fencing |
| Liverpool John Moores University | 2 | Archery, Boxing |
| University of Glamorgan | 2 | Archery, Football |

*(Continued)*

**Table 67 (Continued)**

| University | Sports | Individual sports |
|---|---|---|
| University of Hull | 2 | Archery, Fencing |
| University of Winchester | 1 | Athletics |
| University of Southampton | 1 | Sailing |
| University of St Andrews | 1 | Football |
| Aberystwyth University | 1 | Cycling (Mountain Bike) |
| Sheffield Hallam University | 1 | Volleyball (Indoor) |
| London South Bank | 1 | Tae Kwon Do |
| University of Liverpool | 1 | Fencing |
| Anglia Ruskin University | 1 | Fencing |
| University of Bedfordshire | 1 | Archery |
| King's College London | 1 | Archery |
| University of York | 1 | Archery |
| University of Gloucestershire | 1 | Badminton |
| University of Teesside | 1 | Table Tennis |

Source: www.london2012.com

# Shake it up – get yourself fitter

Now, of course, most of us are mere mortals rather than the gilded gods of international- or national-level competition sport. There's nothing wrong with a bit of a leisurely non-league kickabout on the five-a-side football pitch on a Sunday morning, and most universities have teams for those who are beginners, not all that competitive or not all that talented.

Meanwhile, the real growth area in university leisure is in fitness and well-being training, rather than in competitive sport. Interest in a healthy lifestyle has never been greater, and levels of obesity are at a record high, so there's an enormous demand for things to help keep you toned and relaxed or simply less encumbered by those pesky bingo wings and beer guts. Many students like activities where they can just turn up and start, rather than having to wait for the rest of the team, or they want to have non-competitive fun with a class or a group of friends – and universities are going out of their way to provide this. The newest sports facilities tend to contain gyms, weights rooms, studios for a variety of fitness classes, and cross-trainers, exercise bikes and treadmills for burning fat and improving aerobic fitness.

Table 68 looks at the all-round sports and leisure facilities at different universities. Those in the top tables provide plenty of variety, with something for everyone, with extra points being given for inclusiveness and easy access to lots of fitness machines and classes. Some, but not all, also excel at national-level sport. Take your pick.

**Table 68 The best and worst UK universities for sport and fitness**

**The top-class universities**

| | A | B | C | D | E | F | G | H | I | J | K |
|---|---|---|---|---|---|---|---|---|---|---|---|
| Aberdeen University | ✓ | ✓ | ✓ | ✓ | ✓ | ✓ | ✓ | ✓ | ✓ | ✓ | |
| Aberystwyth University | ✓ | ✓ | ✓ | ✓ | | ✓ | | ✓ | ✓ | ✓ | ✓ |
| Aston University | ✓ | ✓ | ✓ | ✓ | | ✓ | ✓ | ✓ | ✓ | | ✓ |
| Bangor University | ✓ | ✓ | ✓ | ✓ | ✓ | | ✓ | ✓ | | ✓ | ✓ |
| University of Bath | ✓ | ✓ | ✓ | ✓ | ✓ | ✓ | ✓ | ✓ | ✓ | | ✓ |
| University of Birmingham | ✓ | ✓ | ✓ | ✓ | ✓ | ✓ | ✓ | ✓ | ✓ | ✓ | ✓ |
| University of Cambridge | ✓ | ✓ | ✓ | ✓ | ✓ | ✓ | ✓ | ✓ | | ✓ | |
| Cardiff University | ✓ | ✓ | ✓ | ✓ | | ✓ | ✓ | ✓ | ✓ | ✓ | |
| University of Dundee | ✓ | ✓ | ✓ | ✓ | | ✓ | ✓ | ✓ | ✓ | ✓ | |
| Durham University | ✓ | ✓ | ✓ | ✓ | ✓ | | ✓ | ✓ | ✓ | ✓ | |
| University of East Anglia | ✓ | ✓ | ✓ | ✓ | ✓ | ✓ | ✓ | ✓ | ✓ | | ✓ |
| Edge Hill University | ✓ | ✓ | ✓ | ✓ | ✓ | ✓ | ✓ | ✓ | ✓ | | |

**Key:**
A = Fitness centre, weights room, cardio training
B = Grass pitches
C = All-weather pitches
D = Gymnasium or sports hall
E = Athletics or running track
F = Swimming pool
G = Tennis courts
H = Squash courts
I = Dance studio
J = Rowing, sailing, canoeing
K = Climbing or bouldering wall

*(Continued)*

**Table 68 (Continued)**

|  | A | B | C | D | E | F | G | H | I | J | K |
|---|---|---|---|---|---|---|---|---|---|---|---|
| University of Edinburgh | ✓ | ✓ | ✓ | ✓ | ✓ | ✓ | ✓ | ✓ | ✓ | ✓ | ✓ |
| University of Essex | ✓ | ✓ | ✓ | ✓ |  |  | ✓ | ✓ | ✓ | ✓ | ✓ |
| University of Exeter | ✓ | ✓ | ✓ | ✓ | ✓ | ✓ | ✓ | ✓ | ✓ | ✓ | ✓ |
| Imperial College London | ✓ | ✓ | ✓ | ✓ |  | ✓ | ✓ | ✓ | ✓ | ✓ | ✓ |
| Lancaster University | ✓ | ✓ | ✓ | ✓ |  | ✓ | ✓ | ✓ | ✓ |  | ✓ |
| Leeds Metropolitan University | ✓ | ✓ | ✓ | ✓ | ✓ | ✓ | ✓ | ✓ | ✓ |  | ✓ |
| Loughborough University | ✓ | ✓ | ✓ | ✓ | ✓ | ✓ | ✓ | ✓ | ✓ |  | ✓ |
| Newcastle University | ✓ | ✓ | ✓ | ✓ |  |  | ✓ | ✓ | ✓ | ✓ | ✓ |
| University of Nottingham | ✓ | ✓ | ✓ | ✓ |  | ✓ | ✓ | ✓ | ✓ | ✓ |  |
| University of Oxford | ✓ | ✓ | ✓ | ✓ | ✓ | ✓ | ✓ | ✓ |  | ✓ | ✓ |
| Oxford Brookes University | ✓ | ✓ | ✓ | ✓ |  | ✓ | ✓ | ✓ | ✓ | ✓ | ✓ |
| Queen's University Belfast | ✓ | ✓ | ✓ | ✓ |  | ✓ |  | ✓ | ✓ | ✓ | ✓ |
| University of St Andrews | ✓ | ✓ | ✓ | ✓ | ✓ |  | ✓ | ✓ | ✓ |  | ✓ |
| University of Sheffield | ✓ | ✓ | ✓ | ✓ |  | ✓ | ✓ | ✓ | ✓ | ✓ | ✓ |
| University of Southampton | ✓ | ✓ | ✓ | ✓ |  | ✓ | ✓ | ✓ | ✓ | ✓ | ✓ |
| University of Stirling | ✓ | ✓ | ✓ | ✓ | ✓ | ✓ | ✓ | ✓ |  | ✓ |  |
| University of Wales Institute Cardiff | ✓ | ✓ | ✓ | ✓ | ✓ | ✓ | ✓ | ✓ | ✓ |  |  |

**Key:**

A = Fitness centre, weights room, cardio training  
B = Grass pitches  
C = All-weather pitches  
D = Gymnasium or sports hall  
E = Athletics or running track  
F = Swimming pool  
G = Tennis courts  
H = Squash courts  
I = Dance studio  
J = Rowing, sailing, canoeing  
K = Climbing or bouldering wall

**Table 68 (Continued)**

| | A | B | C | D | E | F | G | H | I | J | K |
|---|---|---|---|---|---|---|---|---|---|---|---|
| University of Wales Swansea | ✓ | ✓ | ✓ | ✓ | ✓ | ✓ | ✓ | ✓ | ✓ | ✓ | ✓ |
| University of Warwick | ✓ | ✓ | ✓ | ✓ | ✓ | ✓ | ✓ | ✓ | ✓ | | ✓ |
| **Excellent universities** | | | | | | | | | | | |
| University of Central Lancashire | ✓ | ✓ | ✓ | ✓ | ✓ | | ✓ | ✓ | ✓ | | |
| University of Glamorgan | ✓ | ✓ | ✓ | ✓ | | | ✓ | ✓ | ✓ | | ✓ |
| University of Hertfordshire | ✓ | ✓ | ✓ | ✓ | | ✓ | | ✓ | ✓ | | ✓ |
| University of Hull | ✓ | ✓ | ✓ | ✓ | ✓ | | ✓ | ✓ | | ✓ | ✓ |
| Keele University | ✓ | ✓ | ✓ | ✓ | ✓ | | ✓ | ✓ | ✓ | | ✓ |
| University of Leicester | ✓ | ✓ | ✓ | ✓ | ✓ | | ✓ | ✓ | ✓ | | |
| University of Liverpool | ✓ | ✓ | ✓ | ✓ | | ✓ | ✓ | ✓ | ✓ | | ✓ |
| Liverpool John Moores | ✓ | ✓ | ✓ | ✓ | | ✓ | ✓ | | ✓ | | ✓ |
| University of Manchester | ✓ | ✓ | ✓ | ✓ | | ✓ | ✓ | ✓ | ✓ | ✓ | |
| Manchester Metropolitan University | ✓ | ✓ | ✓ | ✓ | | ✓ | ✓ | ✓ | ✓ | | |
| University of Reading | ✓ | ✓ | ✓ | ✓ | | | ✓ | ✓ | ✓ | ✓ | |
| University of Salford | ✓ | ✓ | ✓ | ✓ | | ✓ | ✓ | ✓ | | ✓ | ✓ |
| University of Surrey | ✓ | ✓ | ✓ | ✓ | | | ✓ | ✓ | ✓ | | ✓ |
| University of Teesside | ✓ | ✓ | ✓ | ✓ | | | | ✓ | ✓ | ✓ | ✓ |
| University of Wolverhampton | ✓ | ✓ | ✓ | ✓ | ✓ | ✓ | ✓ | ✓ | ✓ | | |
| University of York | ✓ | ✓ | ✓ | ✓ | ✓ | | ✓ | ✓ | ✓ | ✓ | |

**Key:**

A = Fitness centre, weights room, cardio training  
B = Grass pitches  
C = All-weather pitches  
D = Gymnasium or sports hall  
E = Athletics or running track  
F = Swimming pool  
G = Tennis courts  
H = Squash courts  
I = Dance studio  
J = Rowing, sailing, canoeing  
K = Climbing or bouldering wall  

*(Continued)*

**Table 68 (Continued)**

| | A | B | C | D | E | F | G | H | I | J | K |
|---|---|---|---|---|---|---|---|---|---|---|---|
| **Good universities** | | | | | | | | | | | |
| Birmingham City University | ✓ | ✓ | ✓ | | | | ✓ | ✓ | ✓ | | |
| University of Bradford | ✓ | ✓ | ✓ | ✓ | | ✓ | | ✓ | ✓ | | |
| University of Bristol | ✓ | ✓ | ✓ | ✓ | | ✓ | | ✓ | | | |
| Brunel University | ✓ | ✓ | ✓ | ✓ | ✓ | | | ✓ | | | ✓ |
| University of Chichester | ✓ | ✓ | ✓ | | ✓ | | ✓ | | | | ✓ |
| University of Cumbria | ✓ | ✓ | ✓ | ✓ | | | ✓ | ✓ | | | ✓ |
| University of Glasgow | ✓ | ✓ | ✓ | ✓ | | ✓ | | ✓ | ✓ | | |
| Heriot-Watt University | ✓ | ✓ | ✓ | ✓ | | | ✓ | ✓ | | | ✓ |
| University of Kent | ✓ | ✓ | ✓ | ✓ | | | ✓ | ✓ | ✓ | | |
| King's College London | ✓ | ✓ | ✓ | | | ✓ | ✓ | ✓ | | | |
| University of Leeds | ✓ | ✓ | ✓ | ✓ | | | | ✓ | | | ✓ |
| University of Lincoln | ✓ | ✓ | ✓ | ✓ | | | | ✓ | ✓ | | |
| Liverpool Hope University | ✓ | ✓ | ✓ | ✓ | | | ✓ | ✓ | | | |
| Middlesex University | ✓ | ✓ | ✓ | ✓ | | ✓ | ✓ | | | | |
| Nottingham Trent University | ✓ | ✓ | ✓ | ✓ | | | | ✓ | ✓ | | |
| University of Plymouth | ✓ | ✓ | | ✓ | | | ✓ | ✓ | | ✓ | |
| University of Portsmouth | ✓ | ✓ | ✓ | ✓ | | | ✓ | | ✓ | | |
| Queen Mary, London | ✓ | ✓ | | ✓ | | | | ✓ | ✓ | ✓ | |

**Key:**

A = Fitness centre, weights room, cardio training
B = Grass pitches
C = All-weather pitches
D = Gymnasium or sports hall
E = Athletics or running track
F = Swimming pool

G = Tennis courts
H = Squash courts
I = Dance studio
J = Rowing, sailing, canoeing
K = Climbing or bouldering wall

**Table 68 (Continued)**

|  | A | B | C | D | E | F | G | H | I | J | K |
|---|---|---|---|---|---|---|---|---|---|---|---|
| Royal Holloway | ✓ | ✓ |  | ✓ |  |  | ✓ | ✓ | ✓ |  |  |
| Sheffield Hallam University | ✓ | ✓ | ✓ | ✓ |  |  | ✓ |  | ✓ |  |  |
| Staffordshire University | ✓ | ✓ | ✓ | ✓ |  |  | ✓ |  | ✓ |  |  |
| University of Strathclyde | ✓ | ✓ | ✓ | ✓ |  |  |  | ✓ | ✓ |  |  |
| University of Sussex | ✓ | ✓ | ✓ | ✓ |  |  | ✓ | ✓ | ✓ |  |  |
| University of Ulster | ✓ | ✓ | ✓ | ✓ |  |  | ✓ | ✓ | ✓ |  |  |
| University of West of England | ✓ |  | ✓ | ✓ |  |  | ✓ | ✓ |  |  | ✓ |
| University of Westminster | ✓ | ✓ | ✓ | ✓ |  |  | ✓ |  | ✓ | ✓ |  |
| University of Winchester | ✓ | ✓ | ✓ | ✓ | ✓ |  |  | ✓ | ✓ |  |  |
| University of Worcester | ✓ | ✓ | ✓ | ✓ |  |  | ✓ |  | ✓ |  |  |
| **Fair universities** |  |  |  |  |  |  |  |  |  |  |  |
| Bournemouth University | ✓ | ✓ | ✓ | ✓ |  |  |  |  |  |  | ✓ |
| University of Brighton | ✓ | ✓ | ✓ | ✓ |  | ✓ |  |  |  |  |  |
| University of Chester | ✓ |  | ✓ | ✓ |  | ✓ |  | ✓ |  |  |  |
| University of Derby | ✓ | ✓ |  | ✓ | ✓ |  |  |  |  |  |  |
| University of East London | ✓ |  |  | ✓ |  | ✓ | ✓ | ✓ |  |  |  |
| Edinburgh Napier University | ✓ |  |  |  |  |  |  |  |  |  |  |
| Glyndŵr University | ✓ | ✓ | ✓ | ✓ |  |  |  |  | ✓ |  |  |
| Goldsmiths, London | ✓ | ✓ |  | ✓ |  |  | ✓ |  | ✓ |  |  |

**Key:**

| | |
|---|---|
| A = Fitness centre, weights room, cardio training | G = Tennis courts |
| B = Grass pitches | H = Squash courts |
| C = All-weather pitches | I = Dance studio |
| D = Gymnasium or sports hall | J = Rowing, sailing, canoeing |
| E = Athletics or running track | K = Climbing or bouldering wall |
| F = Swimming pool | *(Continued)* |

**Table 68 (Continued)**

| | A | B | C | D | E | F | G | H | I | J | K |
|---|---|---|---|---|---|---|---|---|---|---|---|
| University of Greenwich | ✓ | ✓ | | ✓ | | | ✓ | | ✓ | | |
| Kingston University | ✓ | ✓ | ✓ | | | | ✓ | | ✓ | | |
| Lampeter (University of Wales) | ✓ | ✓ | | ✓ | | | | ✓ | | | |
| London School of Economics | ✓ | ✓ | | ✓ | | | ✓ | | | | |
| University of Northampton | ✓ | ✓ | | ✓ | | | ✓ | | ✓ | | |
| University of Northumbria | ✓ | ✓ | ✓ | ✓ | | | | ✓ | | | |
| Queen Margaret University | ✓ | | ✓ | ✓ | | | | | ✓ | | |
| Robert Gordon University | ✓ | | | ✓ | | ✓ | | | ✓ | | ✓ |
| Roehampton University | ✓ | ✓ | | ✓ | | | ✓ | | ✓ | | |
| Southampton Solent University | ✓ | ✓ | | ✓ | | | ✓ | | | ✓ | |
| University College London | ✓ | ✓ | | | | | | ✓ | ✓ | | |
| University of Wales Newport | ✓ | ✓ | | ✓ | | | ✓ | | | | |
| University of West of Scotland | ✓ | ✓ | ✓ | ✓ | | | | | | | |
| York St John University | ✓ | ✓ | ✓ | ✓ | | | | | | | ✓ |
| **Poor universities** | | | | | | | | | | | |
| Abertay Dundee University | ✓ | | | | | | | | | | |
| Anglia Ruskin University | ✓ | ✓ | | ✓ | | | | | | | |
| Arts London | | | | | | | | | | | |

**Key:**
A = Fitness centre, weights room, cardio training
B = Grass pitches
C = All-weather pitches
D = Gymnasium or sports hall
E = Athletics or running track
F = Swimming pool
G = Tennis courts
H = Squash courts
I = Dance studio
J = Rowing, sailing, canoeing
K = Climbing or bouldering wall

**Table 68 (Continued)**

| | A | B | C | D | E | F | G | H | I | J | K |
|---|---|---|---|---|---|---|---|---|---|---|---|
| Bath Spa University | | | | | | | | | | | |
| Bedfordshire University | ✓ | | | ✓ | | | | | ✓ | | |
| Bolton University | ✓ | | | ✓ | | | | | | | ✓ |
| Bucks New University | ✓ | ✓ | | ✓ | | | | | | | |
| Canterbury CC University | ✓ | | | ✓ | | | ✓ | | | | |
| City University, London | ✓ | ✓ | | | | | | ✓ | | | |
| Coventry University | ✓ | | | ✓ | | | | | ✓ | | |
| University for Creative Arts | | | | ✓ | | | | | | | |
| De Montfort University | ✓ | | | ✓ | | | | ✓ | | | |
| Glasgow Caledonian University | ✓ | | | ✓ | | | | | ✓ | | |
| University of Gloucestershire | ✓ | | | ✓ | | | | | | | |
| University of Huddersfield | ✓ | | | ✓ | | | | ✓ | | | |
| London Metropolitan | ✓ | | | ✓ | | | | | ✓ | | |
| London South Bank | ✓ | ✓ | | ✓ | | | | | | | |
| SOAS | ✓ | | | | | | | ✓ | | | |
| University of Sunderland | ✓ | | | ✓ | | ✓ | | | | | |
| Swansea Metropolitan | ✓ | | | ✓ | | | | | | | |
| Thames Valley University | ✓ | ✓ | | ✓ | | | | | | | |

**Key:**

A = Fitness centre, weights room, cardio training
B = Grass pitches
C = All-weather pitches
D = Gymnasium or sports hall
E = Athletics or running track
F = Swimming pool

G = Tennis courts
H = Squash courts
I = Dance studio
J = Rowing, sailing, canoeing
K = Climbing or bouldering wall

It's worth noting that some of the universities in the 'poor' category above have made arrangements with nearby colleges so that they can share facilities, or they're very close to commercial or council-run sports and fitness facilities that offer comprehensive services to students at a hefty discount. If in doubt, contact the university to find out whether these sorts of arrangement exist.

The Inclusive Fitness Initiative aims to get everyone more active, whether they're disabled or non-disabled. They support the creation of accessible facilities, the purchase of inclusive fitness equipment, and staff training, and have accredited the following universities as Inclusive Fitness Sites.

- ► University of Bath (Sports Training Village)
- ► Edge Hill University (Sporting Edge)
- ► Sheffield Hallam University (Club Hallam, City Campus)
- ► University of Hull
- ► University of Lincoln
- ► University of Teesside
- ► University of York

It's also worth noting that the University of Wales Institute, Cardiff, has a designated centre specifically designed for the varied fitness needs of students with disabilities, in addition to accessible general facilities.

For more information, you can download IFI's Student Information Pack: www.inclusivefitness.org/images/catimages/IFI_Student_Information_Pack.pdf.

# Arts and entertainment – get involved

You might prefer to get creative with your interests in your free time. This can be a lot of fun, and it's a great way to meet new people. It's also an invaluable opportunity to learn a variety of new skills, some of which – since many job openings require relevant work experience – can enhance your future career prospects. You can try your hand at student media such as newspapers, magazines, websites, blogs and radio, or look for theatre, dance and music groups if you'd like to get involved with performances.

If you fancy yourself as a newshound, the student newspaper is the best place to offer your services, but if you'd like to contribute more diverse styles of writing and types of content you can also look to university magazines and websites. Some national award winners are listed below.

**Table 69 *Guardian* student newspaper award winners 2001–2008**

| Year/status | University | Publication |
|---|---|---|
| 2008 winner | Imperial College London | *Felix* |
| 2008 runner up | University of York | *Nouse* |
| 2007 winner | University of York | *York Vision* |
| 2007 runner up | Univesrity of Oxford | *The Oxford Student* |
| 2006 winner | Imperial College London | *Felix* |
| 2006 runner up | University of Sheffield | *Sheffield Steel Press* |
| 2005 winner | Cardiff University | *Gair Rhydd* |
| 2005 runner up | University of York | *Nouse* |
| 2004 winner | University of York | *York Vision* |
| 2004 runner up | University of Leeds | *Leeds Student* |
| 2003 winner | University of York | *York Vision* |
| 2003 runner up | University of Warwick | *Warwick Boar* |
| 2002 winner | University of York | *York Vision* |
| 2002 runner up | University College Dublin | *The University Observer* |
| 2001 winner | University of Oxford | *The Oxford Student* |
| 2001 runner up | St Andrews University | *The Saint* |

Source: Guardian Student Media Awards

**Table 70 *Guardian* student magazine award winners 2001–2008**

| Year/status | University | Publication |
|---|---|---|
| 2008 winner | University of Cardiff | *Quench* |
| 2008 runner up | Imperial College London | *I, Science* |
| 2007 winner | Tower Hamlets Summer University | *Nang* |
| 2007 runner up | University of Nottingham | *Impact* |
| 2006 winner | University of Cardiff | *Quench* |
| 2006 runners up | Imperial College and London University of Oxford | *I, Science* *Isis* |
| 2005 winner | University of Cardiff | *Quench* |
| 2005 runner up | University of Nottingham | *Impact* |
| 2004 winner | University of Oxford | *Isis* |
| 2004 runner up | University of Cardiff | *Quench* |
| 2003 winner | UK medical schools | *Student BMJ* |
| 2003 runner up | University of Portsmouth | *Pugwash* |
| 2002 winner | UK medical schools | *Student BMJ* |
| 2002 runner up | University of the West of England | *Westworld* |
| 2001 winner | University of Nottingham | *Impact* |
| 2001 runner up | Bournemouth University | *Nerve* |

Source: Guardian Student Media Awards

**Table 71 Guardian student website award winners 2001–2008**

| Year/status | University | Website |
|---|---|---|
| 2008 winner | University of Oxford | Cherwell |
| 2008 runner up | University of York | Nouse |
| 2007 winner | Imperial College London | live.cgcu.net |
| 2007 runner up | University of York | Nouse |
| 2006 winner | University of Warwick | Warwick Boar |
| 2006 runner up | University College Falmouth | www.bloc-online.com |
| 2005 winner | London School of Economics | Pulsefm.co.uk |
| 2005 runner up | University of Warwick | Warwick Boar |
| 2004 winner | University of Southampton | www.wessexscene.co.uk |
| 2004 runner up | Lancaster University | www.lusu.co.uk/scan |
| 2003 winner | Cardiff University | Blunt |
| 2003 runner up | University of Southampton | Wessex Scene |
| 2002 winner | University of York | York Vision Online |
| 2002 runner up | University of Cambridge | Varsity |
| 2001 winner | University of Central Lancashire | Preston 2000 |
| 2001 runner up | University of York | York Vision Online |

Source: Guardian Student Media Awards

**Table 72 National student radio awards winners 2005–2008**

| Year/status | University | Station |
|---|---|---|
| 2008 Gold | University of Nottingham | URN |
| 2008 Silver | University of Westminster | Smoke Radio |
| 2008 Bronze | Nottingham Trent University | Fly FM |
| 2007 Gold | University of Cambridge and Anglia Ruskin University | CUR1350 |
| 2007 Silver | University of Westminster | Smoke Radio |
| 2007 Bronze | De Montfort University | Demon FM |
| 2006 Gold | University of Nottingham | URN |
| 2006 Silver | University of Warwick | RaW |
| 2006 Bronze | University of Westminster | Smoke Radio |
| 2005 Gold | University of York | URY |
| 2005 Silver | Royal Holloway, London | 1287AM Insanity |
| 2005 Bronze | University of Leeds | LSR FM |

Source: www.studentradio.org.uk

If student radio sounds more like your sort of thing, get involved and try your hand at producing, presenting and more. If your university of choice doesn't have a radio station you could try setting one up, or try contacting the university website to see whether they support podcasts and other media. See Table 72 for some award-winning university radio stations.

**Table 73 NaSTA Best Broadcaster Award winners 2005–2009**

| Year | University | Station |
|------|------------|---------|
| 2009 | University of Leeds | LSTV |
| 2008 | Oxford Brookes University | Brookes TV |
| 2007 | University of Leeds | LSTV |
| 2006 | Imperial College London | stoic tv |
| 2005 | University of Leeds | LSTV |

Source: www.nasta.tv

Some universities also have their own television stations, which could be particularly useful if you're considering a career in broadcasting, or just fancy trying your hand writing scripts, producing or editing, or making short films. Contact the National Student Television Association (NaSTA) to find out which universities regularly enter its annual range of awards (www.nasta.tv).

If making your own radio or TV programmes doesn't appeal, perhaps you'd prefer to get your face on national television instead. The TV quiz show *University Challenge* has been taxing student brains since 1963, and if your general knowledge is top notch you could always give it a go. To try out for a team, contact your student union around Christmas time when Granada Television send out their invitations to apply. If you succeed in getting onto the show you'll be in good company – previous contestants have included Stephen Fry, Sebastian Faulkes, Malcolm Rifkind, Clive James, Miriam Margolyes, John Simpson, Julian Fellowes and David Starkey.

Maybe you'd like to tread the boards and try some acting, or to get involved with some of the offstage work that is also an essential part of student drama, such as set design, play writing, lighting, directing or wardrobe. Many universities have very active student theatre or drama societies and often they win prestigious awards in national competitions, as well as enjoying the spotlight in their own town.

To find out more about drama societies at universities you're considering applying to, begin by contacting the students' union (websites all listed at the back of this book) at the relevant institution. Generally speaking, the larger the university, the more likely it is to have one or more performing arts groups. They may even offer a choice of groups that perform comedy, classics, new plays, or musical theatre.

**Table 74 University Challenge winners since 1995**

| Year | Institution | Year | Institution |
|---|---|---|---|
| 1995 | Trinity College, Cambridge | 2003 | Birkbeck College, London |
| 1996 | Imperial College, London | 2004 | Magdalen College, Oxford |
| 1997 | Magdalen College, Oxford | 2005 | Corpus Christi, Oxford |
| 1998 | Magdalen College, Oxford | 2006 | University of Manchester |
| 1999 | Open University | 2007 | University of Warwick |
| 2000 | University of Durham | 2008 | Christ Church, Oxford |
| 2001 | Imperial College, London | 2009 | University of Manchester* |
| 2002 | Somerville College, Oxford | | |

Sources: www.ukgameshows.com and www.blanchflower.org
*In 2009 the original winners, Corpus Christi, Oxford, were controversially disqualified after one of the team was declared a non-student and thus ineligible.

**Table 75 National Student Drama Festival winners 2001–2009**

| Year | University | Production title |
|---|---|---|
| 2009 | University of Edinburgh<br>University of Hull | 'Normal'<br>'Never Enough' |
| 2008 | University of York | 'Metamorphosis' |
| 2007 | University of Edinburgh | 'Radio' |
| 2006 | University of Edinburgh | 'Enola' |
| 2005 | Dartington College | 'Tea Without Mother' |
| 2004 | Liverpool Insititute for Performing Arts | 'Beautiful Thing' |
| 2003 | University of Exeter | 'The Freudian Slip' |
| 2001 | University of York | 'Pull My Strings' |

Source: Festgoers' Prize awards, National Student Drama Festival

# Arts and entertainment – enjoy

The types of entertainment students are most likely to spend their money on are nightclubs, pubs, live music and cinema. Here's a brief guide to what students think are the most entertaining cities and towns in Britain. Since nearly all towns and cities have at least one local cinema playing the current blockbusters, the acid test of good local film is whether or not the place has its own art house cinema showing more unusual films. Don't despair if a town or city you're considering hasn't got much by way of nightlife – you may find that the main source of nearby entertainment is actually at the university itself, or in a neighbouring city a short bus or car journey away.

**Table 76 Local nightlife**

| Town/city | Local nightclubs | Local pubs and bars | Live music | Arts cinema |
|---|---|---|---|---|
| Birmingham | excellent | excellent | excellent | yes |
| Brighton | excellent | excellent | excellent | yes |
| Bristol | excellent | excellent | excellent | yes |
| Cardiff | excellent | excellent | excellent | yes |
| Glasgow | excellent | excellent | excellent | yes |
| Leeds | excellent | excellent | excellent | yes |
| Liverpool | excellent | excellent | excellent | yes |
| London | excellent | excellent | excellent | yes |
| Manchester | excellent | excellent | excellent | yes |
| Newcastle upon Tyne | excellent | excellent | excellent | yes |
| Nottingham | excellent | excellent | excellent | yes |
| Edinburgh | good | excellent | excellent | yes |
| Leicester | good | excellent | excellent | yes |
| Sheffield | good | excellent | excellent | yes |
| Aberdeen | okay | excellent | good | yes |
| Bath | okay | excellent | good | yes |
| Cambridge | okay | excellent | good | yes |
| Oxford | okay | excellent | good | yes |
| Plymouth | okay | excellent | good | yes |
| Southampton | good | good | excellent | yes |
| Swansea | good | excellent | good | yes |
| York | good | excellent | good | yes |
| Portsmouth | good | good | excellent | yes |
| Aberystwyth | okay | good | good | yes |
| Lancaster | okay | good | good | yes |
| Belfast | okay | good | good | yes |
| Bournemouth | good | good | okay | yes |
| Bradford | okay | good | okay | yes |
| Newport | okay | good | good | yes |
| Derby | okay | good | okay | yes |
| Dundee | okay | good | good | yes |
| Exeter | okay | good | good | yes |
| Guildford[1] | okay | good | okay | yes |

*(Continued)*

**Table 76 (Continued)**

| Town/city | Local nightclubs | Local pubs and bars | Live music | Arts cinema |
|-----------|------------------|---------------------|------------|-------------|
| Lincoln | okay | good | okay | yes |
| Northampton | okay | good | good | yes |
| Norwich | okay | good | good | yes |
| Reading | good | good | good | yes |
| Stoke[2] | okay | good | okay | yes |
| Wolverhampton | okay | good | good | yes |
| Coventry | good | good | good | no |
| Hull | good | good | good | no |
| Middlesbrough | good | good | good | no |
| Bangor | okay | good | okay | no |
| Bolton | okay | good | okay | no |
| Carlisle | okay | good | okay | no |
| Cheltenham[3] | good | good | okay | no |
| Colchester[4] | okay | good | good | no |
| Durham | okay | good | poor | no |
| Huddersfield | okay | good | poor | no |
| Loughborough | okay | good | poor | no |
| Luton | okay | okay | okay | no |
| St Andrews | okay | good | okay | no |
| Stirling | okay | good | okay | no |
| Sunderland | okay | good | okay | no |
| Canterbury | poor | good | okay | yes |
| Chelmsford[5] | okay | good | okay | no |
| Chester | okay | good | okay | no |
| Chichester | okay | good | poor | yes |
| Preston[6] | okay | good | okay | no |
| Uxbridge[7] | poor | okay | okay | no |
| Winchester | poor | good | okay | yes |
| Worcester | okay | good | okay | no |
| Wrexham[8] | okay | okay | okay | no |
| Coleraine[9] | poor | okay | poor | no |
| Egham, Surrey[10] | poor | okay | poor | no |
| Hatfield[11] | poor | poor | poor | no |

**Table 76 (Continued)**

| Town/city | Local nightclubs | Local pubs and bars | Live music | Arts cinema |
|---|---|---|---|---|
| High Wycombe[12] | poor | okay | poor | no |
| Lampeter (University of Wales) | poor | poor | poor | no |
| Ormskirk[13] | poor | poor | poor | no |

*Source: Student questionnaire*

**Notes**

1. University of Surrey
2. Staffordshire University
3. University of Gloucestershire
4. University of Essex
5. Anglia Ruskin University
6. University of Central Lancashire
7. Brunel University
8. Glyndŵr University
9. University of Ulster
10. Royal Holloway
11. University of Hertfordshire
12. Buckinghamshire New University
13. Edge Hill University

Many universities and students' unions own excellent facilities for entertainment, and have gained good reputations for providing enjoyable ways to spend your leisure time. Some places are so well served and popular that their students don't venture into nearby towns and cities all that often for a night out.

At the time of writing this book, university and student union entertainment facilities were in a state of flux at various institutions. At some places this was because they were in the middle of renovating older facilities or building new ones, but at others financial problems were threatening closures or sales.

**Table 77 University/student union-owned entertainment facilities**

| University | Bars/ pubs | Nightclubs/ dancefloors | Live music venues | Theatre/ studio | Student cinema |
|---|---|---|---|---|---|
| Aberdeen University | 0 | 0 | 0 | 0 | 0 |
| Abertay Dundee University | 2 | 1 | 1 | 0 | 1 |
| Aberystwyth University | 2 | 1 | 2 | 1 | 1 |
| Anglia Ruskin University | 1 | 1 | 1 | 1 | 0 |
| University of the Arts, London | 3 | 0 | 1 | 0 | 1 |
| Aston University | 1 | 1 | 1 | 0 | 0 |
| Bangor University | 2 | 1 | 1 | 0 | 0 |
| Bath Spa University | 2 | 1 | 1 | 1 | 0 |
| University of Bath | 2 | 1 | 1 | 1 | 0 |
| Bedfordshire University | 1 | 1 | 1 | 2 | 1 |
| Birmingham City University | 4 | 1 | 1 | 1 | 0 |

*(Continued)*

**Table 77 (Continued)**

| University | Bars/ pubs | Nightclubs/ dancefloors | Live music venues | Theatre/ studio | Student cinema |
|---|---|---|---|---|---|
| University of Birmingham | 3 | 1 | 1 | 1 | 0 |
| Bolton University | 1 | 0 | 1 | 0 | 0 |
| Bournemouth University | 3 | 1 | 2 | 1 | 1 |
| University of Bradford | 5 | 1 | 3 | 1 | 1 |
| University of Brighton | 0 | 0 | 0 | 1 | 0 |
| University of Bristol | 5 | 2 | 3 | 1 | 0 |
| Brunel University | 3 | 1 | 2 | 1 | 0 |
| Buckinghamshire New University | 1 | 1 | 1 | 0 | 0 |
| Canterbury Christ Church University | 1 | 0 | 1 | 0 | 0 |
| Cardiff University | 7 | 2 | 3 | 1 | 0 |
| University of Central Lancashire | 3 | 2 | 2 | 1 | 1 |
| University of Chester | 3 | 1 | 1 | 1 | 0 |
| University of Chichester | 2 | 0 | 1 | 1 | 0 |
| City University, London | 1 | 0 | 0 | 0 | 0 |
| Coventry University | 1 | 0 | 1 | 1 | 0 |
| University of Cumbria | 3 | 0 | 3 | 1 | 0 |
| De Montfort University | 1 | 1 | 1 | 1 | 0 |
| University of Derby | 1 | 0 | 1 | 0 | 0 |
| University of Dundee | 4 | 2 | 2 | 0 | 1 |
| Durham University | 4 | 4 | 3 | 1 | 0 |
| University of East Anglia | 3 | 1 | 2 | 1 | 0 |
| University of East London | 1 | 0 | 1 | 1 | 0 |
| Edge Hill University | 0 | 0 | 0 | 2 | 0 |
| University of Edinburgh | 12 | 2 | 3 | 1 | 0 |
| Edinburgh Napier University | 1 | 0 | 0 | 1 | 0 |
| University of Essex | 4 | 2 | 1 | 1 | 0 |
| University of Exeter | 2 | 1 | 1 | 1 | 1 |
| University of Glasgow | 9 | 1 | 2 | 1 | 0 |
| Glasgow Caledonian University | 0 | 0 | 0 | 0 | 0 |
| University of Gloucestershire | 4 | 0 | 2 | 0 | 0 |
| Goldsmiths, London | 1 | 1 | 1 | 1 | 0 |
| University of Greenwich | 2 | 1 | 1 | 1 | 0 |

**Table 77 (Continued)**

| University | Bars/ pubs | Nightclubs/ dancefloors | Live music venues | Theatre/ studio | Student cinema |
|---|---|---|---|---|---|
| Heriot-Watt University | 1 | 1 | 2 | 1 | 0 |
| University of Hertfordshire | 3 | 1 | 1 | 1 | 0 |
| University of Huddersfield | 1 | 0 | 1 | 1 | 0 |
| University of Hull | 3 | 1 | 1 | 1 | 0 |
| Imperial College London | 3 | 1 | 3 | 0 | 1 |
| Keele University | 4 | 1 | 2 | 1 | 0 |
| University of Kent | 2 | 1 | 1 | 1 | 0 |
| King's College London | 2 | 1 | 2 | 1 | 0 |
| Kingston University | 3 | 1 | 3 | 1 | 0 |
| Lampeter (University of Wales) | 3 | 1 | 2 | 1 | 0 |
| Lancaster University | 9 | 1 | 3 | 1 | 1 |
| University of Leeds | 5 | 3 | 3 | 2 | 0 |
| Leeds Metropolitan University | 2 | 0 | 2 | 0 | 0 |
| University of Leicester | 7 | 1 | 1 | 1 | 0 |
| University of Lincoln | 4 | 2 | 1 | 1 | 1 |
| University of Liverpool | 4 | 1 | 2 | 1 | 0 |
| Liverpool Hope University | 1 | 0 | 0 | 1 | 0 |
| Liverpool John Moores | 2 | 1 | 1 | 1 | 0 |
| London Metropolitan University | 2 | 1 | 1 | 1 | 0 |
| London School of Economics | 2 | 1 | 2 | 1 | 0 |
| London South Bank University | 1 | 1 | 1 | 1 | 0 |
| Loughborough University | 9 | 3 | 1 | 0 | 1 |
| University of Manchester | 7 | 2 | 4 | 1 | 0 |
| Manchester Metropolitan University | 1 | 1 | 1 | 0 | 0 |
| Middlesex University | 0 | 0 | 0 | 0 | 0 |
| Newcastle University | 6 | 1 | 2 | 1 | 0 |
| University of Northampton | 3 | 1 | 1 | 1 | 0 |
| University of Northumbria | 4 | 2 | 3 | 1 | 1 |
| University of Nottingham | 1 | 0 | 1 | 1 | 1 |
| Nottingham Trent University | 3 | 1 | 1 | 1 | 0 |
| Oxford Brookes University | 3 | 1 | 2 | 1 | 0 |
| University of Plymouth | 4 | 2 | 2 | 1 | 0 |
| University of Portsmouth | 3 | 1 | 2 | 1 | 0 |

*(Continued)*

155

**Table 77 (Continued)**

| University | Bars/ pubs | Nightclubs/ dancefloors | Live music venues | Theatre/ studio | Student cinema |
|---|---|---|---|---|---|
| Queen Margaret University | 1 | 0 | 1 | 1 | 1 |
| Queen Mary, London | 3 | 1 | 2 | 1 | 0 |
| Queen's University Belfast | 5 | 1 | 2 | 0 | 1 |
| University of Reading | 3 | 1 | 1 | 1 | 1 |
| Robert Gordon University | 2 | 1 | 2 | 0 | 0 |
| Royal Holloway | 1 | 1 | 3 | 1 | 0 |
| University of St Andrews | 3 | 2 | 2 | 2 | 0 |
| University of Salford | 2 | 1 | 1 | 1 | 0 |
| University of Sheffield | 5 | 4 | 4 | 1 | 1 |
| Sheffield Hallam University | 4 | 3 | 1 | 1 | 0 |
| SOAS | 1 | 0 | 0 | 0 | 0 |
| University of Southampton | 6 | 1 | 2 | 1 | 1 |
| Southampton Solent University | 2 | 1 | 1 | 1 | 0 |
| Staffordshire University | 3 | 2 | 2 | 1 | 1 |
| University of Stirling | 4 | 1 | 1 | 0 | 0 |
| University of Strathclyde | 4 | 1 | 1 | 0 | 0 |
| University of Sunderland | 1 | 0 | 1 | 1 | 0 |
| University of Surrey | 5 | 2 | 1 | 0 | 0 |
| Swansea Metropolitan University | 1 | 0 | 0 | 1 | 0 |
| University of Teesside | 3 | 1 | 1 | 1 | 0 |
| University College London | 5 | 2 | 2 | 1 | 0 |
| University of Wales Institute Cardiff | 3 | 0 | 2 | 1 | 0 |
| University of Wales Newport | 1 | 1 | 1 | 1 | 0 |
| University of Wales Swansea | 3 | 2 | 2 | 1 | 1 |
| University of Warwick | 5 | 2 | 2 | 2 | 0 |
| University of West of England | 2 | 1 | 1 | 1 | 1 |
| University of West of Scotland | 4 | 2 | 2 | 0 | 1 |
| University of Wolverhampton | 0 | 0 | 0 | 1 | 0 |
| University of Worcester | 1 | 0 | 1 | 1 | 0 |
| University of York | 6 | 1 | 2 | 0 | 1 |

*Source: Student union questionnaire*

# Join our club – clubs and societies

We've seen what the nearest cities have to offer, and we've looked at what universities themselves can provide by way of entertainment and fitness facilities, but there's also what the students themselves have set up: the clubs and societies. These can cover anything including sports, politics and green issues, cultural and international groups, academic, arts and entertainment, religions, and general recreational and social societies. As some universities support over 300 clubs

## Universities with People & Planet groups

University of Aberdeen
University of Abertay Dundee
Aberystwyth University
Aston University
Bangor University
University of Bath
University of Birmingham
University of Bristol
Brunel University
University of Cambridge
Cardiff University
University of Central Lancashire
University of Chester
University of Derby
University of Dundee
Durham University
University of East Anglia
University of Edinburgh
University of Glasgow
Goldsmiths, University of London
Heriot-Watt University
University of Hull
Imperial College London
Keele University
Kingston University
Lancaster University
University of Leeds
University of Leicester
University of Liverpool

London School of Economics
London South Bank University
Loughborough University
University of Manchester
Manchester Metropolitan
    University
Newcastle University
University of Nottingham
University of Oxford
Oxford Brookes University
University of Reading
Roehampton University
Royal Holloway, University
    of London
School of Oriental And
    African Studies
University of Sheffield
University of St Andrews
University of Stirling
University of Strathclyde
University of Surrey
Swansea University
University College London
University of Warwick
University of West of England,
Bristol
University of Westminster
University of York
York St John University

and societies there simply isn't enough room to fit them all into this book, so you should try looking at the students' union websites of universities that you're interested in to gain some idea of what's on offer in each place. Remember that if you can't see exactly what you're looking for, provided you can get four or five other students to join you, you can always set up your own group, often for free.

If you'd like to join a People & Planet group, they are active at the universities listed in the box above. You could also help to start a group yourself if you decide to attend a university that doesn't already have one.

## University Officer Training Corps (UOTC)

Many universities offer the chance to join a branch of the University Officer Training Corps (UOTC). According to the Ministry of Defence, the mission of the UOTC is to 'develop the leadership potential of selected university students through enjoyable and challenging training in order to communicate the values, ethos and career opportunities of the British Army'. What this translates into is paid work, mainly at weekends: students undergo army training and take part in military exercises and community projects. The army lends students full kit for free, and you may even be able to travel abroad on some assignments, although you won't be placed in any combat situations. There's no obligation to join the army on graduation and students can resign from the corps at any time, but it can be very helpful if you're considering a military-related career. It's also very sociable and can help you to improve your fitness levels. For more information look at: www.army. mod.uk/UOTC/5458.aspx.

There are currently 19 UK centres for university officer training.

## UK centres for university officer training

| | |
|---|---|
| Aberdeen | University, Loughborough |
| Belfast | University and University of |
| Birmingham | Lincoln) |
| Bristol | Edinburgh |
| Cambridge | Exeter |
| East Midlands (serves Nottingham | Glasgow and Strathclyde |
|     University, Nottingham Trent | Leeds |
|     University, Leicester University, | Liverpool |
|     Derby University, De Montfort | London |

| | |
|---|---|
| Manchester | Tayforth (serves Dundee, Stirling, |
| Northumbrian (based in | St Andrews) |
| Newcastle) | Wales (bases in Cardiff, Swansea, |
| Oxford | Bangor, Aberystwyth and |
| Sheffield | Wrexham) |
| Southampton | |

## Student volunteering

If you're thinking about doing some volunteering, nearly every established university has its own volunteering service, usually called 'Student Community Action', 'Student Volunteer Centre' or something similar. Often these groups are individually registered UK charities or societies within a student union, and there's a network of SCA groups all over the country belonging to the Student Volunteers Network. This consists of over 125 universities, with over 15,000 volunteers, which aim to 'empower and enable students to initiate, plan and manage their own volunteering projects, and encourage students to work with organisations within their communities'. The parent body provides opportunities, training, resources and support, and it's been administered by Volunteering England since 2007.

See: www.volunteering.org.uk/WhatWeDo/Student+Volunteering/
There are many benefits that you can gain from volunteering. For example, you can:

▶ experience diversity and integration with the community
▶ meet like-minded people and make new friends
▶ make a difference in the community
▶ increase levels of self-confidence, awareness and life skills
▶ build an impressive-looking CV
▶ gain a sense of achievement and personal satisfaction.

To find out more about student volunteering possibilities at any university you might be considering, start by contacting the relevant students' union (their websites are listed in the resources section of this book). In the unlikely event of a university being unable to offer any suitable volunteering opportunities, you can still try a local volunteer centre, sign up with TimeBank UK (www.timebank.org. uk) or directly approach any organisation you would like to volunteer with.

# Chapter 6

# Thinking long term – your prospects

For most students, their primary motivation for entering higher education is to improve their career prospects, and a degree can certainly do that. According to a recent Universities UK and PricewaterhouseCoopers report, the average graduate can expect to add an extra 20–25% to their earnings over a working lifetime, compared to people who leave school after A levels. This premium is even greater for subjects such as medicine, engineering, maths and business. There's less of a premium for humanities and arts graduates, but there is still increased earning potential. A degree can also allow you to enter some careers that are only open to people who hold professional qualifications – you can't work your way up through the ranks to eventually become a vet, for example.

The 2009 Graduate Market Employment Survey carried out by Highfliers found the following:

► the UK's largest graduate employers had decreased their 2009 recruitment targets by 17%

► the sectors preparing to employ the most graduates in 2009 were accountancy, the public sector, and the armed forces

► although there are fewer jobs in total, starting salaries for 2009 were expected to rise by 5.9%, taking the average starting package to £27,000.

The Association of Graduate Recruiters' Graduate Recruitment Winter Survey 2009 painted a similar picture, but they were less optimistic about starting salaries.

- ▶ The engineering sector may buck the trend with an expected 8.3% rise in jobs but there may be a shortfall of graduates to fill them.
- ▶ The highest starting salaries are currently found in law, investment banking, business and financial services, and IT.
- ▶ Employers have urged struggling graduates to research jobs and prepare for interviews more thoroughly than ever as competition intensifies.

Whatever the economic situation, however, there are various things you can do to improve your chances of getting a good job after you graduate.

Before you apply, bear the following points in mind.

- ▶ Pick a university with a good general reputation (it's not fair, but snob value still goes a long way). See Chapter 1 for more on this.
- ▶ Pick a university that top employers are known to target in general (see Table 83).
- ▶ If you have a set career in mind, research the main employers in that field to find out about the particular university departments they target.
- ▶ Take a course with a good reputation  (see Chapter 2).
- ▶ Pick a subject that has high levels of graduate employment, and is likely to continue to do so – see later in this chapter for more details.
- ▶ Work hard to get good A level or Higher results, so you have a better range of universities and course choices open to you.
- ▶ Consider getting sponsored, especially if there's work experience involved and a possibility of a graduate job at the end of the course – see Chapter 3 for more information.

You can continue to improve your prospects once at university too:

- ▶ work hard to get a good class of degree award
- ▶ get relevant work experience at university, such as part-time jobs, overseas study, sandwich courses, volunteering
- ▶ build up proof of the skills employers want – do extra courses, join societies, be a representative or team leader, organise events, enter for awards
- ▶ make the most of the university's career service for CV and interview tips and information about who's hiring
- ▶ start looking for graduate jobs earlier than the rest of the crowd
- ▶ treat getting a job as a job in itself – be organised and persistent.

# What employment sectors do students want to work in?

The employment aspirations of students have changed over time. Here's the latest list of career sectors that appeal to students who are nearing graduation.

**Table 78 Most popular types of work for final-year students in 2009**

| Work type | % of students | Work type | % of students |
|---|---|---|---|
| Teaching | 13.7% | General management | 6.0% |
| Media | 13.6% | Human resources | 6.0% |
| Marketing | 12.6% | Finance | 5.0% |
| Charity or voluntary work | 10.4% | Retailing | 4.7% |
| Accountancy | 10.0% | IT | 3.7% |
| Consulting | 9.8% | Armed forces | 3.1% |
| Research and development | 9.6% | Buying or purchasing | 2.9% |
| Law | 8.9% | Police | 2.5% |
| Investment banking | 8.7% | Property | 2.2% |
| Engineering | 8.5% | Transport or logistics | 2.0% |
| Sales | 6.4% | Actuarial work | 1.8% |

Source: High Fliers, based on 16,357 face-to-face interviews on 30 different university campuses around the UK in February 2009

It's interesting to note that some of these careers can be accessed by further study that's not related to a student's original undergraduate degree, and others don't require specific qualifications.

# Graduate prospects at different universities

Students from different universities have different graduate prospects. This can be for a variety of reasons: the university's general reputation; an intake of particularly bright and capable students; graduates who are well-rounded people rather than purely academically gifted; the majority of courses offered being in areas with high graduate employment; excellent links with businesses; and helpful student careers centres. The list goes on.

In Tables 79 and 80, you can see the top and bottom universities for graduate prospects. Here, 'good graduate prospects' are taken to be the combined percentage of students who are in graduate-type jobs or in further study within six months of graduation. The lists exclude students who are in general non-graduate type work, unable to work, or who are assumed to be unemployed.

**Table 79 The top universities for graduate jobs/further study after graduation**

| Rank | University | % in graduate job or further study |
|------|------------|-----------------------------------|
| =1 | University of Cambridge | 86 |
| =1 | Imperial College London | 86 |
| 3 | London School of Economics | 85 |
| 4 | Newman University College | 81 |
| 5 | University of Oxford | 80 |
| =6 | University of Bath | 79 |
| =6 | University of Bristol | 79 |
| 8 | University College London | 78 |
| 9 | King's College London | 77 |
| 10 | Robert Gordon University | 76 |
| =11 | Aston University | 75 |
| =11 | University of Surrey | 75 |
| =11 | Aberdeen University | 75 |
| =11 | Edinburgh Napier University | 75 |
| =15 | University of Edinburgh | 73 |
| =15 | Durham University | 73 |
| =15 | University of Nottingham | 73 |
| =15 | University of Glasgow | 73 |
| =15 | Newcastle University | 73 |
| =15 | Queen's University of Belfast | 73 |
| =21 | University of Warwick | 72 |
| =21 | City University, London | 72 |
| =21 | University of Strathclyde | 72 |
| =21 | Cardiff University | 72 |
| =25 | University of Dundee | 71 |
| =25 | Nottingham Trent University | 71 |
| =25 | Queen Mary, London | 71 |
| =25 | Heriot-Watt University | 71 |
| =25 | University of Bradford | 71 |
| =30 | Loughborough University | 70 |
| =30 | University of Southampton | 70 |
| =30 | University of Sheffield | 70 |

*Source: The Guardian University Guide 2009*

**Table 80 The bottom universities for graduate jobs/further study after graduation**

| Rank | University | % in graduate job or further study |
|---|---|---|
| 1 | Buckinghamshire New University | 42 |
| 2 | University of Derby | 45 |
| =3 | University of Winchester | 46 |
| =3 | University of Westminster | 46 |
| =5 | University of Lincoln | 47 |
| =5 | Lampeter (University of Wales) | 47 |
| =5 | Bolton University | 47 |
| =8 | University of the Arts, London | 48 |
| =8 | Abertay Dundee University | 48 |
| =10 | University of Huddersfield | 50 |
| =10 | London South Bank University | 50 |
| =12 | Staffordshire University | 51 |
| =12 | Swansea Metropolitan University | 51 |
| =14 | University of Plymouth | 52 |
| =14 | University of Wales Institute, Cardiff | 52 |
| =14 | University of Chichester | 52 |
| =17 | University of Glamorgan | 53 |
| =17 | Bath Spa University | 53 |
| =17 | Aberystwyth University | 53 |
| =17 | University of Northampton | 53 |
| =17 | University of Teesside | 53 |
| =17 | Bedfordshire University | 53 |
| =17 | Roehampton University | 53 |
| =17 | York St John University | 53 |
| =17 | Southampton Solent University | 53 |
| =17 | University of East London | 53 |
| =17 | University of Wolverhampton | 53 |

*Source: The Guardian University Guide 2009*

**Table 81 Average salary of full-time first degree leavers entering full-time graduate\* employment by institution 2007–2008**

| Institution | Average salary (excludes unknown salaries) |
| --- | --- |
| University of Aberdeen | £19,676 |
| University of Abertay Dundee | £20,350 |
| Aberystwyth University | £19,264 |
| Anglia Ruskin University | £20,337 |
| University of the Arts, London | £19,609 |
| Aston University | £20,284 |
| Bangor University | £17,752 |
| University of Bath | £24,247 |
| Bath Spa University | £17,979 |
| University of Bedfordshire | £20,367 |
| University of Birmingham | £22,719 |
| Birmingham City University | £19,890 |
| University College Birmingham | £18,154 |
| Bishop Grosseteste University College Lincoln | £19,361 |
| University of Bolton | £20,667 |
| Arts Institute at Bournemouth | £18,889 |
| Bournemouth University | £20,997 |
| University of Bradford | £19,462 |
| University of Brighton | £20,759 |
| University of Bristol | £23,802 |
| Brunel University | £23,402 |
| University of Buckingham | — |
| Buckinghamshire New University | £20,786 |
| University of Cambridge | £25,218 |
| Canterbury Christ Church University | £20,912 |
| Cardiff University | £21,923 |
| University of Wales Institute, Cardiff | £19,961 |
| University of Central Lancashire | £18,409 |
| Central School of Speech and Drama | £16,737 |
| University of Chester | £18,185 |
| University of Chichester | £20,400 |
| City University | £23,138 |
| Conservatoire for Dance and Drama | £21,724 |

**Table 81 (Continued)**

| Institution | Average salary (excludes unknown salaries) |
|---|---|
| Coventry University | £20,552 |
| University for the Creative Arts | £17,000 |
| University of Cumbria | £19,955 |
| Dartington College of Arts | — |
| De Montfort University | £19,604 |
| University of Derby | £18,913 |
| University of Dundee | £24,122 |
| University of Durham | £22,168 |
| University of East Anglia | £20,932 |
| University of East London | £23,048 |
| Edge Hill University | £20,134 |
| University of Edinburgh | £23,270 |
| Edinburgh College of Art | £19,000 |
| University of Essex | £20,050 |
| University of Exeter | £21,332 |
| University College Falmouth | £15,741 |
| University of Glamorgan | £19,916 |
| University of Glasgow | £23,125 |
| Glasgow Caledonian University | £20,231 |
| Glasgow School of Art | £15,088 |
| University of Gloucestershire | £19,351 |
| Glyndŵr University | £20,994 |
| Goldsmiths College | £21,833 |
| University of Greenwich | £22,306 |
| Guildhall School of Music and Drama | — |
| Harper Adams University College | £20,311 |
| Heriot-Watt University | £21,510 |
| University of Hertfordshire | £21,667 |
| Heythrop College | — |
| University of Huddersfield | £18,616 |
| University of Hull | £20,000 |
| Imperial College of Science, Technology and Medicine | £29,409 |
| University of Keele | £19,764 |
| University of Kent | £22,214 |

*(Continued)*

**Table 81 (Continued)**

| Institution | Average salary (excludes unknown salaries) |
|---|---|
| King's College London | £25,489 |
| Kingston University | £22,021 |
| Lampeter (University of Wales) | — |
| University of Lancaster | £19,931 |
| University of Leeds | £20,693 |
| Leeds College of Music | £15,294 |
| Leeds Metropolitan University | £19,028 |
| Leeds Trinity and All Saints | £19,043 |
| University of Leicester | £21,178 |
| University of Lincoln | £18,159 |
| University of Liverpool | £22,090 |
| Liverpool Institute for Performing Arts | £18,857 |
| Liverpool John Moores University | £19,119 |
| London South Bank University | £23,396 |
| London School of Economics and Political Science | £30,559 |
| Loughborough University | £23,012 |
| University of Manchester | £22,496 |
| Manchester Metropolitan University | £19,538 |
| Middlesex University | £21,761 |
| Napier University | £20,948 |
| Newcastle University | £21,578 |
| Newman University College | £20,438 |
| University of Wales, Newport | £21,035 |
| University of Northampton | £19,175 |
| University of Northumbria at Newcastle | £19,089 |
| Norwich University College of the Arts | £16,000 |
| University of Nottingham | £22,651 |
| Nottingham Trent University | £19,784 |
| University of Oxford | £26,045 |
| Oxford Brookes University | £21,136 |
| University of Plymouth | £20,724 |
| University College Plymouth St Mark and St John | £19,644 |
| University of Portsmouth | £20,903 |

**Table 81 (Continued)**

| Institution | Average salary (excludes unknown salaries) |
|---|---|
| Queen Margaret University, Edinburgh | £20,542 |
| Queen Mary, University of London | £25,522 |
| Queen's University Belfast | £20,014 |
| Ravensbourne College of Design and Communication | £19,636 |
| University of Reading | £21,478 |
| Robert Gordon University | £21,582 |
| Roehampton University | £21,434 |
| Rose Bruford College | £17,000 |
| Royal Agricultural College | £19,737 |
| Royal Holloway and Bedford New College | £22,900 |
| Royal Scottish Academy of Music and Drama | £20,000 |
| Royal Veterinary College | £23,857 |
| University of St Andrews | £21,894 |
| St George's Hospital Medical School | £26,000 |
| St Mary's University College | £21,163 |
| St Mary's University College, Twickenham | £22,247 |
| University of Salford | £19,565 |
| School of Oriental and African Studies | £22,514 |
| School of Pharmacy | £19,500 |
| Scottish Agricultural College | — |
| University of Sheffield | £21,145 |
| Sheffield Hallam University | £19,930 |
| University of Southampton | £22,307 |
| Southampton Solent University | £19,411 |
| Staffordshire University | £18,226 |
| University of Stirling | £19,009 |
| Stranmillis University College | £18,750 |
| University of Strathclyde | £22,302 |
| University Campus Suffolk | £20,873 |
| University of Sunderland | £18,885 |
| University of Surrey | £22,643 |
| University of Sussex | £20,030 |
| Swansea University | £19,774 |

*(Continued)*

**Table 81 (Continued)**

| Institution | Average salary (excludes unknown salaries) |
| --- | --- |
| Swansea Metropolitan University | £18,772 |
| University of Teesside | £20,266 |
| Thames Valley University | £21,317 |
| Trinity College, Carmarthen | £17,556 |
| Trinity Laban | — |
| UHI Millennium Institute | £17,500 |
| University of Ulster | £19,510 |
| University College London | £26,474 |
| University of Warwick | £24,564 |
| University of the West of England, Bristol | £20,584 |
| University of the West of Scotland | £20,692 |
| University of Westminster | £21,150 |
| University of Winchester | £19,588 |
| University of Wolverhampton | £18,942 |
| University of Worcester | £18,567 |
| Writtle College | £19,786 |
| University of York | £22,239 |
| York St John University | £19,000 |
| **Mean Salary** | £21,293 |

Source: HESA Destinations of Leavers Survey 2007/08
Note: "—" indicates a suppressed average based upon a population of 7 or fewer students
* Graduate employment as defined in Elias & Purcell's report 'SOC (HE) A Classification of occupations for studying the graduate labour market'

# Graduate prospects for different subjects

It goes without saying that graduate prospects are better for students on some courses at particular universities. Again, this could be due to excellent teaching standards, overall reputation, bright students, good links with employers, or a whole range of other factors. If you already have specific subject areas in mind, and have a list of universities you're currently considering, you can get information about graduate prospects for your chosen combination at www.unistats.com; and you can look up the UCAS entry points that the last set of first-years achieved before they started the course to see whether you stand a good chance of getting in. Remember to cross-reference this with the course entry requirements on the UCAS website, and the average degree course offers the department makes to applicants. See *Heap 2010: University Degree Course Offers* by Brian Heap, published by Trotman, for more detailed information.

Courses such as medicine and dentistry have always traditionally had very high rates of employment after graduation because they are vocational subjects, but for many other subjects it's less easy to predict patterns of post-graduation work. There are fluctuations year upon year, as markets and other factors change. Table 82 shows results from a study published at the end of 2008, which means that the data are from surveys done in 2007. It can't predict what the workforce will be like in the year that you graduate, but it can be used as a guide.

When all the subjects below are looked at together, on average:

► 63.3% of graduates were in a job within six months of finishing their degree
► 13.9% had gone on to further study or training
► 9.1% were combining work and study
► 5.5% were unemployed.

It's interesting to see which subjects score higher and lower than this. In the category marked 'other', a number of students had become self-employed.

Should you study a subject that you're less keen on, just because it has better employment prospects? Only you can decide, but do remember that you might get better grades and more enjoyment from studying a different subject that you love and have a talent for.

**Table 82 Destinations of recent graduates, by subject studied**

| Rank | Subject | % in a job | % in further study | % working and studying | % unemployed | % other |
|------|---------|-----------|------------|-----------|-----------|---------|
| 1 | Marketing | 74.9 | 3.6 | 5.0 | 6.3 | 10.2 |
| 2 | Civil engineering | 74.3 | 6.2 | 12.5 | 2.4 | 4.6 |
| 3 | Media studies | 71.7 | 6.1 | 4.9 | 8.2 | 9.2 |
| 4 | Business and management | 68.9 | 6.7 | 9.0 | 6.0 | 9.3 |
| 5 | Mechanical engineering | 68.2 | 10.5 | 7.7 | 6.5 | 7.1 |
| 6 | IT and computing | 68.1 | 8.2 | 5.7 | 9.5 | 8.4 |
| 7 | Art and design | 67.2 | 6.5 | 6.0 | 8.5 | 11.7 |
| 8 | Electrical and electronic engineering | 66.1 | 11.6 | 7.8 | 7.7 | 6.7 |
| 9 | Sociology | 66.0 | 12.1 | 7.3 | 5.5 | 9.2 |
| 10 | Architecture and building | 65.8 | 9.2 | 15.4 | 2.9 | 6.8 |
| 11 | Performing arts | 63.5 | 15.2 | 7.8 | 5.7 | 7.7 |

*(Continued)*

**Table 82 (Continued)**

| Rank | Subject | % in a job | % in further study | % working and studying | % unemployed | % other |
|------|---------|------------|--------------------|------------------------|--------------|---------|
| 12 | Sport science | 62.0 | 16.3 | 9.7 | 3.9 | 8.0 |
| 13 | Psychology | 59.7 | 15.3 | 10.7 | 5.6 | 8.7 |
| 14 | Politics | 58.0 | 19.9 | 6.7 | 6.2 | 9.1 |
| 15 | Modern languages | 57.5 | 20.5 | 7.6 | 5.2 | 9.2 |
| 16 | Environmental/ physical/ geographical/ earth science | 57.2 | 20.2 | 7.7 | 5.0 | 9.8 |
| 17 | English | 56.3 | 20.6 | 8.2 | 6.0 | 8.9 |
| 18 | Geography | 55.7 | 20.3 | 8.2 | 5.3 | 10.5 |
| 19 | Economics | 55.6 | 13.4 | 15.2 | 5.8 | 10.0 |
| 20 | History | 53.6 | 20.6 | 8.2 | 6.0 | 8.9 |
| 21 | Accountancy | 53.0 | 5.7 | 25.6 | 7.4 | 8.3 |
| 22 | Biology | 52.4 | 24.1 | 7.9 | 6.7 | 8.9 |
| 23 | Mathematics | 47.4 | 22.9 | 15.4 | 5.9 | 8.5 |
| 24 | Chemistry | 43.3 | 34.4 | 7.6 | 6.2 | 6.4 |
| 25 | Physics | 41.3 | 33.9 | 10.3 | 7.0 | 7.5 |
| 26 | Law | 35.6 | 41.5 | 11.0 | 3.7 | 8.1 |

Source: HESA, Destinations of Leavers from Higher Education (DLHE) Survey 2006/07, published in 2008

# Which universities do the top 100 employers target?

If you've already looked at the graduate prospects shown in Table 79, it might come as a bit of a surprise when you see which universities are most actively targeted by the major graduate recruiters. This targeting involves on-campus events as well as other recruitment methods, and there is some interesting reasoning behind their planning. Manchester and London both have huge numbers of students studying a wide variety of subjects, and it's easy to arrange fairs, presentations and local advertising. Warwick apparently has a reputation for training go-getters, and Cambridge and Oxford have a worldwide reputation for academic quality.

The employers in the survey were from *The Times Top 100 Graduate Employers*, which were voted for by final-year students. They include the Arcadia Group, Cancer Research UK, Deutsche Bank, the Foreign Office, GlaxoSmithKline,

**Table 83 Universities most targeted by top employers in 2008–2009**

| Rank | University | Previous year's rank |
|---|---|---|
| 1 | University of Manchester | 1 |
| 2 | University of London | 3 |
| 3 | University of Warwick | 5 |
| 4 | University of Cambridge | 2 |
| 5 | University of Oxford | 4 |
| 6 | University of Bristol | 7 |
| 7 | Durham University | 10 |
| 8 | University of Nottingham | 6 |
| 9 | University of Bath | 12 |
| 10 | University of Leeds | 11 |
| 11 | University of Birmingham | 9 |
| 12 | University of Edinburgh | 8 |
| 13 | University of Sheffield | 13 |
| 14 | Loughborough University | 17 |
| 15 | University of Southampton | 18 |
| 16 | Cardiff University | 16 |
| 17 | University of Glasgow | — |
| 18 | Newcastle University | 14 |
| 19 | University of York | 20 |
| 20 | University of St Andrews | — |

Source: *The Graduate Market in 2009, published by High Fliers*

Thomson Reuters and many others. To view the full list of these employers, see page 8 of *The Graduate Market in 2009*, published by High Fliers, which can be accessed by using this link: www.highfliers.co.uk/download/GraduateMarket09.pdf.

If you're thinking about maybe working for one of the top 100 employers, this list is certainly something to consider when looking ahead, but also remember that your dream job might be with one of the hundreds of other companies that weren't in the survey and who recruit differently.

# Sandwich degrees

Sandwich programmes offer undergraduates a chance to spend time gaining vital work experience, often with a year at a time being spent in industry. Direct experience of employment can considerably enhance your career prospects, and it looks fantastic on a CV. Most of these positions are also paid work, which can make it easier for some students to support themselves.

The Association for Sandwich Education and Training (ASET) says that approximately 112,000 students go on sandwich placements each year. Currently, around 6.5% of all UK undergraduates are studying sandwich courses, and certain subject areas offer the most scope if you're considering this mode of study. For more information contact ASET, The Work-Based and Placement Learning Association, Department for Innovation, Universities and Skills (DIUS), W11 Moorfoot, Sheffield, S1 4PQ, tel: 0114 221 2902, or visit www.asetonline.org.

**Table 84 Number of students on sandwich courses studying each main subject**

| Rank | Subject area of sandwich degree | Total number of students | Female students | Male students |
|------|----------------------------------|--------------------------|-----------------|---------------|
| 1 | Business and administrative studies | 36,685 | 18,385 | 18,300 |
| 2 | Computer science | 16,210 | 2,450 | 13,760 |
| 3 | Engineering and technology | 15,645 | 2,745 | 12,900 |
| 4 | Architecture, building and planning | 9,325 | 2,355 | 6,965 |
| 5 | Biological sciences | 7,055 | 4,420 | 2,635 |
| 6 | Creative arts and design | 5,930 | 3,430 | 2,500 |
| 7 | Subjects allied to medicine | 5,485 | 4,225 | 1,260 |
| 8 | Physical sciences | 4,035 | 1,950 | 2,085 |
| 9 | Social studies | 3,445 | 1,655 | 1,790 |
| 10 | Languages | 2,755 | 1,885 | 870 |
| 11 | Agriculture and related subjects | 1,850 | 1,110 | 740 |
| 12 | Law | 1,845 | 1,195 | 650 |
| 13 | Mathematical sciences | 1,500 | 590 | 915 |
| 14 | Mass communications and documentation | 1,215 | 825 | 390 |
| 15 | Combined | 685 | 415 | 270 |
| 16 | Historical and philosophical studies | 290 | 175 | 115 |
| 17 | Education | 55 | 25 | 30 |
| 18 | Medicine and dentistry | 15 | 10 | 5 |

*Source: HESA, Students in Higher Education Institutions 2007/2008*
**Notes:** numbers are rounded up to newest 5.

# Chapter 7

# The tables – your personal university rankings

If you've looked through the whole of this guide you'll probably have a few good ideas about what you'd like to study, and where you'd like to be spending the next few years as an undergraduate. What you consider the most important factors in this very big decision is entirely up to you, but it often helps to write down a few of the most significant things so that you can compare them more easily.

Your choices are completely individual, and there's room in the following tables for you to add a mixture of academic and non-academic factors. Have a look at the following example, and try making up one or more of your own. You'll probably find that after doing this, you'll have one or two clear favourites, and a few others that look like good second choices, and that's going to help you target a few open day visits and/or some UCAS form entries.

*Example:* Andy expects to get high grades and wants to study history somewhere with good career prospects, maybe in a big exciting city. He looks at Chapter 2 of this book to find out about drop-out rates, and at the Unistats.com website for the other statistics.

**Table 85a Example table**

| Important factors: | Course title: History | | | | | | |
|---|---|---|---|---|---|---|---|
| | Oxford | Manchester | York | Leeds | Durham | Cardiff | Edinburgh |
| High entry grades (UCAS points) | 480 | 420 | 440 | 400 | 480 | 390 | 436 |
| Good graduate prospects | 86% | 87% | 87% | 88% | 85% | 85% | 89% |
| Low drop-out rate | 1% | 5% | 4% | 6% | 3% | 5% | 5% |
| Students satisfied with course | — | 75% | 90% | 91% | 95% | 93% | 84% |
| University in or near city? | yes | yes | yes | yes | yes | yes | yes |
| Excellent nightlife? | ok | yes | yes | yes | no | yes | good |

**Notes:**

**Table 85b**

| | Course title: | | | | | | |
|---|---|---|---|---|---|---|---|
| **Important factors:** | | | | | | | |
| | | | | | | | |
| | | | | | | | |
| | | | | | | | |
| | | | | | | | |
| | | | | | | | |
| | | | | | | | |
| **Notes:** | | | | | | | |
| | | | | | | | |

# Appendix

## Useful books

*Getting Into Oxford & Cambridge 2010 Entry* by Sarah Alakija. Published by Trotman.
*The Guardian University Guide 2010* by Alice Wignall. Published by Guardian Books.
*Guide to Student Money 2010* by Gwenda Thomas. Published by Trotman.
*Guide to UK Universities 2010* by Klaus Boehm and Jenny Lees-Spalding. Published by Trotman.
*Heap 2010: University Degree Course Offers* by Brian Heap. Published by Trotman.
*The Insider's Guide to Applying to University* by Karla Fitzhugh. Published by Trotman.
*The Times Good University Guide 2010* by John Leary. Published by Times Books.
*University Scholarships, Awards & Bursaries* by Brian Heap. Published by Trotman.
*The Virgin 2010 Guide to British Universities* by Piers Dudgeon. Published by Virgin Books.

## Useful research websites

**The Complete University Guide** (in association with the *Independent*)
www.thecompleteuniversityguide.co.uk
Online league tables that allow website users to compare universities and courses, with useful click-through links to summary pages about life at different universities.

**Connexions Direct**
www.connexions-direct.com/jobs4u
Profiles of job families, and online chat with trained careers advice officers. You can also text, phone or email your questions in.

**Directgov**
www.direct.gov.uk
Has a Higher Education section to help you work out which university and course are right for you. Also contains information and advice about student life, and funding and personal finance.

**Graduate Prospects**
www.prospects.ac.uk
Contains a tool called Prospects Planner that allows you to look at what would motivate you in a job, identify your skills, generate job ideas and explore jobs in greater detail.

### High Fliers
www.highfliers.co.uk
Undertakes regular research into patterns of graduate recruitment at some of
the UK's largest universities. Website contains reports such as careers surveys, and
recruiters' questionnaires.

### Opendays
www.opendays.com
A well-kept up-to-date calendar of university open days all around Britain. Go and
see what you might be getting yourself into.

### Quality Assurance Agency for Higher Education (QAA) Reviews
www.qaa.ac.uk/reviews
Get the official low-down on the standards and quality of any courses you might
be considering.

### Research Assessment Exercise (RAE)
http://submissions.rae.ac.uk/results/
Carried out every few years on behalf of the UK higher education funding
councils to evaluate the quality of research undertaken by British higher education
institutions. The last RAE was carried out in 2008, and used a four-point quality
scale.

### Student Finance
www.direct.gov.uk/studentfinance
Where to start when you're applying for financial help with your studies, such
as grants. See also www.delni.gov.uk, www.studentfinancewales.co.uk and www.
student-support-saas.gov.uk.

### UCAS
*Online Prospectus Ordering Service*
http://ucas.prospectusuk.com
Comprehensive range of UK prospectuses available to order for free, to help you
find out more about specific universities, departments and courses.
*UCAS Conventions*
www.ucasevents.com/conventions
Details of all the UK conventions, which are free to attend. Also contains good
advice about how to prepare for a convention or fair, and how to get the most out
of the occasion while you're there.

### Unistats
www.unistats.com
A 'one-stop shop' for official university information, covering subject areas rather
than specific courses. Allows prospective students to compare different universities
by looking at Student Satisfaction Survey results, UCAS entry points, Quality

Assurance Agency for Higher Education report results, and graduate prospects. Owned by HEFCE (the Higher Education Funding Council for England) and featuring a website created and maintained by UCAS and Hotcourses Ltd.

# Official bodies

**Department for Innovation, Universities and Skills (DIUS)**
Castle View House
East Lane
Runcorn WA7 2GJ
Tel: 020 7215 5555
Email: info@dius.gsi.gov.uk
Website: www.dius.gov.uk/higher_education
Provides a list of all the recognised UK degrees.

**National Union of Students (NUS)**
NUS HQ
Centro 3
19 Mandela Street
London NW1 0DU
Tel: 0871 221 8221
Text phone: 020 7380 6649
Fax: 0871 221 8222
Email: nusuk@nus.org.uk
Website: www.nus.org.uk
The NUS is the national voice of students, helping them to campaign, get cheap student discounts and get the best advice on living student life to the full.

**Skill: National Bureau for Students with Disabilities**
Unit 3, Floor 3
Radisson Court
219 Long Lane
London SE1 4PR
Main tel and textphone: 020 7450 0620
Fax: 020 7450 0650
Email: skill@skill.org.uk
Website: www.skill.org.uk
Skill Information Service
Tel: 0800 328 5050
Textphone: 0800 068 2422
Email: info@skill.org.uk
A national independent charity that promotes opportunities for people in learning and entry to employment. Helps young people and adults over 16 years of age with

any kind of impairment, including physical and sensory disabilities, learning and mental health difficulties, throughout the UK.

**Student Loans Company**
Headquarters
100 Bothwell Street
Glasgow G2 7JD
Tel: 0141 306 2000; General helpline: 0845 607 7577
Fax: 0141 306 2005
Website: www.slc.co.uk
The government-subsidised financial company that administers government-funded loans and grants to students throughout the United Kingdom.

**UCAS**
PO Box 28
Cheltenham
GL52 3LZ
Tel (Customer Service Unit): 0871 468 0 468
Email: enquiries@ucas.ac.uk
Website: www.ucas.ac.uk
Responsible for managing applications to higher education courses in the UK; processes more than two million applications for full-time undergraduate courses every year. The website contains online application forms, course details and entry requirements, institution guides and more.

# Student websites

**The Student Room**
www.thestudentroom.co.uk
Big commercial website with busy message boards, some of it serious, some of it funny. Also has a handy wiki for university-related information.

**YouGoFurther**
http://yougo.co.uk
Run by UCAS, and you can swap messages with trained advisers. Good for making a few new friends before you arrive at your chosen university.

**WhatUni**
www.whatuni.com
An attractive, easy to use website containing thousands of reviews of different universities. They include academic factors, and more about location and lifestyle.

# University contacts list

(Including student union websites and contact emails.)

**University of Aberdeen**
King's College
Aberdeen AB24 3FX
Tel: 0122 427 2000
Fax: 0122 427 2034
Email: sras@abdn.ac.uk
Website: www.abdn.ac.uk
*Aberdeen University Students' Association*
Website: www.ausa.org.uk

**University of Abertay Dundee**
Bell Street
Dundee DD1 1HG
Tel: 01382 308080
Fax: 01382 308081
Email: sro@abertay.ac.uk
Website: www.abertay.ac.uk
*University of Abertay Dundee Students' Association*
Website: www.abertaystudents.com

**Aberystwyth University** (Prifysgol Aberystwyth)
Old College
King Street
Aberystwyth SY23 2AX
Tel: 01970 622021
Fax: 01970 627410
Email: ug-admissions@aber.ac.uk
Website: www.aber.ac.uk
*University of Aberystwyth Guild of Students*
Website: http://union.aber.ac.uk

**American InterContinental University**
110 Marylebone High Street
London W1U 4RY
Tel: 020 7467 5640
Fax: 020 7467 5641
Email: admissions@aiulondon.ac.uk
Website: www.aiulondon.ac.uk

**Anglia Ruskin University**
Bishop Hall Lane

Chelmsford CM1 1SQ
Tel: 0845 271 3333
Fax: 01245 251789
Email: answers@anglia.ac.uk
Website: www.anglia.ac.uk
*Anglia Ruskin University Students' Union*
Website: www.angliasu.com

## University of the Arts, London

65 Davies Street
London W1K 5DA
Tel: 020 7514 6000 ext 6197
Fax: 020 7514 6198
Email: c.anderson@arts.ac.uk
Website: www.arts.ac.uk
*University of the Arts London Students' Union*
Website: www.suarts.org

## Aston University

Aston Triangle
Birmingham B4 7ET
Tel: 0121 204 4444
Fax: 0121 204 3696
Email: admissions@aston.ac.uk
Website: www.aston.ac.uk
*Aston Students' Guild*
Website: www.astonguild.org.uk

## Bangor University (Prifysgol Bangor)

Bangor LL57 2DG
Tel: 01248 382016/382017
Fax: 01248 370451
Email: admissions@bangor.ac.uk
Website: www.bangor.ac.uk
*Bangor, University of Wales Students' Union*
Website: www.undeb.bangor.ac.uk

## University of Bath

Claverton Down
Bath BA2 7AY
Tel: 01225 383019
Fax: 01225 386366
Email: admissions@bath.ac.uk
Website: www.bath.ac.uk
*University of Bath Students' Union*
Website: www.bathstudent.com

**Bath Spa University**
Newton Park
Newton St Loe
Bath BA2 9BN
Tel: 01225 875875
Fax: 01225 875444
Email: enquiries@bathspa.ac.uk
Website: www.bathspa.ac.uk
*Bath Spa University Students' Union*
Website: www.bathspasu.co.uk

**University of Bedfordshire**
Park Square
Luton LU1 3JU
Tel: 01582 743500
Fax: 01582 489323
Email: admission@beds.ac.uk
Website: www.beds.ac.uk
*Bedfordshire Students' Union*
Website: www.ubsu.co.uk

**Birkbeck College**
Birkbeck, University of London
Malet Street
London WC1E 7HX
Tel: 020 7631 6000
Fax: 020 7631 6270
Email: info@bbk.ac.uk
Website: www.bbk.ac.uk
*Birkbeck College, London Students' Union*
Website: www.bbk.ac.uk/su

**University of Birmingham**
Edgbaston
Birmingham B15 2TT
Tel: 0121 415 8900
Fax: 0121 414 7159
Email: admissions@bham.ac.uk
Website: www.bham.ac.uk
*Birmingham University Guild of Students*
Website: www.bugs.bham.ac.uk

**Birmingham City University** (former Uni of Central England, Birmingham)
Perry Barr
Birmingham B42 2SU
Tel: 0121 331 5595

Fax: 0121 331 7994
Email: choices@bcu.ac.uk
Website: www.bcu.ac.uk
*Birmingham City Students' Union*
Website: www.birminghamcitysu.com

## University of Bolton
Deane Road
Bolton BL3 5AB
Tel: 01204 900600
Fax: 01204 399074
Email: enquiries@bolton.ac.uk
Website: www.bolton.ac.uk
*University of Bolton Students' Union*
Website: www.bisu.co.uk

## Bournemouth University
Talbot Campus
Fern Barrow
Poole BH12 5BB
Tel: 01202 524111
Fax: 01202 962736
Email: askBU@bournemouth.ac.uk
Website: www.bournemouth.ac.uk
*Bournemouth University Students' Union*
Website: www.subu.org.uk

## University of Bradford
Richmond Road
Bradford BD7 1DP
Tel: 0800 073 1225
Fax: 01274 235585
Email: course-enquiries@bradford.ac.uk
Website: www.bradford.ac.uk
*University of Bradford Students' Union*
Website: www.ubuonline.co.uk

## University of Brighton
Mithras House
Lewes Road
Brighton BN2 4AT
Tel: 01273 644644
Fax: 01273 642607
Email: admissions@brighton.ac.uk
Website: www.brighton.ac.uk

*University of Brighton Students' Union*
Website: www.ubsu.net

## University of Bristol
Senate House
Tyndall Avenue
Bristol BS8 1TH
Tel: 0117 928 9000
Fax: 0117 925 1424
Email: ug-admissions@bristol.ac.uk
Website: www.bristol.ac.uk
*University of Bristol Students' Union*
Website: www.ubu.org.uk

## Brunel University
Uxbridge UB8 3PH
Tel: 01895 265265
Fax: 01895 269790
Email: admissions@brunel.ac.uk
Website: www.brunel.ac.uk
*Brunel Students' Union*
Website: www.brunelstudents.com

## University of Buckingham
Yeomanry House
Hunter Street
Buckingham MK18 1EG
Tel: 01280 820313
Fax: 01280 822245
Email: info@buckingham.ac.uk
Website: www.buckingham.ac.uk
*University of Buckingham Students' Union*
Website: www.buckingham.ac.uk/life/social/su

## Buckinghamshire New University
Queen Alexandra Road
High Wycombe HP11 2JZ
Tel: 0800 0565 660
Fax: 01494 605023
Email: admissions@bucks.ac.uk
Website: www.bucks.ac.uk
*Bucks Students' Union*
Website: www.bucksstudent.com

**University of Cambridge**
Cambridge Admissions Office
Fitzwilliam House
32 Trumpington Street
Cambridge CB2 1QY
Tel: 01223 333308
Fax: 01223 366383
Email: admissions@cam.ac.uk
Website: www.cam.ac.uk/admissions/undergraduate
*Cambridge University Students' Union*
Website: www.cusu.cam.ac.uk

**Canterbury Christ Church University**
North Holmes Road
Canterbury CT1 1QU
Tel: 01227 782900
Fax: 01227 782888
Email: admissions@canterbury.ac.uk
Website: www.canterbury.ac.uk
*Canterbury Christ Church University Students' Union*
Website: www.ccsu.co.uk

**Cardiff University** (Prifysgol Caerdydd)
PO Box 927
30–36 Newport Road
Cardiff CF24 0DE
Tel: 029 2087 9999
Fax: 029 2087 6982
Email: admissions@cardiff.ac.uk
Website: www.cardiff.ac.uk
*Cardiff Students' Union*
Website: www.cardiffstudents.com

**University of Wales Institute, Cardiff** (Athrofa Prifysgol Cymru Caerdydd)
PO Box 377
Llandaff Campus
Western Avenue
Cardiff CF5 2SG
Tel: 029 2041 6070
Fax: 029 2041 6286
Email: admissions@uwic.ac.uk
Website: www.uwic.ac.uk
*University of Wales Institute, Cardiff Student Union*
Website: www.uwicsu.co.uk

**University of Central Lancashire**
Preston PR1 2HE
Tel: 01772 201201
Fax: 01772 894954
Email: uadmissions@uclan.ac.uk
Website: www.uclan.ac.uk
*University of Central Lancashire Students' Union*
Website: www.yourunion.co.uk

**University of Chester**
Parkgate Road
Chester CH1 4BJ
Tel: 01244 511000
Fax: 01244 511260
Email: enquiries@chester.ac.uk
Website: www.chester.ac.uk
*University of Chester Students' Union*
Website: www.chestersu.com

**University of Chichester**
Bognor Regis Campus
Upper Bognor Road
Bognor Regis PO21 1HR
Tel: 01243 816002
Fax: 01243 812104
Email: admissions@chi.ac.uk
Website: www.chiuni.ac.uk
*University of Chichester Students' Union*
Website: www.chisu.org

**City University**
Northampton Square
London EC1V 0HB
Tel: 020 7040 5060
Fax: 020 7040 8995
Email: ugadmissions@city.ac.uk
Website: www.city.ac.uk
*City University Students' Union*
Website: www.citysu.com

**Coventry University**
The Student Centre
Coventry University
1 Gulson Rd
Coventry CV1 2JH
Tel: 024 7615 2222

Fax: 024 7615 2223
Email: studentenquiries@coventry.ac.uk
Website: www.coventry.ac.uk
*Coventry University Students' Union*
Website: www.cusu.org

## University for the Creative Arts
Falkner Road
Farnham
Surrey GU9 7DS
Tel: 01252 892696
Fax: 01252 892624
Email: admissions@ucreative.ac.uk
Website: www.ucreative.ac.uk
*University for the Creative Arts Students' Union*
Website: www.uccasu.com

## University of Cumbria
Registered Office
University of Cumbria
Fusehill Street
Carlisle CA1 2HH
Tel: 01228 616234
Fax: 01228 616235
Email: Use form on website
Website: www.cumbria.ac.uk
*University of Cumbria Students' Union*
Website: www.thestudentsunion.org.uk

## De Montfort University
The Gateway
Leicester LE1 9BH
Tel: 0116 255 1551
Fax: 0116 250 6204
Email: enquiries@dmu.ac.uk
Website: www.dmu.ac.uk
*De Montfort University Students' Union*
Website: www.mydsu.com

## University of Derby
Kedleston Road
Derby DE22 1GB
Tel: 08701 202330
Fax: 01332 597724
Email: askadmissions@derby.ac.uk
Website: www.derby.ac.uk

*University of Derby Students' Union*
Website: www.udsu.co.uk

## University of Dundee
Dundee DD1 4HN
Tel: 01382 384160
Fax: 01382 388150
Email: srs@dundee.ac.uk
Website: www.dundee.ac.uk/admissions/undergraduate/
*Dundee University Students' Association*
Website: www.dusa.co.uk

## Durham University
University Office
Durham DH1 3HP
Tel: 0191 334 2000
Fax: 0191 334 6055
Email: admissions@durham.ac.uk
Website: www.durham.ac.uk
*Durham University Students' Union*
Website: www.dsu.org.uk

## University of East Anglia
Norwich NR4 7TJ
Tel: 01603 456161
Fax: 01603 458596
Email: admissions@uea.ac.uk
Website: www.uea.ac.uk
*University of East Anglia Students' Union*
Website: www.ueastudent.com

## University of East London
Docklands Campus
University Way
London E16 2RD
Tel: 020 8223 2835
Fax: 020 8223 2978
Email: admiss@uel.ac.uk
Website: www.uel.ac.uk
*University of East London Students' Union*
Website: www.uelsu.net

## Edge Hill University
Ormskirk L39 4QP
Tel: 0800 195 5063
Fax: 01695 584355

Email: enquiries@edgehill.ac.uk
Website: www.edgehill.ac.uk
*Edge Hill Students' Union*
Website: www.edgehill.ac.uk/ProspectiveStudents/StudentLife/StudentUnion.htm

## University of Edinburgh
Student Recruitment and Admissions
21 Buccleuch Place
Edinburgh EH8 9LN
Tel: 0131 650 4360
Fax: 0131 651 1236
Email: sra.enquiries@ed.ac.uk
Website: www.ed.ac.uk/studying/undergraduate/
*Edinburgh University Students' Association*
Website: www.eusa.ed.ac.uk

## Edinburgh Napier University
Craiglockhart Campus
Edinburgh EH14 1DJ
Tel: 08452 60 60 40
Fax: 0131 455 6464
Email: info@napier.ac.uk
Website: www.napier.ac.uk
*Napier University Students' Association*
Website: www.napierstudents.com

## University of Essex
Wivenhoe Park
Colchester CO4 3SQ
Tel: 01206 873666
Fax: 01206 873423
Email: admit@essex.ac.uk
Website: www.essex.ac.uk
*University of Essex Students' Union*
Website: www.essexstudent.com

## University of Exeter
Level 8
Laver Building
North Park Road
Exeter EX4 4QE
Tel: 01392 263855
Fax: 01392 263857
Email: ug-ad@exeter.ac.uk
Website: www.ex.ac.uk

*University of Exeter Guild of Students*
Website: www.exeterguild.org

**University of Glamorgan** (Prifysgol Morgannwg)
Enquiries and Admissions Unit
Pontypridd CF37 1DL
Tel: 0800 716925
Fax: 01443 654050
Email: enquiries@glam.ac.uk
Website: www.glam.ac.uk
*University of Glamorgan Students' Union*
Website: www.glamsu.com

**University of Glasgow**
The Fraser Building
65 Hillhead Street
Glasgow G12 8QQ
Tel: 0141 330 6062
Fax: 0141 330 2961
Email: ugenquiries@gla.ac.uk
Website: www.gla.ac.uk
*Glasgow University Students' Union*
Website: www.guu.co.uk

**Glasgow Caledonian University**
City Campus
Cowcaddens Road
Glasgow G4 0BA
Tel: 0141 331 3000
Fax: 0141 331 3449
Email: admissions@gcal.ac.uk
Website: www.gcal.ac.uk
*Glasgow Caledonian University Students' Association*
Website: www.caledonianstudent.com

**University of Gloucestershire**
Hardwick Campus
St Paul's Road
Cheltenham GL50 4BS
Tel: 01242 714501
Fax: 01242 543334
Email: admissions@glos.ac.uk
Website: www.glos.ac.uk
*University of Gloucestershire Students' Union*
Website: www.yourstudentsunion.com

**Glyndŵr University** (Prifysgol Glyndŵr)
Plas Coch
Mold Road
Wrexham LL11 2AW
Tel: 01978 293439
Fax: 01978 290008
Email: sid@glyndwr.ac.uk
Website: www.glyndwr.ac.uk
*Glyndŵr University Students' Guild*
Website: www.glyndwr.ac.uk/Studentsupportservices/en/StudentsGuild

**Goldsmiths College**
Lewisham Way
London SE14 6NW
Tel: 020 7919 7766
Fax: 020 7919 7509
Email: admissions@gold.ac.uk
Website: www.goldsmiths.ac.uk
*Goldsmith's Students Union*
Website: www.goldsmithsstudents.com

**University of Greenwich**
Greenwich Campus
Old Royal Naval College
Park Row
London SE10 9LS
Tel: 0800 005006
Fax: 020 8331 8145
Email: courseinfo@gre.ac.uk
Website: www.gre.ac.uk
*University of Greenwich Students' Union*
Website: www.suug.co.uk

**Heriot-Watt University**
Edinburgh Campus
Edinburgh EH14 4AS
Tel: 0131 449 5111
Fax: 0131 451 3630
Email: ugadmissions@hw.ac.uk
Website: www.hw.ac.uk
*Heriot-Watt University Students' Association*
Website: www.hwusa.org

**University of Hertfordshire**
University Admissions Service

College Lane
Hatfield AL10 9AB
Tel: 01707 284800
Fax: 01707 284870
Website: www.herts.ac.uk
*University of Hertfordshire Students' Union*
Website: www.uhsu.herts.ac.uk

## University of Huddersfield

Queensgate
Huddersfield HD1 3DH
Tel: 01484 473969
Fax: 01484 472765
Email: admissionsandrecords@hud.ac.uk
Website: www.hud.ac.uk
*University of Huddersfield Students' Union*
Website: www.huddersfieldstudent.com

## University of Hull

Cottingham Road
Hull HU6 7RX
Tel: 01482 466100
Fax: 01482 442290
Email: admissions@hull.ac.uk
Website: www.hull.ac.uk
*Hull University Union*
Website: www.hullstudent.com

## Imperial College London

Registry
South Kensington Campus
London SW7 2AZ
Tel: 020 7589 5111
Fax: 020 7594 8004
Email: registry.advice@imperial.ac.uk
Website: www.imperial.ac.uk
*Imperial College Students' Union*
Website: www.union.ic.ac.uk

## Keele University

Keele ST5 5BG
Tel: 01782 584005
Fax: 01782 632343
Email: undergraduate@keele.ac.uk

Website: www.keele.ac.uk
*Keele University Students' Union*
Website: www.kusu.net

## University of Kent
Registry
Canterbury CT2 7NZ
Tel: 01227 827272
Fax: 01227 827077
Email: recruitment@kent.ac.uk
Website: www.kent.ac.uk
*University of Kent Students' Union*
Website: www.kentunion.co.uk

## King's College London
The Strand
London WC2R 2LS
Tel: 020 7836 5454
Fax: 020 7836 1799
Email: ucas.enquiries@kcl.ac.uk
Website: www.kcl.ac.uk
*King's College London Students' Union*
Website: www.kclsu.org

## Kingston University
Student Information and Advice Centre
Cooper House
40–46 Surbiton Road
Kingston upon Thames KT1 2HX
Tel: 020 8547 7053
Fax: 020 8547 7080
Email: aps@kingston.ac.uk
Website: www.kingston.ac.uk
*Kingston University Students' Union*
Website: www.kusu.co.uk

## Lampeter (University of Wales)  (Prifysgol Cymru, Llanbedr Pont Steffan)
The Academic Registry SA48 7ED
Tel: 01570 424831
Fax: 01570 424978
Email: admissions@lamp.ac.uk
Website: www.lamp.ac.uk
*Lampeter (University of Wales) Students' Union*
Website: www.lamp.ac.uk/su

**University of Lancaster**
Lancaster LA1 4YW
Tel: 01524 592029
Fax: 01524 846243
Email: ugadmissions@lancaster.ac.uk
Website: www.lancs.ac.uk
*Lancaster University Students' Union*
Website: www.lusu.co.uk

**University of Leeds**
Leeds LS2 9JT
Tel: 0113 343 3999
Fax: 0113 244 3923
Email: admissions@adm.leeds.ac.uk
Website: www.leeds.ac.uk
*Leeds University Union*
Website: www.luuonline.com

**Leeds Metropolitan University**
Course Enquiries Office
Civic Quarter
Leeds LS1 3HE
Tel: 0113 81 23113
Fax: 0113 81 23129
Email: course-enquiries@leedsmet.ac.uk
Website: www.leedsmet.ac.uk
*Leeds Metropolitan University Students' Union*
Website: www.lmusu.org.uk

**University of Leicester**
University Road
Leicester LE1 7RH
Tel: 0116 252 5281
Fax: 0116 252 2447
Email: admissions@le.ac.uk
Website: www.le.ac.uk
*Leicester University Students' Union*
Website: www.leicesterstudent.org

**University of Lincoln**
Admissions
Brayford Pool
Lincoln LN6 7TS
Tel: 01522 886097
Fax: 01522 886146
Email: admissions@lincoln.ac.uk

Website: www.lincoln.ac.uk
*University of Lincoln Students' Union*
Website: www.lincolnsu.com

## University of Liverpool
The Foundation Building
Brownlow Hill
Liverpool L69 7ZX
Tel: 0151 794 2000
Fax: 0151 708 6502
Email: ugrecruitment@liv.ac.uk
Website: www.liv.ac.uk
*University of Liverpool Guild of Students*
Website: www.lgos.org

## Liverpool Hope University
Hope Park
Liverpool L16 9JD
Tel: 0151 291 3295
Fax: 0151 291 2050
Email: admission@hope.ac.uk
Website: www.hope.ac.uk
*Liverpool Hope University Students' Union*
Website: www.hopesu.co.uk

## Liverpool John Moores University
Roscoe Court
4 Rodney Street
Liverpool L1 2TZ
Tel: 0151 231 5090
Fax: 0151 231 3462
Email: recruitment@ljmu.ac.uk
Website: www.ljmu.ac.uk
*Liverpool Students' Union*
Website: www.l-s-u.com

## University of London
Information Centre
Stewart House
32 Russell Square
London WC1B 5DN
Tel: 020 7862 8360/8361/8362
E-mail: enquiries@london.ac.uk
Website: www.london.ac.uk
*University of London Union*
Website: www.ulu.co.uk

**London Metropolitan University**
166–220 Holloway Road
London N7 8DB
Tel: 020 7133 4200
Email: admissions@londonmet.ac.uk
Website: www.londonmet.ac.uk
*London Metropolitan University Students' Union*
Website: www.londonmetstudents.com

**London School of Economics and Political Science**
Houghton Street
London WC2A 2AE
Tel: 020 7955 7125/7769
Fax: 020 7955 6001
Email: ug-admissions@lse.ac.uk
Website: www.lse.ac.uk
*London School of Economics Students' Union*
Website: www.lsesu.com

**London South Bank University**
103 Borough Road
London SE1 0AA
Tel: 020 7815 6100
Fax: 020 7815 8273
Email: course.enquiry@lsbu.ac.uk
Website: www.lsbu.ac.uk
*South Bank University Students' Union*
Website: www.lsbsu.org

**University College London**
Gower Street WC1E 6BT
Tel: 020 7679 3000
Fax: 020 7679 3001
Email: sclo@ucl.ac.uk
Website: www.ucl.ac.uk
*University College London Students' Union*
Website: www.uclu.org

**Loughborough University**
Loughborough LE11 3TU
Tel: 01509 223522
Fax: 01509 223905
Email: admissions@lboro.ac.uk
Website: www.lboro.ac.uk
*Loughborough University Students' Union*
Website: www.lufbra.net

**University of Manchester**
Oxford Road
Manchester M13 9PL
Tel: 0161 275 2077
Fax: 0161 275 2106
Email: ug-admissions@manchester.ac.uk
Website: www.manchester.ac.uk
*University of Manchester Students' Union*
Website: www.umu.man.ac.uk

**Manchester Metropolitan University**
Admissions Office
All Saints (GMS)
All Saints
Manchester M15 6BH
Tel: 0161 247 2000
Fax: 0161 247 6335
Email: admissions@mmu.ac.uk
Website: www.mmu.ac.uk
*Manchester Metropolitan University Students' Union*
Website: www.mmunion.co.uk

**Middlesex University**
The Burroughs
London NW4 4BT
Tel: 020 8411 5555
Fax: 020 8411 5649
Email: admissions@mdx.ac.uk
Website: www.mdx.ac.uk
*Middlesex University Students' Union*
Website: www.musu.mdx.ac.uk

**Newcastle University**
6 Kensington Terrace
Newcastle upon Tyne NE1 7RU
Tel: 0191 222 5594
Fax: 0191 222 6143
Email: enquiries@ncl.ac.uk
Website: www.ncl.ac.uk
*Newcastle University Students' Union*
Website: www.unionsociety.co.uk

**University of Wales, Newport** (Prifysgol Cymru, Casnewydd)
Caerleon Campus
Lodge Road
Newport NP18 3QT

Tel: 01633 432030
Fax: 01633 432850
Email: admissions@newport.ac.uk
Website: www.newport.ac.uk
*Newport Students' Union*
Website: www.newportunion.com

## University of Northampton

Park Campus
Boughton Green Road
Northampton NN2 7AL
Tel: 0800 358 2232
Fax: 01604 722083
Email: admissions@northampton.ac.uk
Website: www.northampton.ac.uk
*University of Northampton Students' Union*
Website: www.northamptonunion.com

## Northumbria University, Newcastle

Trinity Building
Northumberland Road
Newcastle upon Tyne NE1 8ST
Tel: 0191 243 7420
Fax: 0191 227 4561
Email: er.admissions@northumbria.ac.uk
Website: www.northumbria.ac.uk
*Northumbria University Students' Union*
Website: www.mynsu.co.uk

## University of Nottingham

Admissions Office
University of Nottingham
University Park
Nottingham NG7 2RD
Tel: 0115 951 5151
Fax: 0115 951 4668
Website: www.nottingham.ac.uk
*University of Nottingham Students' Union*
Website: www.su.nottingham.ac.uk

## Nottingham Trent University

Dryden Centre
Burton Street
Nottingham NG1 4BU
Tel: 0115 941 8418
Fax: 0115 848 6063

Email: admissions@ntu.ac.uk
Website: www.ntu.ac.uk
*Nottingham Trent University Union of Students*
Website: www.trentstudents.org

## Open University
Student Registration and Enquiry Service
PO Box 197
Milton Keynes MK7 6BJ
Tel: 0845 300 6090
Fax: 01908 654914
Email: use website query form
Website: www.open.ac.uk

## University of Oxford
Undergraduate Admissions Office
Wellington Square
Oxford OX1 2JD
Tel: 01865 288000
Fax: 01865 280125
Email: undergraduate.admissions@admin.ox.ac.uk
Website: www.admissions.ox.ac.uk
*Oxford University Students' Union*
Website: www.ousu.org

## Oxford Brookes University
Admissions Office
Headington Campus
Gipsy Lane
Oxford OX3 0BP
Tel: 01865 483040
Fax: 01865 483983
Email: admissions@brookes.ac.uk
Website: www.brookes.ac.uk
*Oxford Brookes Students' Union*
Website: www.thesu.com

## University of Plymouth
Drake Circus
Plymouth PL4 8AA
Tel: 01752 588037
Fax: 01752 588050
Email: admissions@plymouth.ac.uk
Website: www.plymouth.ac.uk
*University of Plymouth Student's Union*
Website: www.upsu.plym.ac.uk

**University of Portsmouth**
Academic Registry
University House
Winston Churchill Avenue
Portsmouth PO1 2UP
Tel: 023 9284 8484
Fax: 023 9284 3082
Email: admissions@port.ac.uk
Website: www.port.ac.uk
*University of Portsmouth Students' Union*
Website: www.upsu.net

**Queen Margaret University, Edinburgh**
Queen Margaret University Drive
Edinburgh EH21 6UU
Tel: 0131474 0000
Fax: 0131 474 0001
Email: admissions@qmu.ac.uk
Website: www.qmu.ac.uk
*Queen Margaret University Edinburgh Students' Union*
Website: www.qmusu.org.uk

**Queen Mary, University of London** (formerly Queen Mary and Westfield
College)
London E1 4NS
Tel: 020 7882 5555
Fax: 020 7882 5500
Email: admissions@qmul.ac.uk
Website: www.qmul.ac.uk
*Queen Mary Students' Union*
Website: www.qmsu.org

**Queen's University Belfast**
University Road
Belfast BT7 1NN
Tel: 028 9097 2727
Fax: 028 9097 2828
Email: admissions@qub.ac.uk
Website: www.qub.ac.uk
*Queen's University Belfast Students' Union*
Website: www.qubsu.org

**University of Reading**
PO Box 217
Reading RG6 6AH
Tel: 0118 378 8619
Fax: 0118 378 8924

Email: student.recruitment@reading.ac.uk
Website: www.reading.ac.uk
*Reading University Students' Union*
Website: www.reading.ac.uk/RUSU

### Richmond American International University
Queens Road
Richmond TW10 6JP
Tel: 020 8332 9000
Fax: 020 8332 1596
Email: enroll@richmond.ac.uk
Website: www.richmond.ac.uk

### Robert Gordon University
Schoolhill
Aberdeen AB10 1FR
Tel: 01224 262728
Fax: 01224 262147
Email: admissions@rgu.ac.uk
Website: www.rgu.ac.uk
*Robert Gordon University Students' Association*
Website: www.rguunion.co.uk

### Roehampton University
Erasmus House
Roehampton Lane
London SW15 5PU
Tel: 020 8392 3232
Fax: 020 8392 3470
Email: enquiries@roehampton.ac.uk
Website: www.roehampton.ac.uk
*Roehampton University Students' Union*
Website: www.roehamptonstudent.com

### Royal Holloway, University of London
Egham TW20 0EX
Tel: 01784 434455
Fax: 01784 473662
Email: Admissions@rhul.ac.uk
Website: www.rhul.ac.uk
*Royal Holloway University of London Students' Union*
Website: www.su.rhul.ac.uk

### University of St Andrews
St Katharine's West

The Scores
St Andrews KY16 9AX
Tel: 01334 462150
Fax: 01334 463330
Email: admissions@st-andrews.ac.uk
Website: www.st-and.ac.uk
*University of St Andrews Students' Union*
Website: www.yourunion.net

## University of Salford
Salford M5 4WT
Tel: 0161 295 4545
Fax: 0161 295 3126
Email: ugadmissions-exrel@salford.ac.uk
Website: www.salford.ac.uk
*Salford University Students' Union*
Website: www.salfordstudents.com

## School of Oriental and African Studies
Thornhaugh Street
Russell Square
London WC1H 0XG
Tel: 020 7074 5106
Fax: 020 7898 4039
Email: undergradadmissions@soas.ac.uk
Website: www.soas.ac.uk
*School of Oriental and African Studies Students' Union*
Website: www.soasunion.org

## University of Sheffield
9 Northumberland Road
Sheffield S10 2TT
Tel: 0114 222 1255
Fax: 0114 222 8032
Email: ask@sheffield.ac.uk
Website: www.sheffield.ac.uk
*Sheffield University Students' Union*
Website: www.shef.ac.uk/union

## Sheffield Hallam University
City Campus
Howard Street
Sheffield S1 1WB
Tel: 0114 225 5555
Fax: 0114 225 2167

Email: admissions@shu.ac.uk
Website: www.shu.ac.uk
*Sheffield Hallam University Students' Union*
Website: www.hallamunion.com

## University of Southampton
Highfield
Southampton SO17 1BJ
Tel: 023 8059 4732
Fax: 023 8059 3037
Email: admissions@soton.ac.uk
Website: www.southampton.ac.uk
*Southampton University Students' Union*
Website: www.susu.org

## Southampton Solent University
East Park Terrace
Southampton SO14 0RT
Tel: 023 8031 9039
Fax: 023 8022 2259
Email: admissions@solent.ac.uk
Website: www.solent.ac.uk
*Southampton Solent University Students' Union*
Website: www.solentsu.co.uk

## Staffordshire University
College Road
Stoke on Trent ST4 2DE
Tel: 01782 292753
Fax: 01782 292740
Email: admissions@staffs.ac.uk
Website: www.staffs.ac.uk
*Stafford University Students' Union*
Website: www.staffsunion.com

## University of Stirling
Stirling FK9 4LA
Tel: 01786 467044
Fax: 01786 466800
Email: admissions@stir.ac.uk
Website: www.stir.ac.uk
*University of Stirling Students' Association*
Website: www.susaonline.org.uk

**University of Strathclyde**
Glasgow G1 1XQ
Tel: 0141 552 4400
Fax: 0141 552 0775
Email: scls@strath.ac.uk
Website: www.strath.ac.uk
*University of Strathclyde Students' Association*
Website: www.strathstudents.com

**University of Sunderland**
Student Recruitment
The Student Gateway
Chester Road
Sunderland SR1 3SD
Tel: 0191 515 3000
Fax: 0191 515 3805
Email: student-helpline@sunderland.ac.uk
Website: www.sunderland.ac.uk
*University of Sunderland Students' Union*
Website: www.sunderlandsu.co.uk

**University of Surrey**
Stag Hill
Guildford GU2 7XH
Tel: 01483 689305
Fax: 01483 689388
Email: admissions@surrey.ac.uk
Website: www.surrey.ac.uk
*University of Surrey Students' Union*
Website: www.ussu.co.uk

**University of Sussex**
Undergraduate Admissions
Sussex House
Brighton BN1 9RH
Tel: 01273 678416
Fax: 01273 678545
Email: ug.admissions@sussex.ac.uk
Website: www.sussex.ac.uk
*University of Sussex Students' Union*
Website: www.ussu.info

**Swansea University** (Prifysgol Abertawe)
Singleton Park
Swansea SA2 8PP

Tel: 01792 295111
Fax: 01792 295110
Email: admissions@swansea.ac.uk
Website: www.swansea.ac.uk
*University of Swansea Students' Union*
Website: www.swansea-union.co.uk

**Swansea Metropolitan University** (Prifysgol Fetropolitan Abertawe)
Mount Pleasant Campus
Swansea SA1 6ED
Tel: 01792 481000
Fax: 01792 481061
Email: gemma.garbutt@smu.ac.uk
Website: www.smu.ac.uk
*Swansea Metropolitan Students' Union*
www.metsu.org

**University of Teesside**
Middlesbrough TS1 3BA
Tel: 01642 218121
Fax: 01642 384201
Email: registry@tees.ac.uk
Website: www.tees.ac.uk
*University of Teesside Students' Union*
Website: www.tees.ac.uk/sections/studentlife/students_union.cfm

**Thames Valley University**
St Mary's Road
London W5 5RF
Tel: 0800 036 8888
Fax: 020 8566 1353
Email: learning.advice@tvu.ac.uk
Website: www.tvu.ac.uk
*Thames Valley University Students' Union*
Website: www.tvusu.co.uk

**UHI Millennium Institute**
UHI Executive Office
Ness Walk
Inverness IV3 5SQ
Tel: 01463 279000
Fax: 01463 279001
Email: info@uhi.ac.uk
Website: www.uhi.ac.uk

**University of Ulster**
Coleraine
Co. Londonderry BT52 1SA
Tel: 028 7032 4221
Fax: 028 7032 4908
Email: online@ulster.ac.uk
Website: www.ulster.ac.uk
*University of Ulster Students' Union*
Website: www.uusu.org

**University of Wales** (Prifysgol Cymru)
University Registry
King Edward VII Avenue
Cardiff CF10 3NS
Tel: 029 2037 6999
Fax: 029 2037 6980
Email: use form on website
Website: www.wales.ac.uk

**University of Warwick**
Coventry CV4 8UW
Tel: 024 7652 3723
Fax: 024 7652 4649
Email: ugadmissions@warwick.ac.uk
Website: www.warwick.ac.uk
*University of Warwick Students' Union*
Website: www.sunion.warwick.ac.uk

**University of the West of England, Bristol**
Frenchay Campus
Coldharbour Lane
Bristol BS16 1QY
Tel: 0117 328 3333
Fax: 0117 328 2810
Email: admissions@uwe.ac.uk
Website: www.uwe.ac.uk
*University of the West of England Students' Union*
Website: www.uwesu.net

**University of the West of Scotland** (formerly Paisley University)
Paisley PA1 2BE
Tel: 0800 027 1000
Fax: 0141 848 3623
Email: uni-direct@uws.ac.uk
Website: www.uws.ac.uk

*Students' Association of the University of the West of Scotland*
Website: www.sauws.org.uk

## University of Westminster
35 Marylebone Road
London NW1 5LS
Tel: 020 7911 5000
Fax: 020 7911 5858
Email: admissions@westminster.ac.uk
Website: www.westminster.ac.uk
*University of Westminster Students' Union*
Website: www.uwsu.com

## University of Winchester
Winchester SO22 4NR
Tel: 01962 827234
Fax: 01962 827288
Email: course.enquiries@winchester.ac.uk
Website: www.winchester.ac.uk
*Winchester University Students' Union*
Website: www.winchesterstudents.co.uk

## University of Wolverhampton
Admissions Unit
MX207, Camp Street
Wolverhampton WV1 1AD
Tel: 01902 321000
Fax: 01902 321896
Email: admissions@wlv.ac.uk
Website: www.wlv.ac.uk
*University of Wolverhampton Students' Union*
Website: www.wolvesunion.org

## University of Worcester
Henwick Grove
Worcester WR2 6AJ
Tel: 01905 855111
Fax: 01905 855377
Email: admissions@worc.ac.uk
Website: www.worcester.ac.uk
*University of Worcester Students' Union*
Website: www.worcsu.com

**University of York**
Admissions and Schools Liaison
Heslington
York YO10 5DD
Tel: 01904 433533
Fax: 01904 433538
Email: admissions@york.ac.uk
Website: www.york.ac.uk
*University of York Students' Union*
Website: www.yusu.org

**York St John University**
Lord Mayor's Walk
York YO31 7EX
Tel: 01904 876598
Fax: 01904 876940/876921
Email: admissions@yorksj.ac.uk
Website: www.yorksj.ac.uk
*York St John Students' Union*
Website: www.ysjsu.com